HOUSECRAFT

ACCOMMODATION OPERATIONS

Valerie Paul, *Leeds Polytechnic*
and Christine Jones

Series Editor: Roy Hayter, Hotel and Catering Training Board

MACMILLAN

First published 1989

Published by
MACMILLAN EDUCATION LTD
Houndmills, Basingstoke, Hampshire RG21 2XS
and London
Companies and representatives
throughout the world

Printed in Great Britain by
Scotprint Ltd, Musselburgh

British Library Cataloguing in Publication Data
Paul, Valerie
  Housecraft
  1. Buildings. Interiors. Cleaning
  I. Title   II. Jones, Christine
  648'.5

ISBN 0–333–46340–4

CONTENTS

CONTENTS

Housecraft

Linen and its care

Specialist cleaning routines

CONTENTS

ACKNOWLEDGEMENTS

Macmillan Education and the Hotel and Catering Training Board are grateful to Mary James and Melvyn Teare who were responsible for setting up the structure and scope of this book, to Jessica Kuper who undertook much of the final editing, and to Gill Verstage and Elaine Cappas who briefed the photographic sessions at the London Tara Hotel and the Royal Marsden Hospital.

The publishers would also like to express their sincere thanks to the following for their help in supplying photographs and illustrations:

Allibert Leisure Furniture (unit 7)

Amtico, Coventry (unit 24)

The Architect's Journal Information Library of 24 April 1968 (illustrations in unit 12, which originally appeared in *Hotel User Study* by Phyllis Allen)

Association of British Laundry Cleaning and Rental Services (unit 41)

Audio Visual Aids Unit, University of Surrey (units 4 and 12)

Barbican Centre, London (unit 13, photographer Clive Totman)

Catherine Blackie (picture research and photography in units 1, 14 and 21)

BMK Ltd, Kilmarnock (illustrations in unit 25)

British Red Cross, St Andrew's Ambulance Association and St John Ambulance for permission to adapt the illustrations in unit 54 from *First Aid Manual*, 1987

Brook Hotel, Felixstowe (units 1, 2 and 19, photographer Edward Morgan)

Broughton Park Hotel, Preston (unit 60, photographer Mark Lovesey)

BUPA (unit 5)

Canberra Cruises Ltd (unit 44)

Cliveden Hotel Ltd (unit 3)

Columbus Dixon, Luton (units 21, 22, 23 and 26)

Commonwealth Hotels International Co. (illustrations in unit 20)

Crest Hotels Ltd (unit 2)

Alexia Cross (photography at the London Tara Hotel and the Royal Marsden Hospital)

English Tourist Board and Holiday Care Service for permission to adapt the illustration in unit 8 from *Providing for Disabled Visitors*, 1985

Format Photographers Ltd (unit 1, photographer Sheila Gray; units 15, 37 and 46, photographer Jenny Matthews; units 17, 32 and 47, photographer Maggie Murray; unit 26, photographer Joanne O'Brien; and unit 11, photographer Brenda Prince)

Guidepost Hotel, Bradford (units 42 and 51, photographer Robin Matthams)

James Halstead Ltd, Manchester (units 5, 24 and 31)

Holiday Inns (UK) Incorporated (unit 44)

Hoover Commercial, Witney (units 22 and 23)

Hotel, Catering and Institutional Management Association for access to its library and permission to adapt the illustrations in unit 9 from *HCIMA Reference Book 1985/86*, 'Trends in Hotel Planning' by Mel Gickman and John Harrison of the Webb Zerafa Menkes Housden Partnership, Toronto, Canada

Hutchinson & Co (Publishers) Ltd, London for permission to base the illustration in unit 43 on that published in *Accommodation and Cleaning Science, Volume 1: Operations* by David M Allen, 1983

The International Wool Secretariat to adapt the illustrations in unit 25 from *Facts about Contract Carpeting*

Alfred Kärcher GmbH & Co, Winnenden, W. Germany (units 29 and 52)

Kirton Designs Ltd (unit 11)

Kleidienst/Association of British Laundry Cleaning and Rental Services (unit 41)

London Tara Hotel (units 17, 18, 20, 21, 30, 31, 33, 38, 40, 41, 43, 44, 45, 49, 53 and 57)

Macdonald/Aldus Archive (unit 44, photographer Geg Germany)

Oundle School (unit 6)

Rentokil Environmental Services Division (unit 57)

The Royal Marsden Hospital (units 21, 22, 45, 49, 54, 59, 61 and 62)

Science Photo Library (unit 15; and unit 16, photographer Dr Tony Brain; unit 11, photographer James Stevenson)

Selsdon Park Hotel, Purley (unit 52)

Shire Bathrooms, Leeds (unit 31)

Sinclair (Contract Furnishers) Ltd, London (unit 10)

Sundour Fabrics, Bolton (unit 9)

Thistle Hotels Ltd (units 13, 48 and 49)

Thorpe Park (unit 4)

Transmedia (cover photograph and unit 48)

The aims of the book

When people go into a building other than their own home, whether it be for a few hours or for many days and nights, they have certain expectations of the standards of cleanliness and of the level of comfort. This book deals with the issues that determine how successfully these expectations are met and which are common to the various types of hotel and catering operation:

- hotels and guesthouses, clubs, restaurants and pubs, conference, leisure and sports centres, ships, ferries, trains and planes
- hospitals, homes for the elderly, convalescent and homeless, schools, students halls of residence, hostels and hospices, prisons and remand centres.

The starting point for all is the customer, that is the guest, patient, resident, member, student etc. who uses the building and its facilities. Different customers have different needs.

Secondly, an appreciation is required of the design and construction of the building and its fittings. Cleaning routines and procedures can then be adapted and developed so they will prolong the life of these often expensive physical assets, while making the best use of staff time and effort.

Thirdly, customers generally expect areas and surfaces to look attractive, welcoming and well-cared for, but it is also a major responsibility of the housekeeping staff to ensure that cleaning procedures remove as far as possible the harmful bacteria and other micro-organisms which thrive in dust and soilage, in sanitary fittings and on used bedclothes and towels, for example. This means choosing effective cleaning agents and equipment and using them correctly.

The structure of the book

Some 62 double page openings (called units) cover these issues. They are grouped into nine divisions:

The customer—introduces the needs of the different groups of customers in accommodation operations, how they have developed and future trends.

Appreciation of design—how the design of buildings, their decor, the fixtures and furnishings are influenced by the needs of the customers and the staff who service and clean them.

Insight—the principles of cleaning, why hygiene is such an important factor and how these considerations can be reflected in the work of housekeeping staff.

Cleaning agents and equipment—the detergents, mops, brushes and other materials and equipment that will help achieve the necessary standards of cleanliness and hygiene, why they are appropriate, when and how they should be used to do the job effectively.

Housecraft—walls, floors and their coverings, sanitary fittings, furniture and fabrics in common use in the industry and how they are cleaned.

Linen and its care—organisation of linen, removing stains and laundering.

Specialist cleaning routines—how the routines and procedures covered earlier can be applied to the principal types of accommodation unit such as hotel bedrooms, hospital wards, public areas and leisure facilities.

Safety and security—why these are the concern of all housekeeping staff, with practical guidance on reducing hazards, how to deal with accidents, bomb scares and other emergencies.

Customercraft—putting personality to full use in dealings with work colleagues and customers, and how to communicate more effectively.

The division of the material into self-contained units makes access to any particular topic straightforward. References to other units and a comprehensive index mean that related information can be quickly located. Units that will help readers gain Caterbase modules in accommodation operations are identified and the Test Yourself questions at the end of each group of units will assist preparation for theory examinations in this area—particularly those of City and Guilds.

Each unit has a TO DO, a practical activity to encourage interest, to help the reader apply his or her knowledge and develop a deeper understanding.

The book takes to a greater depth those basic skills dealt with in the companion *Housecraft: Operations Workbook*. It is supported by the video *Housecraft: A Key to Operations* and the video and book *Customercraft: Keeping the Customers Satisfied* also include major sections on accommodation operations.

1 THE CUSTOMER

Most people spend some time away from their home through choice. It may be to spend their summer holidays in a hotel or caravan park, or for a day at a leisure centre in the country, or it may be to see Europe, hitchhiking and staying in youth hostels.

Sometimes people have to be away, to attend school, or to go into hospital. They may be elderly and have to be cared for in a state or private residential home. They might have been sent to prison for committing a crime.

Other reasons why people choose or are required to stay away from home include:

- travelling
- conducting business away from home
- attending conferences
- visiting exhibitions
- attending a course
- visiting relatives or friends
- touring to visit places of interest
- celebrating an anniversary, promotion or exam success
- attending a wedding, funeral or speech day
- visiting a person in hospital or prison
- attending college or university
- participating in sporting or other leisure activities
- convalescing from an illness or having a baby
- working or training away from home
- on military duty
- being cared for because they are homeless, infirm or mentally ill.

How long people stay away from home

The length of time people stay away from home is connected with the reasons for having to be away. A business person may need to spend only one night in a hotel in order to attend a meeting or visit a client, whereas a student nurse who comes from a distant town may have to stay in a nurses' residence for the whole period of training. An extreme case of a long, involuntary absence from home is the prisoner serving a ten year jail sentence. On the other hand, an absence from home may only last a few hours. Attending an exhibition or participating in a sporting event need not require an overnight stay. But however long they are away, people who are not at home may need some kind of accommodation, residential or non-residential, and some of the services that home would normally provide.

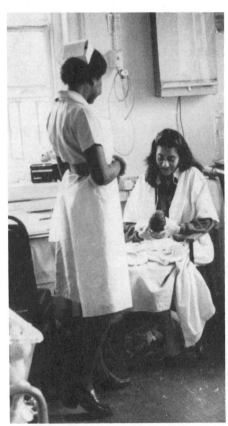

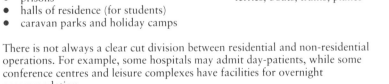

Examples of accommodation establishments

Residential:

- hotels
- hospitals
- hospices
- prisons
- halls of residence (for students)
- caravan parks and holiday camps

Non-residential:

- conference centres
- leisure complexes
- theme parks
- ferries, boats, trains, planes

There is not always a clear cut division between residential and non-residential operations. For example, some hospitals may admit day-patients, while some conference centres and leisure complexes have facilities for overnight accommodation.

Where they stay

There are many different types of establishment, which provide a range of services and facilities for people away from home. These can be classified in a number of ways, the usual being according to whether the establishment is a commercial, profit-making operation, or a non-profit-making one.

A hotel is a commercial operation, whereas a National Health Service hospital is non-profit-making, and it is often referred to as a welfare institution. (A welfare institution may, however, be run on a commercial basis—a private hospital, for instance, being a commercial welfare operation.)

How things are changing

The accommodation industry is growing fast. Tourism, both local and foreign, is increasing every year, and is one of the largest growth industries in the country. More and more people have time and money for leisure activities, both holidays and day trips. Day trippers are being catered for by the huge development of theme parks and leisure centres, some of which also offer residential accommodation. The private hospital sector is also expanding, as more people are insured for private medicine, and offering services on a par with hotels. With the expansion of multi-national companies and the huge growth in general of the business sector, conferences become regular events for businesspeople, and business hotels have developed to cater for their special requirements. The non-business sector is also becoming increasingly specialised, with different facilities catering for special categories of clients. For example, teenagers may earn comparatively little, but a high proportion of their income is spent on leisure activities, and they are some of the main customers of theme parks. At the other end of the age-range, people are living longer as general health and welfare improves, which increases the demand for old age residential homes. Pensioners are travelling too, taking excursions to local attractions and pleasure parks, and going on low-cost coach holidays in the UK (and abroad) during the off-peak season.

Some facts and figures

In 1987, about 15.6 million visitors came to the UK—60% from the USA and 27% from Western Europe. In June alone, visitors to Britain spent £610 million. Although predictions are not always reliable—they cannot take into account terrorist incidents, currency variations, stock market collapses—there is likely to be a huge expansion of foreign tourism by the early 1990s, when it is predicted that overseas visitors will spend about £23 billion in Britain each year.

The British also have more money to spend on leisure than in previous decades. In 1984, for example, 34 million Britons took holidays in the UK and 16 million went abroad. By 1987 the number going abroad had increased to 27.2 million, spending £7240 million. (Interestingly, in 1971, the exact same number of Britons, 34 million, had a holiday in Britain.) Besides holidays, roughly 92% of all adults make at least one leisure day trip during the summer. Many of these are to theme parks and leisure centres.

2 THE CUSTOMER

An accommodation establishment, whether it be a hotel, hospital, leisure centre or hall of residence, commercial or non-commercial, exists to satisfy the needs of its customers.

In order to do this means finding out about the customers—who exactly they are and what they want:

- Is there just one type of customer, or a variety?
- What is the main age group, if any?
- How much money can they afford to spend?
- What are their reasons for using the establishment?
- What are their expectations?
- Do they have alternatives—does hotel B offer the same services for less money or more services for the same money?
- Is there any seasonal variation in the type of customers?

 TO DO

Take any accommodation establishment that you know well, perhaps your own workplace or college, and consider all the different types of customers who use it. Collect as much information as you can about them, using the checklist in this unit.

The following records may be available and help:

- reservation and registration information
- occupancy statistics
- accounting summaries
- guest/patient histories/files
- local tourist board information.

Watching, listening and talking to customers will prove particularly helpful. Members of staff are also likely to be able to describe the characteristics of customers.

Why it is important to know the customer

The owners of the establishment, or their representatives (for example, board of directors, the governors), clearly have an interest in knowing as much as possible about the customer so that services and facilities can be provided at an adequate profit (if it is a commercial venture) or within specific costs (if it is a non-commercial venture):

- What are the customers' needs and requirements?
- What type of accommodation and amount of space must be provided?
- Is existing accommodation adequate?
- What facilities and services are required?
- Are existing facilities and services adequate?
- What price should be charged?
- What standards should be provided?
- What sales and marketing campaigns are required?

But the nature of accommodation operations means that however excellent the facilities, customer needs cannot be fully met without the participation of staff. It is staff who:

- clean and maintain the building, furnishings and equipment, so that it provides a hygienic, pleasing environment which is safe to be in;
- respond to the individual needs of customers, make them feel welcome and care for their well-being;
- are in the best position to know how well customers are satisfied with the services and to report points which cause satisfaction (so that they can be made even better) and dissatisfaction (so they can be put right).

For accommodation operations staff to do their job effectively, it is important that they know the procedures, but it is equally important that they appreciate their role in helping meet customers' expectations. This role is a key one (see the Customercraft units). To perform it effectively means:

- knowing the workplace and what it offers
- knowing the customers and what they want.

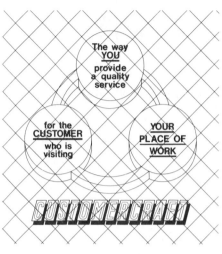

All staff in accommodation establishments play a key role in helping to meet customers' expectations—even those who infrequently or never meet the customers

Finding out about the customers: a checklist

Who are they?

- Business people
- Conference delegates
- Travellers
- Tourists
- Overseas visitors
- Tour groups
- Holidaymakers
- Banqueting guests
- Patients
- Out-patients
- People who have suffered accidents and emergencies
- Hospital visitors
- Students
- Short course delegates
- Others

What type of people are they?

- Are they male or female?
- Are they disabled?
- What is the age range?
- Are they married couples?
- Are they families? (with babies, young children or teenagers)
- What type of occupations do they have? (professional, executive, manual)
- How much do they earn?

Why do they stay/visit?

- Stop over/travelling to another destination
- On business—attending functions/banquets
  attending shows/exhibitions
  attending a conference or short course
  conducting meetings/interviews

- On pleasure—part of a tour group
  on holiday
  attending an event
  attending a function/banquet
- Is it their temporary home?
- Are they ill, terminally ill, convalescing?
- Are they incapable of looking after themselves?

How long do they stay?

- What is the average length of stay?
- What types of people stay for what length of time?

Where do they come from?

- Are they local—from which area?
  from what local businesses or companies?
  from what local organisations, associations or clubs?
- Are they nationals?—from which counties?
- Are they international?—from which countries?

How much do they spend?

Note: in some cases customers may only need to pay directly for extras, for example, hospital patients will perhaps buy newspapers, books, sweets if allowed, or make telephone calls; inclusive tour members may only have to pay for drinks, wines and telephone calls; while in other cases customers will spend a great deal of money, not only on the accommodation, food and drinks but gambling in the casino, for instance.

When do they come?

- What time of the day do they arrive and leave?
- What time of the week do they stay?
- What time of the year do they stay?

Where customers can stay—on business or pleasure

Most customers away from home for one or more nights in the UK have some choice about where they can stay, depending on how much they are prepared to pay. A single room with breakfast in a hotel offering basic facilities can cost as little as £10, but in cities and other areas where property costs are high, the prices are well above this—in 1988 three-star hotels in business/tourist locations were charging £50–60 and the five-star Hyatt Carlton Tower in London was the first hotel to charge over £200 for a standard single room.

Hotels can be classified in a number of different ways, for example by the type of customer:

- **Business hotels** cater largely (but not only) for business people, who use them for overnight stays or for conferences and other business meetings. Most are located in towns and cities.
- **Tourist or resort hotels** are mainly for holiday makers. They are in resort areas—at the seaside, in the mountains, or near special tourist attractions, such as theme parks. Many resort hotels have their own leisure facilities, for example a swimming pool and tennis courts.
- **Residential hotels** are for permanent occupants. They are often called 'Private Hotels'.
- **Motels** or **motor hotels**, are designed for people travelling by car, and therefore must provide parking areas and have easy access to highways.

Hotels can be **licensed** to sell alcoholic beverages or be **unlicensed** (for example temperance hotels, such as the Methodist Holiday Hotels).

A **guesthouse** provides more or less the same services as a hotel or motel, but to residents only. The dining room or restaurant, for example, is not usually open to the public. Prices are generally lower because the facilities and perhaps the degree of comfort are not up to the usual hotel standards.

A **boarding house** offers the same services as a guesthouse but on a long-term basis.

 FOR INTEREST

The first hotels, going back many centuries, were called *inns*, and they were places where travellers on horseback or in stagecoaches could break their journey. Inns offered food and accommodation, and stables for the animals. The word 'inn' is now commonly used instead of hotel, for example Holiday Inn.

The earliest modern-type hotels date back to the last century, to a time when the building of railway lines encouraged travel on a mass scale. Just as inns were located near the highways in medieval times, so 19th century hotels were built near train stations. Later, as air travel became popular, many hotels were built near airports. Nowadays, many hotels belong to the same company or hotel chain. The largest hotel chain in Britain is Trusthouse Forte Ltd. It runs 800 hotels worldwide (including 200 in Britain). Many THF hotels cater for business travellers and people on package tours.

There are an estimated 33,200 hotels, guesthouses, hostels and holiday camps in Britain. Of this, about 19,300 are proprietor or partnership-run.

Looking at the overall picture, about:

- 21,000 are hotels or motels
- 4500 are licensed private hotels or guesthouses
- 500 are holiday camps with catering facilities
- 7000 are unlicensed private hotels, hostels and boarding houses.

✱ FOR INTEREST

Holiday centres are being modernised and improved in an effort to re-establish their position in the holiday market following a number of years in the doldrums. For example, Butlins has recently spent £9 million on the Minehead Centre in Somerset to convert it to a combined theme park and holiday centre called Somerset World.

The largest holiday centre operators are:
- Mecca Leisure/Warners (11 centres)
- Butlins (6 centres selling 750,000 holidays per year)
- Pontins (26 centres and about 200,000 customers)
- Ladbrokes (16 holiday locations, of which 6 are holiday villages, and 3 hotels)

◗ ◗ ◗ TO DO

Get information on either three holiday centres or three caravan parks in any part of the country you choose. Make a comparison of the facilities they offer and the prices they charge. Find out as much as you can about any new facilities they have recently added.

Holiday centres, established in Britain since the 1950s are a popular and cheaper alternative to staying in hotels. The first, and still the most famous, holiday centres were the Butlins Holiday Camps, built (in Billy Butlin's words) "to offer a week's holiday for a week's wages". The image of holiday camps has now changed. Many have gone upmarket, appealing to better-off families and are known as holiday centres, not camps (which suggests 'roughing it' in tents). They try to provide daytime and evening entertainment for the whole family. Most visitors to holiday centres spend at least a week, as the tariff is usually a weekly one. Outside the season, some holiday centres offer weekend rates, or special packages, including for example reduced fares on train services and free entertainment.

Caravan parks are either areas which allocate space to holiday-makers who come with their own touring caravans (rather like tent sites) or else they are parks containing permanently sited caravans (also known as mobile homes), which can be rented by holiday-makers. Some of the larger parks accommodate both touring and static caravans. The small caravan parks for touring caravans usually have only the basic amenities: toilet and washing facilities. Many of the larger parks have shops, restaurants, bars, sanitary and laundry areas, and even provide entertainment (in which case they are little different from holiday camps).

Trends

A number of stately homes, such as Cliveden, the former home of the Astor family, have been converted into hotels.

Some local authorities in London and other large cities find that they have to place homeless families in hotels. This provides a steady income to the hotel over a long period.

Some companies, such as Little Chef, THF's roadside restaurant chain and Granada Motorway Services are building budget hotels or lodges offering basic overnight accommodation at low prices.

Most business travellers, who spend many nights away from the comforts of home, expect hotels to be clean and comfortable. And as city hotels respond to their needs, by providing special facilities for business people (desks, computers etc.), they set a trend which other hotels have to follow.

Several hotel chains have responded to the increase in women executives by providing special rooms for them.

Conference facilities, also expanding rapidly, but often outpacing the demand, have to offer something extra, even luxurious, to keep up.

Transport accommodation

Most people use transport—car, coach, train, plane or boat—purely as a means of getting from one place to another.

However, there are exceptions—the sea cruise holiday, and the train holiday package are two obvious examples.

Regular transport carriers offer day and sometimes also sleeping accommodation, but with far less attention to luxury and with a greatly reduced staff. For example, ferries provide berths which can be booked overnight or for a few nights in the case of longer journeys, or for only a couple of hours during a day crossing.

Like most ferry journeys, plane trips seldom last more than several hours. On long intercontinental hauls, however, people do require sleeping accommodation. Most airlines provide this in the form of reclining seats, supplying a pillow and blanket, while first class passengers are able to recline their seats to a near-horizontal position. Some private jets have beds.

Trains, too, mainly accommodate passengers going on short journeys. If a journey lasts overnight, or over several nights, passengers sleep in berths, which are converted day couches. Some trains provide proper bed linen, others only provide blankets and pillows.

Conference centres

Conference centres are places where conferences, meetings, exhibitions and other big events are held. They range in size from a small office, perhaps a converted hotel bedroom, where several people may be meeting informally, to a huge, purpose-built conference centre with numerous facilities including exhibition halls, auditoriums and a range of up-to-date audio visual and communications services, including simultaneous interpretation.

Conferences may also be held in other forms of accommodation, such as halls of residence, college or university buildings, theatres, holiday centres etc. (in off-peak periods). University conference centres are generally aimed at the more budget conscious, although a number of universities are improving their facilities in order to attract a wider clientele.

* FOR INTEREST

Recently the Venice Simplon-Orient-Express, the Great Maharaja and other famous train services have been revived, offering facilities little different from luxury hotels.

Combining work with leisure

A number of conference centres are being built in country areas where delegates are able to engage in relaxing leisure pursuits in their free time, such as fishing, golfing and walking. Famous examples are the conference venue at Castle Howard, in Yorkshire, the setting for *Brideshead Revisited*, and The Belfry, Wishaw, North Warwickshire, the home of the Ryder Cup, which has conference facilities for up to 300 people, plus two golf courses. Many hotels with conference facilities also have leisure complexes which conference delegates can use.

Theme parks

Theme parks are large commercial entertainment centres, with a common theme linking the different indoor and outdoor entertainments, and sometimes even the buildings, landscapes and staff uniforms. The original, and still the best known, theme park is Disneyland, in California, USA.

The attractions are designed to provide a full day's entertainment for both children and adults. Theme parks also cater to the growing teenager and elderly market, who have more money to spend on leisure than ever before.

Most theme parks are easy to reach by car and coach, and where there is no accommodation at the theme park itself, the area is usually well served with hotels, holiday centres, camping sites and caravan parks.

 FOR INTEREST

Theme parks in Britain are modelled on some of the famous theme parks of Europe and North America. For example, Center Parc Sherwood Forest Village in Nottinghamshire, which incorporates a theme park with a holiday village, takes many of its ideas from the famous parks in the Netherlands.

One of Europe's largest tourist attractions, with 2.3 million visitors every year, is De Efteling in the southern Netherlands. All the rides, gardens, and public buildings incorporate a common theme—the folklore creations for children of Anton Pieck, a famous Netherlands painter. One reason for its success is the park's continual investment in new facilities, such as water attractions, its beautiful parklike landscape, and its immaculate upkeep.

 TO DO

If possible, involve 4 to 6 of your colleagues in this activity. Split into two groups, one with the task of organising a short conference for a company represented by the second group.
  Separately:

- The client group should prepare as many questions as possible to find out about the facilities available.
- The organiser group should prepare a description of what facilities are available (one designed to appeal to the clients and persuade them to confirm the booking), and a checklist of what information is needed.

The groups should then meet, acting out their assumed roles. A note should be kept of questions not included on the client's list and of those not included on the organiser's list. Then add what other questions might be important as a result of the discussions.
  The following headings might help:

General conference details
Delegate details
Guest speakers
Accommodation requirements

- meeting rooms
- sleeping
- meals
- registration/administration

Social/leisure/entertainment activities
Arrangements for food and drinks, teas and coffees
Costs and payment details.

 FOR INTEREST

The theme of Thorpe Park, 21 miles south-west of London, is the history of the British people as a maritime nation. The attractions include a Roman port scene, complete with fighting gallery, Roman bath and temple.
  Below are some facts about Thorpe Park:

- education visits amount to over 10% of total attendance
- 40% of the total number of visitors annually come in August
- 45% of all visitors are children
- the average length of stay is 6 hours, 20 minutes
- the park is available for company days out
- in June the park reduces its prices for senior citizens.

The five biggest conference centres in the UK are:

- Barbican Conference Centre, London
- Brighton Centre
- Harrogate International Conference and Exhibition Centre
- Wembley Conference Centre
- Birmingham's National Exhibition Centre.

Establishments which cater for people who are elderly or unwell include National Health Service (NHS) hospitals, private hospitals and clinics, health care centres, mental institutions, hospices, and residential care homes for the elderly. The patients range from the newborn to the very old, and from the healthy, such as maternity patients, to the senile, who cannot look after themselves, and the dying.

Every type of patient has differing needs, and requires different forms of treatment, care and attention: *out-patients* attend a hospital clinic for treatment, including the accident and emergency wards. Only the *in-patients* are admitted for an overnight (or several nights) stay in the hospital.

Then there are the *day-patients*, who only stay in hospital during the daytime and sleep elsewhere, usually in their own homes. Many of these are mentally handicapped or mentally ill people.

Most of the hospitals in the UK are operated by the National Health Service. Some NHS hospitals have private wings or private wards, where patients pay for accommodation, food and treatment.

Private hospitals offer more luxurious facilities, and from the point of view of decor, furnishings, food and service, are comparable to high-class hotels.

Hospices provide care for the dying, offering control of pain and other symptoms, and psychological support for the patients and their families. Some hospices are funded by the NHS, and others are run by independent charities.

 FOR INTEREST

There are roughly 2000 NHS hospitals, with nearly half a million beds, which treat close to 5.5 million in-patients each year, and 840 health centres (for out-patient treatment).

Of the total number of NHS in-patients, roughly 85,000 are treated privately. In addition, there are 22 million out-patients, and 979,000 day cases. Because of improved methods of treatment, and also reduced funding in many of the NHS hospitals, length of stay in hospitals has declined over the past decade, and more people are being treated as day cases, or are being looked after at home.

The private medical sector has expanded in recent years and 4.5 million people are now insured for private health. It is also used by foreigners who come to Britain for medical treatment. But the private sector is still small compared with the National Health sector. While there are 1200 registered private hospitals in the UK, in England (where most of them are located) only 10% of hospital beds are in private hospitals and nursing homes.

 FOR INTEREST

In a hospital, the domestic service department has almost as many staff as the nursing department. In a hospital with 1000 or more beds, there should be roughly 700 full-time domestic assistants (or the equivalent).

Patient needs A hospital patient expects to be treated, cared-for and nursed. While in hospital, the patient requires clean, hygienic, warm and comfortable surroundings, and staff should by sympathetic, kind, caring and sensitive to their needs. The basic requirements of any hospital patient are a bed, food, somewhere to put away the few possessions that they have with them, and sanitary facilities. As they recover, many patients have time for leisure activities, so television sets, reading material and hospital radio services are usually provided. Most hospitals also have a shop which sells newspapers, books, sweets, notepaper etc., or a trolley of items for sale is taken round from ward to ward.

Long-stay patients may be put into wards which are specially planned for their benefit. Cheerful fabrics and decor make these wards a home-away-from-home for patients deprived of their home surroundings. These patients are also encouraged to bring more of their possessions from home.

Residential care homes

There are many different types, for a wide range of people. Some are privately owned, and others are owned and managed by local authorities. They include:

- convalescent homes
- hostels and shelters for the homeless
- homes for the mentally ill and mentally handicapped
- senior citizens' homes
- homes for the blind
- children's homes.

Length of stay partly depends on the nature of the institution. A person might stay for a night in a Salvation Army Hostel, and then move on somewhere else. The elderly and infirm, who can no longer look after themselves, usually remain in residential care homes until they die, unless they become physically ill and are moved to hospitals for treatment. Some psychiatric patients and mentally handicapped people have lived in residential homes for many years, although there is a growing trend to move them to so-called Halfway Houses, where they live in small groups under the supervision of a warden, before becoming independent.

 TO DO

Staff often use the establishment's services and facilities (such as staff canteen, restrooms etc.) and can also be regarded as customers. A hospital, for example, must cater in various ways not only for patients but for doctors and nurses, who must be fed and perhaps even housed, and for visitors, tradespeople and maintenance staff, who may need waiting rooms, canteen services, toilets and so on.

The types of customer at a typical hospital can therefore be split into two groups:

Patients	*Other users*
Patients staying on the wards (in-patients)	Resident staff
Patients visiting clinics	Nursing and medical staff
Accident and emergency patients } (out-patients)	Visitors
	Tradespeople
	Maintenance staff
Patients visiting on a daily basis and returning home at night (day patients)	Delivery people

Make your own list of the main customer groups and other users for either a hotel or a hall of residence at a college or university.

Schools

The total school-going population in the UK is just under ten million. Around 94% of school children attend one of the 36,500 schools supported by local education authorities. The balance (some 500,000) go to the 2500 private, or independent, fee-paying schools.

Most school children attend school while living at home. But there are boarding schools where children live during the term (or week, in the case of weekly boarders). There they are housed, fed and looked after, at fees of up to £2500 per term in private schools.

Colleges, polytechnics, and universities

Post-school educational institutions are universities, polytechnics, colleges of further education and higher education, art colleges, agricultural colleges, colleges of technology, secretarial schools and other specialist establishments. The term 'further education' refers to all post-school education apart from the universities and polytechnics, which provide 'higher education'.

Accommodation in educational establishments

Accommodation is provided for tuition (academic accommodation), and in some institutions residential accommodation is also available.

The *academic accommodation* covers lecture rooms or class rooms; specialist rooms such as training kitchens, laboratories; offices; library and media rooms; student union rooms; common rooms for students and for staff; catering facilities and sporting facilities.

Residential accommodation includes

- dormitories (for boarding schools)
- halls of residence with full catering and domestic services
- student flats or apartments
- student houses.

In boarding schools, most children sleep in communal dormitories with several other children. These may be completely open, or divided with partitions or curtains into separate bed spaces or cubicles. At a few public schools, the older children are given their own bedroom-cum-study. Besides sleeping accommodation, there are common rooms, study rooms, sick rooms, dining rooms, staff quarters, sanitary facilities etc.

Universities, polytechnics and other colleges of further education normally put up students not living at home or in private accommodation in halls of residence, either for both men and women students, or single sex. There are some which only take in foreign students. A few rooms in the hall are often used by academic staff, domestic and catering managers, and sometimes by visitors.

Many halls offer a combination of single, twin or triple rooms. Occasionally married quarters are also provided. As students are either on grants or being paid for by their parents, they cannot be expected to pay much for their room, and this is reflected in the standard of accommodation. However, with good planning, the rooms can be made to look very attractive, with enough space to move about with ease and kept warm, draught free, clean and well lit, with private or communal washing facilities with hot running water. A desk or table and chair is necessary for

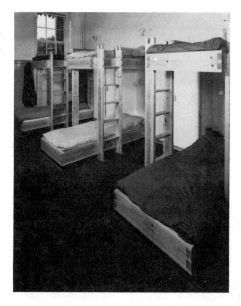

> **✻ FOR INTEREST**
>
> In the mid 1980s, about 972,000 students were enrolled for full-time courses at universities and colleges of further education. There are 47 universities and 30 polytechnics in Britain, as well as a small number of private universities and colleges. Most of the students are between the ages of 18 and 22, but some are older ('mature' students).

study purposes. Students bring many of their own possessions to improve the appearance and comfort.

A hall of residence usually has a laundry, kitchen/pantry facilities for student use, a common room and/or television room, a dining room, and a storage room for trunks and suitcases. Some halls, especially in universities, contain a licensed bar. Some halls provide at least two meals a day, seven days a week; others have facilities for students to cater fully for themselves.

Other facilities are:

- entrance hall or foyer, with porter or caretaker's desk
- areas for entertaining visitors
- pay phone
- library
- games room
- bicycle storage room
- sick bay with nursing and medical facilities.

 TO DO

Many halls of residence are expected to be self-funding, so they supplement their income by offering accommodation for conferences, tourist groups, bed and breakfast and self-catering visitors during the 5-month vacation period.

Write a brief report on how your local university, polytechnic or college supplements its income, describing the sort of activities it gets involved in. What extra action would you suggest to make better use of its accommodation facilities?

Fulfilling customer expectations

Accommodation establishments always have to be ready to respond to customer expectations, and to anticipate future requirements. If guests get what they expect, then the chances are that they will come back again, or recommend the place to their friends and colleagues. If they are dissatisfied, they will not.

Establishments may have to upgrade their facilities in order to keep their position in the market, especially when other establishments are improving theirs. Or they may decide to take the first step to improve standards of service and maintenance. However, before embarking on any expansion or improvement programme, they need to be sure what their market is, what customers expect, and what sort of customers they can hope to attract with additional facilities.

An example of different customer expectations and spending power
A student hall of residence provides accommodation for students studying at that centre of learning. So the establishment has to offer various facilities which the students require and can afford to pay for: basic room and toilet facilities, basic food, meeting centre, pub etc. There is no sense in offering more than students can afford to pay for, as these extra facilities will be wasted. However, in recent years, student residences are being turned into conference venues during the holiday periods when students are away. This means that the residence has in addition to cater for a new type of customer, often with more money and greater expectations of luxury. One way that residences are trying to attract conference convenors is to plan all new buildings with conferences in mind, as well as student requirements. The residences may keep better quality linen for conference users, and provide extra domestic cleaning services during this period. In short, the residence has to be organised with both markets in mind, students with limited resources, and conference organisers with greater resources. Their conflicting requirements may sometimes be difficult to meet.

Test yourself: Units 1–6

City and Guilds

1. Give as many reasons as you can (at least six) why a person may *choose* to stay away from home overnight.
2. State at least three reasons why a person may *have* to stay away from home for one or more nights.
3. For each of the reasons you have given to questions 1 and 2, name one type of residential accommodation establishment where the person might stay.
4. Give five reasons why the owners of an establishment should know about their customers?
5. Describe briefly five different types of hotel.
6. What type of customer do holiday camps mainly cater for?
7. Give an example of the way in which each of the following types of accommodation operation have changed to meet new customer needs: (a) hotels, (b) halls of residence, (c) holiday camps.
8. Name three examples of types of residential home.

First impressions are crucial, and the most powerful first impressions are formed by the looks of an establishment. Design, decoration and furnishings can prejudice customers strongly in favour of an establishment—or equally firmly against it. A customer will be favourably impressed if the outside of a hotel or hospital looks smart and well cared for, and the inside is clean, well planned and attractively furnished. On the other hand, a run-down appearance and careless decor are bound to put customers off, and will immediately raise further doubts—about cleanliness of toilet areas and kitchens, or the quality of the food, or of health care (in the case of hospitals).

The customer's needs

Obviously, not every customer can shop around for the most attractively-packaged accommodation. A prisoner has no choice but to accept the accommodation provided. A person receiving medical treatment in a National Health hospital will be sent to a hospital with the appropriate residential and medical facilities. But an ill person who is covered by medical insurance or who can afford to go to a private hospital for treatment may choose a particular private hospital because the rooms are spacious, comfortable and attractive.

A traveller passing through a one-hotel village will likewise have no option, although there may be a choice of several places to eat—a corner café, an Indian restaurant, a bistro with views of the river, or a country house a few miles outside the village which has been converted into a restaurant.

Where people do have a choice, the quality of the design is decisive. How, for example, does a traveller choose one hotel instead of another? He/she makes a quick check on price and services—and then chooses the establishment which *looks* the most promising.

What interior design covers

The aim of the interior designer is to create a usable area, with an appropriate mood or theme that takes special account of the activities which are to take place in it. Is it going to be used successfully for eating, sleeping, reading the newspaper, or doing physical exercises? Will it be abused or vandalised? Will it be comfortable?

The *practical* or *functional* aspects of the design, such as ease of cleaning or how long the attractive appearance will be retained (see unit 8), must be kept in mind alongside the *psychological* aspects: how will the user of the room react to the design, and will the design contribute to the overall image or theme which the designer is trying to put across?

Time, effort and money may well be wasted if even one element is not right or has been overlooked. An inappropriate picture, or the wrong colour waste paper bin, will spoil the final appearance of the room.

The style selected will also be influenced by the following factors:

- style of architecture, size and shape of building and of the rooms within
- company policy on design
- current fashion relating to themes, materials, colour schemes.

The interior designer may choose one theme for the entire establishment, to give the building a common identity, or select a particular theme for most of the bedrooms for example, but individual themes for the suites, where the guests enjoy a more personal style and will book specific suites.

Standardisation of design

In recent years, many hotels have standardised, in varying degrees, the style of decor, furnishings, furniture and room layout. Some hotel chains have even standardised not just the single bedrooms of a particular hotel, for example, but all bedrooms throughout the chain: a bedroom in the north of England will be exactly the same as a bedroom in London, including the carpet, curtains, bedspread and wallpaper!

Standardisation helps to create what is known as 'corporate image'. Guests begin to recognise a particular style (and standard) and come to expect exactly the same style and standard in all of the chain's hotels.

But many people dislike standardisation because it has eliminated much of the novelty and excitement of travel. Hotels of the same chain may be practically identical, even if one is in Tokyo and the other in Sydney, hence the famous quip, "If it's Sunday, this must be Brussels." One consequence is that many travellers prefer older hotels which retain character and individuality, even if they are not so convenient.

For the owners or operators of establishments, standardisation means they can buy in bulk and get a larger discount. They also need to make fewer decisions about decoration, but standardisation can make the work of the cleaning staff more monotonous.

Effect of design on staff

If the working environment is pleasant and welcoming, staff are more likely to be comfortable, committed and efficient. By contrast, staff who are forced to work in a dirty and drab environment are likely to stop caring about their own appearance and the impression that they make on the customer (see unit 19).

The quality of the working environment also influences staff turnover (how often people leave and have to be replaced), speed and efficiency of work, accident rates, and number of sick days taken.

Designing for appearance: a checklist

Space
Does the room feel crowded, cluttered, empty, spacious?

Colour
1. Do the colours suit the size and shape of the room?
2. How are the colours affected by natural and artificial lighting? Do they reflect or absorb light?

Materials
Does the appearance of the materials selected for curtains, furniture, walls, floors and sanitary fittings contribute to the overall atmosphere of the room?

Furniture
Does the furniture blend in well with the other design features, for example curtains, carpets and lights?

Fittings
1. Do the fittings—doors, windows, sanitary fittings—suit the room's design and layout?
2. How do they contribute to the atmosphere of the room?

Pattern
1. Is the use of pattern satisfactory? Is there too much or too little? Do any of the patterns clash?
2. Is the scale of the patterns satisfactory in relation to the room's size?

Texture
1. Is there an interesting variety of textures?
2. Have natural items, such as wood and brick been used to good effect?

Lighting
Does the lighting contribute to the mood and atmosphere created in the room?

Heating and ventilation
Are the heating appliances and ventilation grilles attractive, or do they mar the room's appearance?

Room accessories
How do the accessories, such as waste bins, ashtrays, pictures and plants, contribute to the room's atmosphere and fit in with the decor?

 **TO DO**

Select an area of a public building such as a bar, a restaurant, a hotel reception or a hospital waiting area. Make a list of the design points you like and those you dislike, with your reasons.

A successful design depends not only on what the building looks like, and the effect that this creates on the user, but also on practical considerations. It must function well, and in order to do so, the designer must be conscious of the following points:

1. Not to lose sight of the kind of establishment and the type of customers. A maternity hospital caters for a different type of user to a hospital for incurables, and must therefore be designed differently.

2. Maintenance: there is little point in installing deep pile carpets at a seaside hotel, as in no time these will become clogged with sand. Textures may be important for their appearance, but they also affect the way in which light and sound are absorbed or reflected.

3. Durability: good materials cost more initially, but last longer than cheaper alternatives. This is particularly important in public buildings as customers are seldom as careful about furniture or furnishings as they are in their own homes.

4. Energy conservation is a crucial consideration. New buildings generally incorporate high standards of insulation in exterior walls, double glazed windows and sometimes sophisticated heat exchange systems so that heat created in kitchens, laundries and similar areas can be used to warm water. Older buildings can be fitted with roof insulation, secondary glazing on the windows and, for example, computerised heating and lighting controls.

5. Ensuring the smooth flow of staff and customers and of goods and services. For example a hospital plan must take into account the needs of the patients themselves, of their visitors, of the medical, catering and domestic staff, so that communications are good and supplies and services can be efficiently organised.

6. Meeting health, hygiene, fire and safety requirements.

7. Security, both of customers and operators. For example, front office staff should be able to keep an eye on all guests entering and leaving the premises.

8. Comfort: the design should always have the size and shape of the user in mind. A chair may fit in perfectly with the decor, but if it is too small or too big for the users, it is likely to cause them discomfort and possible pain. Another consideration is avoidance of fatigue.

9. Flexibility: if an area is designed for several uses, then the furnishings and space arrangements should be flexible.

The functional aspects of design: a checklist

Space
1. How much space is needed for the activities which have to be carried out in the room?
2. Is the most economical use made of it?

Colour
1. Do the colours hide the dirt or not?
2. Is the colour scheme practical—can it be cleaned?

Materials and surfaces
1. Are they likely to last well?
2. Are they resistant to dirt, and hygienic?
3. Are they easy and economical to clean and maintain?
4. Are they fire resistant?

Furniture
1. Is the furniture layout practical? Does it allow for movement and circulation in the area?
2. Is it functional, durable, well constructed, easy to move around, and can it be stacked?
3. Is it comfortable and designed to the recommended dimensions in relation to the body?

Lighting
1. Does the lighting level and distribution of light seem efficient for the activities for which the room was designed?
2. Have the amount of natural light and the direction the room faces been considered?
3. Can the room user control the amount of light required, and can the amount of light be changed in different parts of the room?
4. How easy is the lighting to clean, and can worn-out light bulbs be replaced easily?

Heating and ventilation
1. How is heating lost from the area?
2. Can the room user easily control the temperature of the heating and put it on or off?
3. Is ventilation adequate and easy to operate and control?

Sound insulation
1. Is noise transmitted from the room to other areas, and from outside into the room? If so, how?
2. Have any measures been taken to prevent the transmission of noise, such as the use of sound absorbent materials, double glazing or double doors?

Circulation diagram

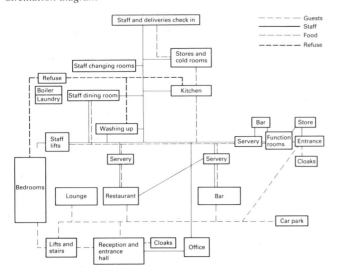

Designing for the disabled: a checklist

Easy access is very important: cars carrying disabled people should be able to stop just outside the main entrance (or an alternative entrance which is well signposted). Reserved parking should be provided for disabled drivers.

Doors should be wide enough for a wheelchair to pass through, and open automatically, or by pressing a conveniently located button, or by a gentle push.

Where a change of level is necessary, a lift (with wide doors and convenient controls) or a ramp should be provided.

Bedroom doors should be fitted with locks that can be easily operated from a wheelchair and entry controlled from the bed.

Special public lavatories should be provided to allow wheelchair access to the WC, wash hand basin, its taps, the mirror, towel dispenser/hand dryer and drinking fountain.

Bedrooms and bathrooms should allow enough space for wheelchairs to move about easily, and the fittings should be at a convenient height, for example low level clothes storage, support rails by the toilet and bath.

Signs should be easy to read with large lettering against a contrasting background, and preferably raised lettering. Fire notices should be provided in Braille.

Wherever possible, warning signals should be visible as well as audible, for example strobe light alarms for the deaf and a vibrator to alert them when they are asleep.

Handrails should be designed to help warn the blind and those with poor vision of approaching corners and the start and end of stairs.

Doors should be hung or fitted with a closing mechanism so that they do not remain half open.

Sharp corners and edges should be avoided.

Glass doors and full length windows should be marked with a contrasting band (roughly at waist height).

Dining room tables and desks should be high enough for the person to not have to be transferred from a wheelchair.

▶ ▶ ▶ TO DO

Using this checklist, make a note of any improvements that should be made to the establishment where you work, or one of your choice.

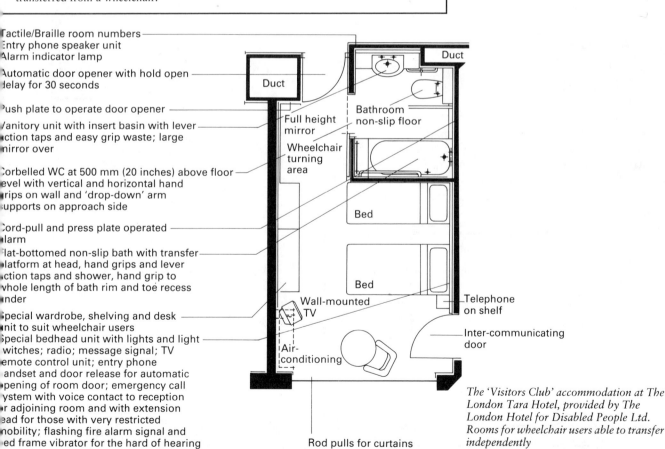

The 'Visitors Club' accommodation at The London Tara Hotel, provided by The London Hotel for Disabled People Ltd. Rooms for wheelchair users able to transfer independently

9 APPRECIATION OF DESIGN

Hotel bedrooms come in a variety of shapes and sizes, particularly in old buildings. On the other hand, the shapes and layouts of bedrooms in many new hotel buildings are standardised, although the rooms themselves can be furnished in a number of different ways. The arrangement is largely dictated by how many beds there are in the room.

Each hotel needs to have its own combination of the various types of bedroom: doubles, singles, suites, family rooms and so forth, depending on the type of guests who patronise it. For example, a hotel whose customers are mostly families will have few, if any, single bedrooms. Where necessary, a twin or double room can be offered at a reduced rate to a single guest. Generally hotels prefer to have more double than single rooms, even those that largely cater for business guests. A room for two takes up little more space than a single room, but offers greater flexibility.

Most modern hotel bedrooms are designed for one to four people, who may all be doing different things: one person may want to sleep, while another may be watching television or getting dressed. An ideal plan would ensure that every occupant has some private space.

A modern hotel bedroom usually has an *en-suite* bathroom, that is its own private bathroom leading directly off the room. The extra space needed for an *en-suite* bathroom is relatively small—a small but adequate bathroom takes up only 1.7 square metres (2 square yards).

The size of a bedroom will depend on the type and standard of hotel, what sort of room it is (that is single, family etc.) and on company policy. It has to fit in with the width and length of the building, which in turn depends on the shape and size of the building site.

Trends in bedroom design

Many of the large hotel chains offer several types of bedroom to suit the different types of customer. The bed and other furnishings are selected to fit in with the image of the room.

For example, bedrooms for business guests aim to create an atmosphere which is suitable both for working and relaxing. As many business guests work in their hotel rooms, there must be a proper desk, with lighting at the correct working height (instead of a dressing table and mirror), as well as the usual colour television, radio and so on. But where there is no one clearly defined target group, bedrooms must be adaptable to suit a range of tastes and requirements so that they can be sold to any customer.

TO DO

Write a short description of the decor and design of a typical bedroom in your local hotel. Suggest some reasons for particular design choices, dividing your list into two categories: practical/ functional and appearance/atmosphere. Are any of the rooms designed for a specific target group? If so what is the intended mood?

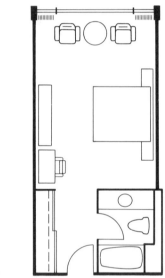

The traditional hotel bedroom is rectangular in shape with the window as a focal point. Dimensions range from 3.8 m (12 ft 6 in) by 7.6 m (25 ft) to 4.3 m (14 ft) by 8.5 m (28 ft) including the bathroom. Deeper rooms often feature a sitting zone by the window or in the window bay. The bathroom provides the only clear private space

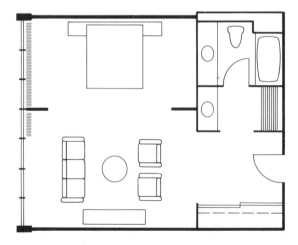

A square room provides a clearer distinction between the private bed area and the sitting area, but requires more space: 41.5–46 square metres (50–55 square yards) compared with 30–37 square metres (36–44 square yards) for the traditional rectangular room. It also takes up two bays (a rectangular room takes up one bay only) and requires about one-third more window space

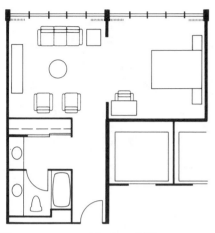

Alcove rooms provide about 20% more space than the square room, yet save the equivalent of half a bay. This shape is therefore ideal for the area adjacent to lifts and stairs

Suites vary considerably in size and shape. A square arrangement (left in the diagram) means both the bedroom and sitting room have an exterior window. The alternative rectangular arrangement (shown right) was developed in all-suite hotels in North America and is spreading in popularity. It is particularly suitable when the access to the room is off an open corridor surrounding a large atrium in the centre of the building. The sitting room then benefits from the natural lighting and landscaped environment created in the atrium

Bedroom design choices for specific target groups
Example: a 150-room city hotel

60 executive twins with all the necessary facilities for male business executives, including a well-equipped and well-lit working area, luxurious mahogany or black ash furniture, smartly decorated in a style appropriate to the guests' lifestyle and self-image.

10 double rooms/meeting rooms with units rather like wardrobe shells in which the bed can be hidden during the daytime, and replaced by a table and chairs for a meeting of up to eight people.

2 twin-bedded rooms for disabled guests with extra-wide doorways to provide wheelchair access, doors which can open and close automatically, low placed switches and fixtures, and enough space between fittings so that wheelchair users can get about.

5 single rooms for lady executives with the same facilities as the male executive rooms, but the fabrics and wallcoverings are more delicate, the furniture is lighter, and there are additional features such as an illuminated make-up mirror in the lid of the desk and a full-length mirror behind the wardrobe door.

73 standard twin-bedded rooms with attractive but relatively plain furniture and decor.

Bed   Beds come in different sizes and are either single, double, queen size or king size. A hotel bed should be of the best quality, constructed to withstand heavy use, and comfortable. The edge must be firm, for many guests will sit on it, even when an armchair is provided. It must be possible to clean underneath the bed, but the bed must not be so high that guests have difficulty getting into it, or so low that bedmaking becomes difficult. Castors are needed so that the bed can be moved for cleaning, but the bed should not move while a guest is in it!

Bedheads are attached to the bed or to the wall, to protect the wall from greasy headmarks.

Bedside table/cabinet/console   A bedside cabinet may be combined with a console, which houses the wake-up call/message system and controls for the television, radio, room lighting and ventilation. The top should be at the same level as the top of the bed so that the guest can easily reach personal items such as books, glasses, his/her watch, and if there is a cabinet with a door, the door should open away from the bed. A double bed will have a bedside table on each side.

Dressing table/desk and stool   This is useful for keeping cosmetics, electric razors and hair brushes. It may also contain drawers or shelves for storing clothes and other personal items. There should be a well illuminated mirror behind the table.

In a small room, the dressing table may double as a desk, so there should be space for papers and documents, and for working. Beverage making facilities may be kept on it.

The dressing table stool should be the right height with adequate knee clearance, so that guests can sit comfortably and see in the mirror. When the table doubles as a desk, a chair with good back support is usually provided instead of a stool.

Luggage rack   Luggage racks avoid the need for guests to leave their suitcases on chairs (this can damage the chair) or on the floor (cleaning is made much more difficult). The rack may be fixed to a wall or be a fold-up portable type (either made of wood or with metal legs and canvas or plastic straps). It should not be too high above the ground, because heavy suitcases are rather difficult to lift.

Storage space for clothes   The amount of storage space provided for clothes depends on the average length of stay of the guests and the degree of luxury provided by the hotel. It should be large enough to store items comfortably, without creasing them, in drawers, or on shelves and by hanging them up. The hanging clothes rail should be strong and fitted with sufficient coat hangers, (preferably the type fixed on to the rail as they cannot be removed).

Wardrobes and chests of drawers are often fitted or built into the room; if not, they should always be sturdy and well balanced, so they cannot easily topple over.

Closed wardrobes and drawers are often preferred to open hanging space and shelves because they give greater privacy, protect clothes from dust, and give the room a tidier appearance. But wardrobes without doors are easier to clean, and guests are less likely to leave clothes behind. A useful wardrobe fixture is an interior light which goes on when the wardrobe is opened.

In some hotels the cupboard units house not only clothes but small safes (guests usually have to pay a small fee to use them and a deposit for the key), vanitory units, mini-bars, even cooking equipment (where self-catering rooms are provided), iron and ironing board.

 ▶ ▶ ▶ TO DO

Find out as much information as you can about the sizes, quality and cost of beds and mattresses that might be suitable for a hotel room of your choice (for example budget room, business executive room, honeymoon suite). Write a report briefly stating your recommendations.

Seating An easy chair may be provided for guests, depending on the size of the room and hotel classification. Larger twin or double rooms usually have at least two chairs and sometimes a settee if guests are likely to have visitors to their room.

Lamps Many hotel rooms do not have a central light. Instead a number of smaller lamps are used to provide localised light: a lamp next to or above the bed (two for a double room), a good standard lamp for reading, a light to illuminate the dressing mirror, and a desk lamp, for example.

Long mirror This is required because many guests like to dress in front of a mirror or at least check their final appearance. The long mirror may be in the wardrobe or attached to the back of the room door.

TV A colour TV is usually provided often with an integral radio and extra channels to show in-house films. Some hotels provide a video. The TV may be placed on an extension of the dressing table, on a table or stand of its own, or mounted on the wall to make the best use of space.

Coffee table This is especially useful when a room has space for easy chairs and room service is provided for snacks and drinks.

Waste bins and ashtrays These must not be overlooked. Guests need somewhere to dispose of their rubbish and (unless it is a designated non-smokers room) their cigarette ends.

Pictures, wall hangings and other ornaments These often play an important role in creating a pleasant appearance. In some hotels the picture frames are fixed to the wall so they cannot be stolen, but de luxe hotels often decorate guest suites with valuable paintings, antiques and delicate china ornaments.

Telephone Most hotel rooms now have a telephone for making in-house calls (for example to request room service), for receiving calls and for making outside calls via the switchboard operator or receptionist. More and more hotel telephones enable guests to dial their own calls, both locally and long-distance. The cost of the call is automatically recorded so it can be added to the guest's bill.

Bathroom furniture and fittings

Bath
A bath may incorporate a shower unit (and shower curtain), giving the guest a choice between taking a bath or a shower.

Shower
A shower unit is sometimes provided instead of a bath where there is not enough space for a full bathroom. (A shower uses less water than a bath, so a hot shower uses less energy than a hot bath.) Most luxury bathrooms have both a bath and a separate shower unit.

Toilet
This may be a pedestal type or fixed to the wall (cantilevered), leaving the floor free and making cleaning easier.

Bidet
Many luxury bathrooms contain a bidet (a low basin that guests can sit on and wash their genitals and anal area).

Wash hand basin
In modern bathrooms, the wash hand basin is usually set into a vanitory unit, giving space around it for toiletries and cosmetics, soap, tooth mugs etc.

Mirror
A mirror with good lighting and a shaver socket is a necessity: for washing, shaving and putting on make-up.

Heated towel rail
This is very useful as it keeps towels warm and dry. It can also be used to dry underwear and other small garments which guests may wish to wash themselves.

Waste bin
Two bins should be provided, one for ordinary rubbish, and one (which must have a lid) for used sanitary towels or tampons.

Washing line
Some bathrooms contain a retractable washing line fixed to the wall, to dry underwear, tights and other small clothing items.

Additional fittings
Depending on the level of luxury provided, these will include such things as a hair dryer, bathroom scales, telephone, tissue holders, double vanitory units and jacuzzi.

Any hospital plan must take into account in-patient accommodation, medical diagnostic and treatment facilities, and consider these two areas in relation to each other so that there can be effective communication between the two areas, and so that supplies and services can be efficiently organised. A plan should also consider the type of patient (elderly, children, orthopaedic, terminally ill, maternity, for example) and the most economical use of staff, space, equipment and services.

Ward areas

Ward areas may be single bedded or multi-bedded. Some private hospitals only provide single rooms and National Health Service hospitals usually have a number for private patients as well as for NHS patients who are likely to infect others, for those who cannot risk being infected because of the nature of their illness or treatment, for the very seriously ill, and for patients who disturb others.

There should be enough space in a single room for the patient who is able to get out of bed to sit, eat and wash, and space for nursing staff to work in and for any medical equipment that is required. Single rooms normally contain a bed, bedside locker, over-bed table, wash hand basin, an easy chair, and one or two upright chairs for visitors. A reading lamp and the radio controls and headphones are fixed to the wall at the head of the bed, within easy reach of the patient. Some single rooms have an attached private bathroom, which may be shared with the adjoining single room. Some hospitals also provide hanging wardrobe space, a television set and telephone.

The room and bed should be arranged in such a way that staff can see the patient at a glance from the door or through a window from the nursing station and easily monitor his or her condition. There is a 'help' button for patient and staff use in each room.

Multi-bedded wards may contain two, four, six, and, in what is known as a Nightingale ward, up to 30 beds lined up on either side of the room. To make the surroundings cosier, more intimate and home like, many of the large open ward areas in older hospitals have been divided into smaller wards. These are known as 'cubiclised' ward areas.

The multi-bedded wards contain the same basic furniture as a single room. Noisy items, such as televisions, are sometimes kept in the day room (a lounge for patients). A pay phone on a mobile trolley can be wheeled from bed to bed and plugged into a wall socket behind the bed.

A cubicle curtain is provided for each bed space, hung on a curtain track around the bed.

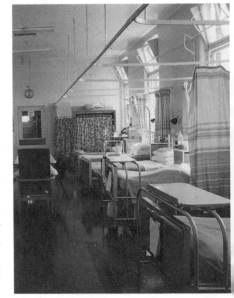

Day areas

The day room offers a change of scenery, which is intended to encourage patients to get out of bed as quickly as possible after an operation or illness. There patients can read, write, watch television, talk and eat meals. Furniture includes easy chairs, a dining table and chairs, side tables and magazine racks. The decor is deliberately bright and cheerful in order to raise patients' spirits. The day room is usually separate from the ward, and has self-closing doors so that the noise does not disturb patients in the ward.

Sanitary facilities for patients

Sanitary facilities are baths, showers, wash hand basins, toilets and bidets. General guidelines recommend how many sanitary fittings there should be, and the amount of space required. There must be enough space and furniture around a bath for nursing staff, who may need to assist patients with bathing. Some patients have to be lifted from the trolley or wheelchair into the bath, either manually or with the aid of a hoist. Some need special 'treatment' baths, and may have to have their dressings replaced before and after bathing, so tables have to be provided or wheeled in.

Hand washing, shaving and hair washing are also done in the sanitary areas, and disabled patients in wheelchairs require special facilities. Safety cannot be ignored: 'help' buttons in every bathroom, toilet, shower and washing area are for patients who find themselves locked into a closed room and need assistance. There should be sanitary facilities at both ends of a large ward, so that patients from each end can get to these areas without difficulty. Male and female patients usually have separate facilities. There must be a toilet near the day room.

In children's wards, sanitary fittings are smaller and placed lower. In wards for elderly or disabled people, various mechanical aids make certain tasks easier, for example, getting in and out of a bath, or on and off a toilet.

▶ ▶ ▶ TO DO

Visit a local hospital and write a brief report on the decor and furniture used in a ward area and day room.

Some of the design considerations for NHS hospital furniture and fittings

Beds
Metal framed for hygiene purposes and ease of damp dusting, with mattress and pillows which are encased in strong polythene covers to protect them from spillages. Height adjustable for ease of access, bedmaking, and to assist recovery for some cases.

Cubicle curtains
Plastic curtain track with curtains made from fibres which can be laundered at high temperatures to kill any germs and which will not shed fibres. There must be enough room inside for staff to work easily when privacy is required and the curtains are drawn.

Easy chairs
Wooden frame with vinyl upholstery to prevent spills soaking in and for easy cleaning. The seat should be the right height for patients to get up out of the chair easily.

Upright chairs
Metal and polypropylene (a type of plastic) stacking chairs.

Wash hand basins
With elbow operated taps in nursing areas to prevent touching with infected hands, and standing waste to allow easier cleaning and prevent build up of hairs in plug hole.

Bedside lockers
Plastic laminate and metal for hygiene and ease of cleaning. Space on top for flowers, cards, fruit, water jug and glass and inside for some clothes, clean nightwear, dressing gown, towel and sponge bag etc. Rubbish bag attached to side.

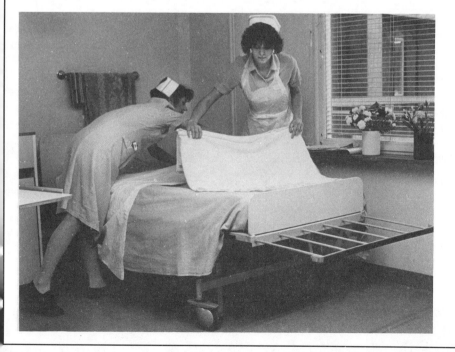

In some halls of residence, rooms are grouped on a corridor or 'hotel' plan with bedrooms arranged on either side of the corridor, and also toilets and bathrooms, pantry and cleaner's room (which contains a sluice and where rubbish is taken for disposal).

Another common arrangement of rooms is around a staircase.

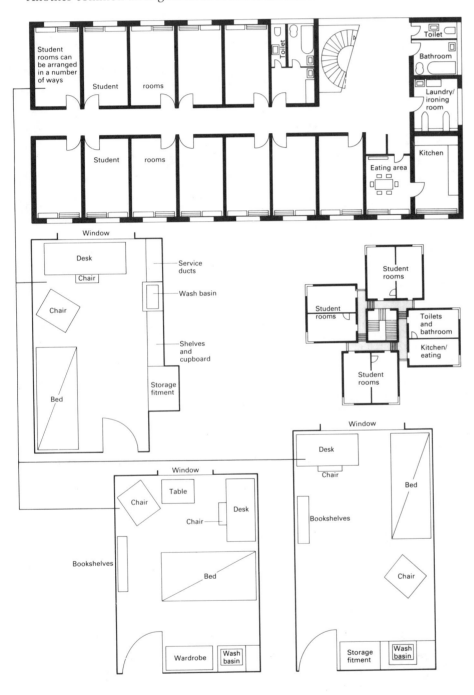

The study bedroom—furnishings and fittings

A study bedroom must be warm and cosy, and must contain the bare essentials. A bed, provided for sleeping, is sometimes also used as a settee during the daytime. In a studio bed arrangement, the bed is in the corner, and a padded head board is attached to the wall along the length of the bed to provide a backrest for people sitting on it.

Where economical use has to be made of space, bunk beds are useful: two people may sleep in the same amount of space required for one bed, or a bed is at the top level, and a desk or work station arrangement is directly underneath.

A worktop or desk is essential. This should be the correct height and large enough to spread out papers and books. It may also double as a dressing table (under the lid there is space for cosmetics and toiletries, and a mirror is attached to the underside of the lid). Another necessity is a wardrobe, and shelf or drawer space where students can keep their clothes.

Wash hand basins may or may not be provided. In some halls, washing facilities are still open and communal, but in halls which also offer conference accommodation, there are usually basins in every room.

If there is space, rooms will also contain an upholstered chair and a coffee table.

✳ FOR INTEREST

Especially in the bigger towns and cities, hostel accommodation is provided for the homeless, for the young, for religious groups, and for those with a shared interest (such as same job or country of origin). The hostels vary in the degree of comfort provided, but many are similar to halls of residence.

➧ ➧ ➧ TO DO

Visit a student hall of residence or hostel and make a plan of a typical student room, including details of the furniture and notes on the furnishings and decor. List any touches or personal belongings the student has used to make the room look more attractive.

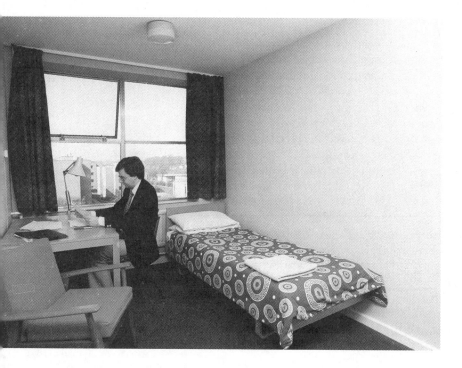

Surfaces These vary, but usually the walls are painted, so that they can be cleaned and redecorated easily and cheaply. Students like to brighten up a room by sticking up posters and photographs. To avoid the walls being damaged it is a good idea to provide a board for these (usually made of cork).

Floor coverings also vary: some rooms have cork, vinyl or linoleum, with or without a rug. Carpets are becoming more common, as they retain the heat, reduce noise levels and are an advantage when trying to attract conferences. (Many halls of residence supplement their income by offering conference accommodation during the holiday periods, see unit 4.)

Public areas include the reception area, lounges, restaurants, bars, reading rooms, banquet rooms and halls, conference and meeting rooms, circulation areas (lifts, stairs, and corridors) and sanitary areas.

The reception area

The reception area is usually the first area that a guest, member, visitor, student or conference delegate enters. It is a principal focal point of most establishments and its design and decor will make an immediate impression. Some large modern hotels, conference centres and private hospitals have achieved this through startling design features such as glass lifts, huge glass atria (creating a feeling of space), the lavish use of foliage plants (often high quality artificial ones), and even waterfalls. But at the same time, given the flow of people through this area, a reception area must be totally functional. Hotel guests, for example, will arrive with luggage, proceed to the reception desk to register, possibly have to wait behind other new arrivals until a receptionist is free, then proceed to their rooms, the restaurant, bars, conference centres and so on.

There must be ample space to cope with this traffic, for storing suitcases and other luggage, for people to wait before departure or to meet friends. The furnishings must be able to withstand the considerable wear and tear. Ideally both guests and staff should be able to see outside so they know when transport has arrived, for example, taxis or coaches. It is also important for security reasons that staff are able to see who is entering and leaving the establishment (see unit 58).

As people will go from the reception area to all other parts of the building, the circulation areas should be clearly signposted and readily accessible, even to those confined to wheelchairs, with no or very poor vision, or otherwise disabled.

Public lounges, TV rooms, reading rooms and bars

With thoughtful design, these areas should provide enough space to cater for large numbers of guests while at the same time allowing for privacy and intimacy. By grouping furniture around focal points, the scale of a large area can be reduced. When these areas are relatively empty, a guest should not feel uncomfortable and exposed.

Guests will be more inclined to use these facilities if the design is enticing and the decor and furnishings are well maintained.

 TO DO

Look in your local or college library at some of the magazines and reference books aimed at conference organisers. List the points that are claimed to be special, or even unique, of the different conference venues which are described in articles, listings or advertisements.

Once you have made your list, rank the items in importance according to your own preference—you might find it helpful to imagine you were put in charge of organising a particular type of conference, for example for eminent surgeons to hear about a new brain scanner, or for local conservationists to express their views on plans to build a new ring road.

Conference and meeting rooms

These vary in size from rooms designed to accommodate a group between two and ten, to rooms large enough for 500 or more people. Some large rooms can be used for two or more smaller functions by pulling across partitions which run on tracks in the floor and ceiling and fold away when not required, either flat against the wall or into a special cupboard. Each area of the room has its own lighting controls and any other necessary facilities.

Ideally a meeting room should not have any pillars, which may restrict viewing in some areas and complicate or limit furniture arrangements.

A platform may be required, a lectern and, of course, the appropriate number of chairs, arranged according to the wishes of the conference organiser (see unit 50).

Good air-conditioning and heating systems are a must. The room should be warm enough for comfort, but it must not be stuffy. Without air-conditioning to remove stale air, delegates are liable to doze off.

The room should be well lit, but the lighting must not be too harsh. Lighting must also be controlled easily so that it can be dimmed, for example if slides, films or videos are shown. If there are windows they should have good quality curtains capable of shutting out all daylight if required.

A good sound amplification system will enable speakers to be heard and good sound insulation will prevent noise spreading to other areas or noise from other areas coming into the conference room.

There must be sufficient power points for all the electrical equipment to be used: overhead projectors, videos, computers, closed television circuits, and so forth.

Large display boards may be required by the organisers, so doors should be wide enough for them to be brought in.

Conference suites and large meeting rooms often have their own washrooms and toilet facilities. Some may even have a small kitchen or pantry so that snacks and refreshments can be quickly prepared and served. Storerooms for spare furniture and equipment should be conveniently located.

Not all exhibitions can be accommodated in regular conference or meeting rooms, so some hotels and the larger conference centres have specially designed halls for very large exhibitions. These have high ceilings, doors that are high and wide enough to get large items in and out, and a floor able to take very heavy equipment. In addition to the usual services, running water, gas, high voltage power points, underfloor TV and computer cabling are provided.

Security

Conference delegates must be safe from possible attack when in the conference room, or when moving between rooms.

Some conference equipment is very valuable and should be carefully protected against theft.

Furniture in conference and meeting rooms

Conference delegates usually have to sit for long periods and pay careful attention, so chairs must be comfortable, and upholstered chairs are often chosen for this reason. Where seats are arranged in rows, the space between rows of chairs must be wide enough for delegates to stretch their legs and make room for others in the same row walking to and from their seats.

Seating may be permanently fixed to the floor, or of the sort that fastens together to form rows, or made up of separate chairs, with or without arms, depending on the degree of flexibility and comfort required and how much storage space is available when the chairs are not needed. Chairs may even have a permanently fixed or removable work table, providing a flat surface for writing on. In some conference rooms, especially where concerts are occasionally held, seating may be tiered. This gives the audience a better view of the stage.

Tables are usually provided for the guest speakers and people chairing sessions, and in some cases also for the delegates. Folding tables or table frames which can take different sizes and shapes of table tops are suitable because they are flexible and easy to store.

Leisure centres, often attached to hotels or conference centres, are a relatively recent development. They include facilities such as a swimming pool, mini-gym, squash courts, racquet ball courts, sauna, massage area, steam room and solarium.

Design and decor

Careful planning is needed to ensure that all the facilities can fit into the allocated space (often rather small), and that related areas are conveniently located in relation to one another. For example, the changing room and sauna should be accessible to the squash court, racquet ball court, swimming pool and gym.

For safety reasons, reception areas should have a view of the swimming pool so that staff can keep a close eye on swimmers. If there is a coffee shop, it should also overlook the pool, so parents and teachers, for example, can keep an eye on their charges and enjoy the view. In some leisure centres there are two sets of changing rooms, a 'wet' changing room for pool, sauna, solarium or steam bath users, and a 'dry' one for people using the squash, gym, and racquet ball facilities.

The emphasis of the design is on relaxation. Leisure centres are places where people can get away from their usual surroundings, have fun and get fit. So an element of the theatre also enters into many of the designs.

Functional considerations in design

The biggest single technical problem in any indoor leisure centre is how to control condensation, otherwise it can destroy the building's fabric and also detract from its appearance. Heating and air-conditioning systems will help to protect the building and only rust-proof equipment and fittings should be used in high moisture areas. Therefore gymnastic equipment located near a swimming pool should be made of stainless steel (which is not affected by moisture). If the equipment is chrome plated (which will rust if condensation forms on it regularly) it must be located in a room or area sectioned off from the pool.

Large extractor fans will draw out the heat and moisture from the swimming pool area, helping to prevent it spreading into adjacent areas. If these areas are kept at a slightly higher temperature, the risk of condensation is reduced further.

To make the best use of the available space, round or octagonal shaped pools are quite common in leisure centres. The shape has the added advantage of creating a rather cosy feel. Since most pool users are middle income business and professional people who just want a bit of healthy exercise in between demanding work sessions, an Olympic-sized pool is not really needed. But any pool has to be large enough to accommodate the maximum number of bathers likely to use it on a regular basis, and to give each bather enough space to move around in.

Dual use of space is another design consideration—for example, if the indoor pool area can be cleared away at night to become a disco.

Service pipes, extractor fans and other unsightly equipment associated with swimming pools can often be disguised by decorative effects, or turned into interesting design features. For example, pipes can be hidden behind an overhead pergola of greenery, and extractor fans painted green and suspended in a ring over the swimming area.

Safety is a most important factor. Most designers take into account the safety standards laid down by the Sports Council and pay great attention to circulation routes around the pool and to and from adjacent areas.

✱ FOR INTEREST

A **sauna** is a wooden cabin with an electric heater or stove which can bring the room temperature to between 80 and 100°C (176 and 212°F).

A sauna may be small enough to seat two people or large enough to seat up to 20 people at the same time. Most saunas are made of untreated kiln-dried pine panels, which are prefabricated and easy to erect. The walls and ceilings are insulated, and the doors are constructed of sturdy warp-free materials. Benches may be positioned at one or two levels, and people can either sit or lie on them. There must be a good ventilation system so that the air can circulate, otherwise it becomes stale and sweaty.

A **Turkish bath** or steam room has internal walls made of glass, PVC, mosaic or tiles. The steam in a Turkish bath also penetrates the respiratory system, so pine or eucalyptus is often added to the water system to provide a refreshing extra touch.

✱ FOR INTEREST

One hotel transports its guests into the classical past, with statues and busts on plinths suggesting the house of a Roman emperor. Tropical themes are popular. The indoor pool at Selsdon Park is built within a white wood structure with red and pink blinds and matching loungers around the pool. Three flamingoes operated by a pneumatic pump can nod their heads, flap their wings and produce flamingo-like sounds. There are palms at the water's edge, and an island built into the middle.

TO DO

Visit a local indoor swimming pool which may or may not be part of a more extensive leisure centre. With the safety checklist for swimming pools, consider the design of the swimming pool and the surrounding space. List what safety points you feel have not been taken into account in its construction? Write a short description of the decor, noting especially any features which have been used to disguise pipes and other ugly equipment.

Indoor swimming pool and surroundings: a safety checklist

1. Staircases should have two handrails if they are more than one metre (3ft 3 inches) wide, and one handrail if less than one metre wide.
2. Stairways and landings should not have open edges which people, particularly young children, could fall through.
3. There should not be any abrupt changes in floor level in 'wet' areas that might cause people to slip or fall, for example, between the changing area and the pool hall, or on the pool surrounds.
4. If there are level changes (which is quite common in many older pools) there should be slip resistant floor surfaces, handrails, clear tread markings and good lighting.
5. Ramps not stairs should be used in wet areas.
6. The access from changing area to the pool should not be near the deep end of the pool. If this cannot be avoided, there should be a barrier rail for the safety of non-swimmers or young children.
7. Where routes to pool facilities take bathers near deep water, special precautions may be needed. Any queueing near deep water is dangerous and must be avoided.
8. Pool surrounds and other circulation routes in wet areas should be wide enough for bathers to pass each other comfortably.
9. Sudden changes in pool depth should be indicated.
10. Grab rails must be provided and situated where bathers jumping or diving in will not strike them. They should not project out of the pool but be recessed into the pool wall.
11. Safety signs (preferably pictorial with writing underneath) should indicate the depth of water in both shallow and deep areas, and where one can or cannot dive etc.
12. Glare-free lighting should be installed which does not reflect off the pool water. The pool base must be visible to lifeguards and bathers. Breakable light fittings should not be used over the water, or if they are, they should be well protected.
13. There should be no electrical installations such as socket outlets in wet areas, no trailing extension leads, and great care must be taken when installing lighting under water.
14. It should be possible to restrict access to the pool area by limiting the number of entrances and positioning them so that they can be easily controlled.

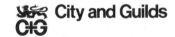

City and Guilds

Test yourself: Units 7–14

1. State two general aims which should be considered by an interior designer hired to refurbish a new or existing establishment.
2. Describe briefly what is meant by standardisation of room design.
3. For a building to function well, its designer must be conscious of a number of points. Briefly describe five.
4. Give four design points that would assist a disabled visitor's stay in a hotel.
5. List three items of furniture usually found in a bedroom in:
   (a) hotels
   (b) students halls of residence.
   For each, give at least two design factors which are important.
6. Describe briefly two design features which are important in a bathroom in a hospital and not usually found in hotel bathrooms.
7. Consider the design of a conference or meeting room and state one important aim for each of the following aspects and briefly describe how it might be achieved:
   (a) ventilation
   (b) lighting
   (c) power points
   (d) chairs
   (e) security.
8. A number of special design points have to be considered for indoor swimming pools. Give at least two general ones and two that relate specifically to safety.

If something is described as 'clean' it generally means that it is free from dust and dirt (known collectively as 'soil'), stains and other unwanted substances or marks. Similarly 'to clean' something generally means to make it free from these unwanted substances by washing, wiping, suction cleaning (often known as vacuum cleaning) dry cleaning (with chemical solvents) or sometimes by brushing. Because the object of cleaning is not only to remove the soil, stain or mark, but to prevent it being carried to another surface, cleaning methods which dissolve or trap the soil in moisture or suck it safely away are preferable to those which try to wipe or brush it aside, such as dry dusting (wiping with a dry cloth) or sweeping.

Types of soil

Soil is made up of dust and dirt:

- *Dust* is loose, dry particles from the air which settle on surfaces. It is trapped in rough surfaces, edges and corners.
- *Dirt* is a mixture of dust and liquid, moisture or grease. It becomes embedded in a surface and may be very difficult to remove, particularly from rough and absorbent surfaces.

Soil may be brought into a building from outside, or it may be produced within the building and then spread from one area to another.

External sources of soil include the readily visible such as mud and dry earth, sand, powdered concrete; as well as those more difficult to detect such as smoke, fumes, salt and pollutants carried in the air.

Internally generated soil includes the obviously unpleasant things produced by the building user such as sewage, mucus from coughing and sneezing (mucus is the liquid produced by some parts of the body, in this case the inside of the nose) and cigarette ash. It also includes the less offensive things such as loose fibres from clothing, wearing carpets and upholstery and minute particles of dead skin. Waste from processes carried on within the building, such as kitchen waste, chalk dust and graffiti, are other sources.

Soil can be transported in the air by draughts, heating or ventilation systems and by building users, particularly on their shoes, but also by hands, clothing, baggage, even hair.

Soil can be spread by creatures like mice, rats, cockroaches and other pests. Poor cleaning methods such as sweeping, mopping or dusting with a dry cloth or brush can transfer soil. Cleaning equipment which has not been properly cleaned and maintained will also spread soil instead of removing it.

How soil can be removed

Soil can be removed by chemical cleaning agents dissolved in water or other liquids. It may also be removed by force (such as pressurised air or water), mechanical pressure (the use of a scrubbing machine), friction (for example, with abrasive pads), agitation (as in the laundry process), suction (dry or wet suction cleaning) and static electricity (using a static mop sweeper). The exact method of soil removal depends on the type and amount of soil present, and the surface on which it has been deposited.

The reasons for cleaning

Cleaning is carried out for a number of reasons. These include:

1. To make a room or area look attractive and inviting, that is to give it aesthetic appeal. With no sign of dust, dirt or rubbish, the appearance of surfaces and items will be pleasing.

See video: *Housecraft: A Key to Operations.*

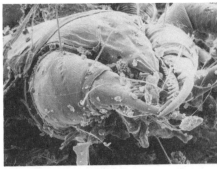

A dust mite foraging among skin scales, cat fur, synthetic and woollen fibres and soil fibres—the typical contents of a suction cleaner after it has been used over a carpet

Cleaning checklist

- Use the appropriate cleaning technique for the task, such as wiping, scrubbing (see units 20–23).
- Use the cleaning agents in the correct concentration (see unit 20).
- Only use chemical disinfectants when instructed and never use instead of cleaning (see unit 16). Areas which have to be disinfected must first be cleaned.
- Use only freshly prepared cleaning solutions (their effectiveness deteriorates with use and time). Never top up cleaning solutions, but discard down sluices or toilets and replace with a new solution.
- Use only clean and suitable cloths and utensils.
- Use separate cloths for cleaning toilets (preferably of a colour designated for this purpose) to avoid spreading bacteria from this high-risk area.
- Thoroughly clean equipment and cloths after use, allow to dry if necessary and store correctly.
- Wear protective uniform for all cleaning tasks, and rubber gloves for cleaning toilets. This will reduce the risk of bacteria being spread from item to item by your body or clothes.
- Wash your hands carefully after each cleaning operation.

2. To create a healthy, germ-free environment. Hygiene is a basic priority, both in the food and non-food areas of all types of accommodation operations. If conditions are not hygienic, bacteria are able to multiply, and as some bacteria are harmful this can cause illness and even death. Food, in particular, is subject to various legal regulations because contaminated food can result in lethal outbreaks of food poisoning. But in the non-food areas, too, there are hazards: infectious diseases are more likely to spread if infected patients' clothes, linen or food utensils are not properly cleaned and disinfected; rats, cockroaches and other pests which thrive in unclean conditions can also carry dangerous bacteria. Cleaning staff may pick up bacteria in the course of their duties—but they can avoid being carriers of these bacteria by paying strict regard to personal hygiene (see unit 19).
3. To look after surfaces and items. Well-cared for furniture, carpets and curtains, for example, are more likely to last longer than they would if neglected. They will look good for longer and not have to be replaced so often.
4. To remove litter, rubbish and spills which could become a fire or safety hazard.

What is considered to be clean

The standard of cleanliness will depend on the condition of surfaces and on the type and amount of usage. The standards of cleanliness will also depend on the number of staff employed to do the cleaning, how experienced they are and what cleaning materials and equipment is made available to them—in effect, on how much money is budgeted for cleaning. This sum should reflect the importance given to the different reasons for cleaning. For example:

- The guests in a five-star hotel will expect a far higher aesthetic standard of cleanliness than pupils at a boarding school. Likewise the management of the hotel will want to extend the life of the expensive furnishings and protect any antiques from damage.
- In kitchens and sanitary areas in all types of establishment, high standards of cleanliness are required for hygiene reasons.
- In hospitals, very high standards are necessary, especially in operating theatres, intensive care units, premature baby units, infectious disease wards, wards for the dangerously ill and any other high risk areas. Not only will cleaning be more thorough and regular, but certain items will also be disinfected.

Design features which can make cleaning easier
- Streamlined areas without ledges to avoid dust traps.
- Skirting boards with rounded edges and corners to prevent soil building up.
- Use of non-absorbent, smooth surfaces, to stop soil penetrating.
- Use of streamlined sanitary fittings which do not have corners or crevices to collect soil.
- An efficient ventilation or air-conditioning system to prevent contaminated air from circulating and a controlled rate of flow so that very little dust is transported from one area to another (three complete changes of air are required every hour).
- Revolving double doors to prevent blasts of air transporting dust into the building.
- Door mats or grids at entrances to the building to remove soil particles from shoes.
- Double glazing to reduce the amount of dust entering through windows.

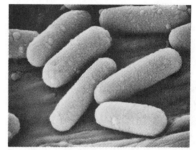
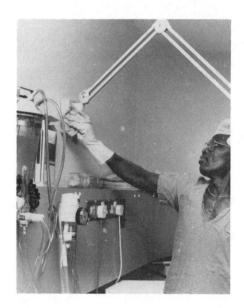

Cleaning improves the appearance of surfaces and areas by removing visible dirt and dust. Bacteria—microscopic organisms that can survive practically anywhere —are usually removed at the same time.

This is fortunate, because bacteria can multiply extremely rapidly. They thrive especially in moist, warm, dirty conditions when the harmful varieties can cause illness and even death.

The removal of bacteria by frequent, thorough cleaning has been a priority in hospitals since their effects began to be understood (see box). Equal importance has been placed on their control, with the development of cleaning procedures and working practices which reduce as far as possible the risk of spreading bacteria from infected sources.

Nowadays, the dangers of bacteria are more widely appreciated. The publicity given to AIDS and Legionnaires' disease, both of which can cause death (see unit 56), means that hygiene is no longer thought of just in terms of food poisoning.

Cross-contamination (the spread of bacteria from infected sources) can occur as easily in accommodation areas as it can in food preparation, and the results can be deadly wherever it occurs.

Cleaning procedures in any type of accommodation operation must therefore pay particular attention to the hygiene aspects. The objective of removing visible dirt and dust so areas look nice must take equal, or even second place, to the removal and control of harmful bacteria so customers and staff are not put at risk.

- A beautifully polished bathroom glass becomes a deadly hazard if it is wiped with a used guest towel.
- Fresh bed linen may carry bacteria if it has been left near soiled linen, for example when the bed was stripped after the last departure.
- A basin may look clean when it has been wiped with a cloth but if the cloth has been used earlier for wiping the toilet seat it is likely to have left harmful bacteria on the basin surface.
- If hands are not washed regularly and particularly after smoking, eating, using the toilet and blowing the nose, then bacteria will be carried to everything that is touched (see unit 19).
- If cloths, mops and similar cleaning equipment are not properly washed and dried after use, bacteria will multiply on them during storage and move to new homes as soon as the equipment is used again.
- If cleaning methods are used which scatter dust, such as dusting with a dry cloth or sweeping, the dust which is not collected may carry bacteria back to surfaces just cleaned.

Cleaning for hygiene

Generally dust can be removed by wiping with damp cloths or mops and as long as they are clean to start with and regularly rinsed out, there is little danger of redepositing bacteria.

Suction cleaning is also satisfactory, so long as the equipment is properly filtered to retain all the dust and it is emptied into an enclosed container or the filled bag sealed and disposed of.

When dirt is embedded in surfaces, the pressure of a damp cloth or mop, or the force of a suction cleaner, will not remove it adequately. It is therefore necessary to dissolve it in a solution of some sort.

Water will dissolve certain types of dirt, but it is not a good wetting agent.

  FOR INTEREST

The fight against harmful bacteria goes back to the 19th century, when doctors and scientists became aware of how infections could be spread. Among them was the English surgeon Joseph Lister, who believed that the so-called 'hospital disease', which many patients suffered from following surgery, was caused by bacteria spread by unclean conditions. He suspected that surgeons and other hospital staff were spreading infections from their hands and clothing to the patients. He insisted that surgical instruments and similar equipment were sterilised before use and that protective clothing and gloves were worn. As a result of these measures, 'hospital disease' has virtually disappeared—but 'cross infection', where patients pick up infections during their stay in hospital, does still occur.

▶ ▶ ▶ **TO DO**

Make a list of other examples of bad practice which can cause bacteria to spread. It may help to concentrate on those types of accommodation operations you are familiar with and to discuss the activity with your colleagues.

Against each item on your list, indicate what you think the correct practice would be.

 HYGIENE

It is not good practice to wash bedroom crockery and glassware in the *en-suite* bathroom, by using the basin as a sink. It will be infected with bacteria and it is too difficult to ensure that sufficiently high rinsing temperatures are used and not practical to let the cups, saucers, teaspoons, coffee/tea pots, glasses etc. air-dry.

These items should be taken to a central washing up area where they can be washed up hygienically.

Surface tension, particularly on hard surfaces, means the water sits on the surface or runs off so quickly it does not dissolve significant amounts of dirt.

Detergents are added to water to overcome the surface tension and so allow the dirt and dust to be dissolved. Many types of detergent have been developed from various chemicals for different purposes (see unit 20) but the oldest example is soap, used for cleaning since around 1000 BC. Today soap is still the most effective method of removing bacteria from the human body.

Special solvents generally have to be used when oils and fat are present, and other cleaners such as abrasive polishes have been developed for cleaning specific surfaces such as metals.

Chemical disinfectants

Chemical disinfectants may seem the obvious agent to use for killing bacteria (and advertising in the media generally supports this view). In most cases, however, they are not usually necessary. If a surface has been cleaned properly, most bacteria will be removed, along with most of the dirt and other matter which encourage the growth of bacteria. (Remember: the surface should be left dry, as moisture also encourages the multiplication of bacteria.)

Occasionally chemical disinfectants are used, for example in hospital wards where infectious patients have received treatment, but then only after cleaning (disinfectants cannot clean surfaces and disinfect at the same time).

Chemical disinfectants designed to kill bacteria will only work if stored and used correctly:

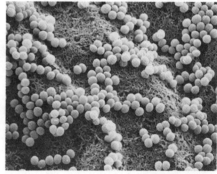

These bacteria (Staphylococcus aureus) are commonly found on healthy human skin so they can be easily transferred to china and glassware, food and other 'clean' surfaces. They are harmful, causing boils, internal abscesses and (by contaminating food) nausea, diarrhoea and vomiting

- The right amount of water must be added according to the instructions given for dilution.
- Disinfectants should never be mixed. To do so can cause a violent chemical reaction or even the release of a dangerous gas, and the disinfectant will lose its effectiveness.
- No single disinfectant is effective on all bacteria, so be sure to find out the correct disinfectant for the specific range of bacteria to be eliminated.
- Disinfectants take time to do their job. Follow instructions carefully.
- Disinfectant solutions should only be made when they are needed. They will lose effectiveness if they are kept, in some cases for more than a few hours.
- Surfaces must first be cleaned.
- Some chemical disinfectants will be inactivated by certain plastics, cork and other materials. Follow instructions.

Using heat to destroy bacteria

Most bacteria are killed at temperatures above 70–75°C (158–167°F) provided they are kept at this temperature for long enough.

Bed linen, towelling and similar items which can carry bacteria should therefore be laundered at these high temperatures.

China and glassware (for example, used in guest bedrooms for tea/coffee and in hospital wards for drinking water and soft drinks kept by the bed) should be washed in a detergent solution at about 60°C (140°F), then rinsed in water at 75–85°C (167–185°F). This is too hot for hands so the items should be placed in a basket and lifted in and out of the water using the basket. The equipment should then be left to dry in the air.

✎ HOUSECRAFT TIP

If you are told to use a chemical disinfectant, always follow instructions carefully, and check with your supervisor if you are unclear on any detail.

Many chemical disinfectants are only intended for specific surfaces. If they come into contact with other surfaces they can lose their effectiveness and can cause permanent damage to the surface. They can also harm you.

Cleaning tasks can be approached in a number of ways to ensure they achieve their objectives with the minimum of human effort, good use of time and without wastage—either of cleaning materials or energy to operate mechanical equipment.

In some establishments, detailed cleaning procedures are laid down for each task covering:

- what cleaning materials to use
- what equipment to use
- the standard to achieve
- how to set about the work
- what sequence to follow
- how long it should take.

Usually whether there are written procedures or not, training is given to new staff and supervisors check that the work is done in the right order and to the standards required.

Quite often the pressures of business and staff shortages mean that it can be difficult for even very experienced staff to complete each task to the right standard. The temptation is to cut corners, but this could mean failing to meet customers' expectations and endangering the health and safety of both customers and staff.

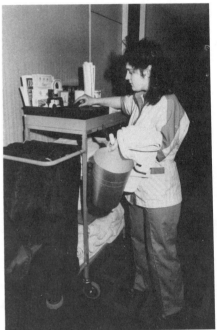

 TO DO

Assume that you have to give a new work colleague some tips on working efficiently. Make a list of about ten reminder points. Keep them as brief as possible.

Make a second list of the points you feel you should remind yourself of. Write them out neatly on a small piece of card and keep them with you to refer to when you think you have been inefficient.

Efficiency checklist

1. *Good organisation*
Whatever the routine, always remember to be methodical. If you start one task, do not switch to another in the middle of doing it. If you do this, you always run the risk of leaving out certain important aspects of the task at hand. By changing your focus of concentration, you are also expending unnecessary energy, and tiring yourself out mentally.

2. *Advance planning*
This is another aspect of good organisation. Select and collect all the items you need for a particular task, and arrange them for convenient use. For example, those items which you use most frequently when cleaning a bedroom should be placed near the front of the trolley. Check that you haven't forgotten anything so that you don't have to waste time returning to stores.

3. *Effectively controlling stocks*
You should be able to plan ahead and order items in advance, so that they are always available when you need them. If you are in charge of reordering, you should work out exactly how much of a particular item you need. If you order too much, the excess items take up storage space, and some items spoil if they are not used within a specified time. If you order too little, you will have to reorder almost immediately, wasting your time and that of the storekeeper, supervisor or supplier. You should know where items are stored, and how they should be stored. If you find anything spoiled or missing, report it immediately. Observing security is another key feature of stock control (see unit 59).

4. *Time*
From knowing how much work has to be done within a given time, you should be able to plan accordingly. An efficient worker paces himself or herself carefully—there is no sense in overworking, and not taking breaks, as you become tired, stop paying attention to detail, and will not do the job properly. If fatigued, you are more likely to have accidents. On the other hand, if you constantly interrupt your work, or allow yourself to be distracted by conversations or 'phone calls, you may find that it is difficult to resume your task without first having to backtrack: "What was I doing?" You may also hold up others, whose work is connected to your task.

5. *Thoroughness*
Any job you undertake should be done thoroughly, so that you don't leave out anything. Check carefully the job procedure and make sure that all steps are followed, but avoid spending too much time and energy on one task, possibly to the detriment of another.

6. *Saving resources*
This involves not using more than you have to of anything, and using it properly, according to the manufacturer's instructions so that it does what it is supposed to do and is not likely to become damaged through being mishandled. If you are cleaning a surface, there is no point in using too much cleaning fluid, as this not only wastes money but can complicate the task at hand. An excess of fluid may be difficult to remove.

Check carefully that you are using the appropriate cleaning agent or equipment. You don't want to have to start with one item, only to discover that you should have used another. This wastes time and money, and there is a danger that you may damage the surface you are cleaning. You can also save resources by carefully cleaning and storing used equipment.

Pay attention to the use of energy. Use hot water in sensible quantities, turning off the hot water tap when it is not required. Report if the heating is too high, turn down or switch off heat or air-conditioning when it is not required. Switch off lights when a room is not being used, and make sure that light bulbs are kept clean (dirty light bulbs require more energy). Turn off all electrical appliances when they are not being used, and close curtains, windows and doors to improve room insulation.

7. *Getting the best use out of equipment*
Use and maintain all items according to instructions. This will prolong their life, and will reduce the risks of accidents, such as fire, which can break out spontaneously if, for example, greasy and oily mops and cloths are stored in poorly ventilated areas (see unit 58) and report promptly any faulty items.

8. *Working as part of a team*
You are likely to be working as part of a team (see unit 61). If you fall behind, you can affect the work of colleagues, who may have to slow down so that you can keep up with them. As a team member, you should be efficient about taking orders, remembering exactly what it is you were asked to do. If you think that instructions are too complicated to keep in your head, make sure to write them down. Similarly, you should be able to pass on information in a clear and concise manner (see unit 62). Always try to maintain a good team spirit, and work hard to establish a good relationship with the other team members.

9. *Looking after your health*
Listlessness and poor performance may result from a poor diet, from not having enough sleep, or from not doing enough exercise to keep fit (see unit 19).

10. *Working without causing unnecessary noise*
Unnecessary noise is irritating, both to the customers and to other staff, particularly in areas which are already noisy, such as entrance lobbies. When you work, be as unobtrusive as possible, but do not ignore people who are trying to communicate with you.

11. *Keeping alert*
Be on your guard against possible dangers from theft, arson or terrorism (see unit 58). Also make sure that the equipment that you are using is safe. Report any suspicious happenings or safety hazards immediately.

Some items and surfaces have to be cleaned several times a day or every time they are used, others just once a day or even once a week. These usually form part of what is referred to as 'routine cleaning'. Examples include:

Several times daily/with use
Emptying ashtrays, wiping food preparation tables, wiping restaurant tables which have hard surfaces, cleaning public toilets.

Daily
Cleaning surfaces and floors of private toilets, bathrooms and kitchens, suction cleaning floors of corridors, dining rooms, public areas, bedrooms which have been occupied overnight.

Weekly
Damp-dusting high shelves and door frames, buffing floors, cleaning mirrors.

Other cleaning tasks, for example, shampooing carpets and upholstery, stripping and polishing floors, dry cleaning or washing curtains and blankets, washing windows, walls, picture glass and chandeliers, are only done periodically. This may mean monthly, annually or even less frequently.

When to clean

The frequency of cleaning, both routine and periodic, depends on three inter-related factors:

1. *The amount of soil that builds up*
This will depend on type of usage (for example, personal washing in bathrooms, food preparation in kitchens) and frequency of usage (for example, busy corridors and entrance halls). It will also depend on the age, condition and design of the various areas and on the location of the building. If it is in an industrial area, the atmosphere is likely to be polluted and by the sea it is likely to be salty.

2. *The required standard of cleanliness*
Special areas such as bathrooms, toilets, kitchens, operating theatres and intensive care units will require a very high standard of cleanliness (sometimes referred to as a 'clinical' standard). Five-star hotels will aim for higher standards of cleanliness than economy tourist hotels. Corridors and administration offices will not require such high standards as wards and bedrooms.

3. *The costs of cleaning*
Almost every type of accommodation establishment has to operate within certain budgets and so the staffing, equipment and material allocated to cleaning will be limited.

Normally it is only the proprietors, governing authority and/or senior management of the establishment that can decide the balance of priorities. They will set the standards of cleanliness which reflect the customers' expectations, ensure hygienic and safe conditions, help prolong the life of decorations and furnishings, and keep within financial resources.

It is the usual practice, therefore, for management to specify how often a task is carried out, by stating, for example, whether it is a daily, weekly, monthly, three-monthly, six-monthly or annual task.

There may be occasions when it may be necessary to vary the frequency of cleaning, for example if a room has had extra-heavy usage or it has been raining a great deal and more soil than usual has been carried into the building on shoes.

USEFUL TERMS

Standard method of performance or **job analysis** is the detailed listing of steps, equipment, materials and time allocations for specific cleaning tasks.

A **work schedule** gives a timetable of the tasks to be undertaken by an individual member of staff within her or his working shift. It will also include breaks for lunch and tea etc. The schedule will cover daily, weekly and periodic tasks.

Some establishments allocate work schedules each week, or even at the start of each shift. In this way the jobs which are considered to be less interesting or even boring can be rotated among several members of staff.

Cleaning can be done by a method known as **block cleaning**. Each member of staff moves from room to room, with responsibility for completing the same task in every room. Block cleaning is a suitable method for a business hotel, where most guests stay only one night and check out early the following morning. It is then possible for a room cleaner to strip the beds in all the rooms allocated to him or her, then resheet all the beds, dust all the rooms and so forth.

In **conventional cleaning** (also known as **orthodox cleaning**), all tasks are completed in one room before proceeding to the next room.

It is possible to combine both procedures. For example, in a hotel all rooms which have been vacated are block cleaned, and the rooms of stayovers (people staying for more than one night) are cleaned by the conventional method.

Team cleaning is where two or more people work together in an area, either on the same task or on different tasks.

  TO DO

Collect examples of room inspection checklists from any accommodation establishments you have a chance to visit or stay in (explain why you are interested).

If you will not have the chance to do so in the near future, try drawing up your own checklist. You might then be able to note improvements you would make to checklists you subsequently collect.

Sometimes however a task can be carried out too often, to the detriment of the item being cleaned. For example, if furniture is polished too often, the surface may become sticky and attract excessive dust. Money has also been wasted through using too much polish and the time might have been spent to better purpose cleaning something else.

Turning cleaning policies into procedures

Cleaning policies will cover:

- the specific standard required
- how often tasks should be done.

Those responsible for cleaning may then be trained in:

- the best methods for each task
- cleaning equipment and cleaning agents to be used
- how long should be spent on each task.

These details are decided on the basis of exactly what surfaces and items have to be cleaned. This can be done from room inventories or schedules which list the types and number of surfaces and items.

The next stage is to break up each task into distinct steps, specifying:

- the order in which they should be carried out
- listing by each step the equipment, cleaning materials and method to be used
- what the finished result should look like, for example: 'the tap will be free from smears'.

More time will be allocated for the standard tasks when they have to be carried out in difficult circumstances, for example, suction cleaning a dining room where heavy furniture obstructs the floor space.

Many of the decisions on what order cleaning tasks are carried out in will reflect principles such as:

- The job should be completed as quickly as possible, with the minimum amount of effort. So, for example, the items to be carried in and out of the bedroom on each journey may be specified: 'take the rubbish out, return with the clean linen'.
- Methods should be standardised as far as possible, to establish uniformity and consistency.
- The varieties of equipment and material required in the establishment should be kept to the minimum to help keep down maintenance and supplies costs.
- Any tasks that will cause dust, for example, stripping the bed should be completed first, and soiled items and rubbish which may carry bacteria removed.
- When cleaning, start with the cleaner areas: if they are cleaned first and the dirtiest last, then dirt is less likely to be transferred from dirty to clean areas.

Monitoring standards

The usual method is for management or supervisors to inspect rooms to check that cleaning tasks have been completed to the correct standard. An inspection checklist is useful provided it is comprehensive, well designed, and the tasks are organised in a systematic layout (sometimes the procedure is to check the room from top to bottom and/ or move around the room in a clockwise direction starting from the door).

Checklists also make it easier for standards to be recorded formally and variations over a period of time to be monitored. A separate column is usually allowed for checking that faults have been put right.

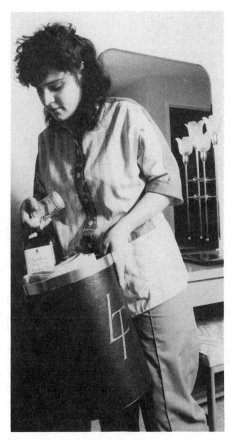

Removing any rubbish is one of the first steps in cleaning a hotel bedroom (see unit 42)

High standards of personal presentation are important:

From the customers' point of view
Customers will notice appearance and what they see may crucially affect their overall impressions of the establishment and of the staff. They are likely to regard untidy, dirty or smelly staff as an indication of even worse standards behind the scenes.

From the establishment's point of view
The appearance of the staff is a direct advertisement of the standards maintained throughout the establishment.

Personal appearance says a lot about members of staff's attitude to:

- their work
- the establishment they work in
- their colleagues
- their customers
- themselves.

If staff are tidy and smart it means:

- their work will be tidy and smart
- their place of work will appear tidy and smart to customers.

A friendly and helpful appearance means their colleagues and customers will be more friendly and helpful.

Hair, face and hands   Hair should be kept clean, neat and appropriately styled: preferably away from the face, with long hair tied back.

If worn, make-up and jewellery should be used sparingly (the establishment's policy must be checked first). Special care should be taken to maintain a clear skin and complexion.

Men should be clean shaven or keep beards and moustaches neatly trimmed.

Hands should be kept clean and well looked after. They must be washed regularly and thoroughly using soap and warm running water, then rinsed downwards from the wrist (so that all lather is removed) and dried, either by hot air or using disposable paper towels.

Fingernails should be kept clean, well looked after and preferably short.

Personal freshness   Any odour will be offensive to customers and work colleagues. Frequent bathing is important and strong scents, perfumes, after-shaves or colognes should be avoided.

Teeth should be regularly brushed and properly looked after. Bad breath should be counteracted with mouth fresheners.

Clothing and footwear   Whether uniforms or personal clothes are worn while on duty, a bad impression will be created if they are dirty or untidy. Uniforms and clothing that have not been put on clean at the beginning of the day or when coming on duty may present a serious hygiene hazard because of the presence of bacteria. Staff should follow workplace instructions on the wearing of uniforms, protective clothing and gloves.

Housekeeping staff spend much of their time on their feet—good quality, strong shoes will prove far more comfortable (and safer!), especially at the end of a long day, than fashionable, lighter shoes. If possible, alternate pairs of shoes—some people find it helps to change shoes during the day.

‼ REMEMBER

If you look good, you will have more self-confidence and are likely to feel good.

And if you feel more confident about the work you are doing so will your customers, your colleagues and your supervisors.

Your customers will be more satisfied with the services your establishment has provided.

Your colleagues will be able to do their jobs better because of the positive effect you have had.

Your supervisors will have more confidence in you and your chances of promotion within the company are increased.

On the other hand if you do your work in a sloppy way, dress in a sloppy way or wear your uniform in a sloppy way and don't keep it clean and well looked after, then you cannot blame your customers, colleagues and supervisors for believing that you are a discredit to the establishment.

Always bear in mind that an untidy appearance instils uncertainty and anxiety, while a well-kept, smart appearance generates confidence.

✳ REMEMBER

The *facial expression* of the housekeeping staff will tell their colleagues in other departments and the customers whether they really are friendly or fed up, bored with the job and letting personal problems get on top of them.

A *smile* immediately creates a friendly, welcoming atmosphere.

Eye contact implies sincerity, interest and trustworthiness.

Slouched, stooping, shuffling about gives a bad impression. A deliberate, upright and alert *posture* implies confidence and enthusiasm.

Grooming is another way in which housekeeping staff can show their concern for the well-being of customers and work colleagues. Clean faces, hair, hands and clothes show that a person is bothered about appearance and therefore more likely to be bothered about the needs of customers and other staff.

Posture A good posture when standing, walking or even sitting, has a good effect on customers and colleagues:

- a tidy posture is controlled, not fidgeting and fussing
- a smart posture is an upright one, not shuffling, with feet dragging.

It is also good for the figure and will help prevent corns, aches and pains.

Ill health Sores must be kept covered with a clean dressing.

Ill health should immediately be reported and attended to. Staff who continue to work when unwell are putting at risk the health of their colleagues and customers.

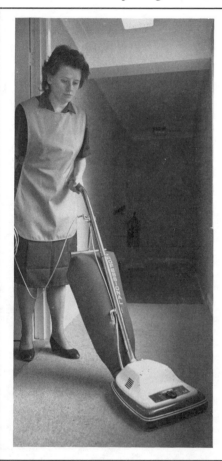

Healthy living guide

Try and regulate the quantity and types of food and drink you consume, so that your body weight is in proportion to your height (your doctor will advise you).

- Eat less fat and avoid fats high in saturates, for example, butter and lard. Look for the label 'high in polyunsaturates' on fats and oils you eat and cook with.
- Eat less sugar and avoid drinks and foods which have a high sugar content.
- Eat more fibre. Choose whole grain cereals and bread in preference to highly refined white bread. Eat more pulses, fruit and vegetables.
- Eat less salt and avoid tinned and processed products that have a high salt content.
- Reduce alcohol consumption to moderation.
- Do not smoke.
- Take regular exercise.
- Get sufficient sleep.
- Try and include periods during the day when you can relax.
- Have regular medical and dental check-ups.

See: *Customercraft* book and video, Mastercraft core book *Health, Hygiene and Safety in the Hotel and Catering Industry* and the video *Foodcraft 8: Catering for Health*.

✓ HOUSECRAFT TIP

Using names when you are talking to colleagues and to customers shows:

- recognition, helping them feel secure
- interest, helping them feel important
- friendliness, helping them feel at home.

but if it's overdone, it can start to sound grovelling.

In hotels, the arrival and departure lists will often give the names of guests. In hospitals, the name of the patient is on the bed or the ward list.

✚ HYGIENE

Wash your hands regularly and always:

- when you come on duty
- after changing into uniform or working clothes
- before and after handling food
- after smoking
- after using the toilet
- after blowing your nose or sneezing
- regularly during and after specific cleaning tasks, particularly those involving items which might be contaminated (such as toilets, soiled linen).

▶ ▶ ▶ TO DO

Make a check on your personal appearance and posture. Ask friends and colleagues for their (frank) comments. Write on a small sheet of card the points you need to improve and keep the card with you so that you can remind yourself from time to time during the day.

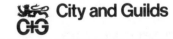 **City and Guilds**

Test yourself: Units 15–19

1. What is soil made up of? Give three examples of external sources of soil and three of internally-generated soil.
2. Give the four principal reasons for cleaning.
3. Give some examples of design features which can make cleaning easier. If possible state four.
4. Suction cleaning is a satisfactory method of hygienic cleaning. Give one condition that must be met for this to be so and name one other satisfactory method.
5. State the main reason why chemical disinfectants are not usually necessary.
6. Briefly describe the most hygienic procedure for cleaning china and glassware from guest bedrooms.
7. If you had to explain to a new member of staff what was important

for her or him to do to clean efficiently, what points would you make? Give six if possible.
8. What is the difference between 'routine' and 'periodic' cleaning tasks? Give two examples of each.
9. When deciding what order to carry out cleaning tasks what are three principles which might be considered? Assume that a cleaning routine has not yet been established.
10. Explain what is meant by 'block cleaning', by 'conventional cleaning' and by 'team cleaning'.
11. Why is a high standard of personal presentation important? Consider the point of view of the customers, the establishment and the individual concerned and give at least one reason for each.
12. What should a member of staff do if he or she feels ill?

Water

The simplest cleaning agent is water. It helps to loosen and dissolve most dirt. However, water by itself does not wet or penetrate a surface properly, instead it forms globules which do not cover the whole surface. If a cleaning agent (soap or detergent) is added to water, then the solution wets the surface more effectively and therefore cleans it better.

Water under pressure is a powerful cleaner. It dislodges dirt and carries it from the surface. Water is also used to rinse out dirt which has been broken up by another cleaning agent, such as soap.

Soap

Soap is made from natural fats, such as palm oil, fish oil or animal fat, mixed with caustic soda (a powerful chemical substance). It is produced in solid, liquid, flake or powder form.

Soap mixed with water is able to emulsify. This means that it can break up most grease or oils into tiny particles, which are then released into the water and can be washed away. To make sure that there are no particles of dirt clinging to the surface, the surface is rinsed.

Unfortunately, when soap is mixed with water it also forms an insoluble scum. This is because water, particularly hard water, contains calcium salts. These salts combine with soap (sodium stearate) to form calcium stearate which adheres to the surface being cleaned, and is difficult to rinse away. This makes soap unsuitable for cleaning surfaces. It is mainly used for personal hygiene.

Synthetic detergents

These are made from a combination of different chemicals, usually derived from petroleum. The active ingredient is called the surface active agent, or surfactant. It can combine with water to form a solution that is able to penetrate the surface and also act on oil-based materials, so making contact with the soil (dirt and dust). The detergent loosens the soil, sometimes enough for it to be released into the solution as a result of chemical action alone, but brushing, agitation or wiping is often necessary to dislodge it completely. It is prevented from falling back on the surface—also by the detergent—until it can be washed away. The final stage is to remove all traces of detergent and soil by rinsing with clean water.

Synthetic detergents do not form a scum in water.

There is a range of synthetic detergents, made from different combinations of chemicals to be suitable for specific cleaning jobs.

Neutral detergents   Sometimes called general purpose detergents, these are the most common. They are often green or straw coloured, and are used for washing dishes, damp dusting and mopping, and for similar routine cleaning tasks. They are made from strong alkalis and weak acids, and are generally safe for all purposes.

Alkali detergents   Also known as hard surface liquid cleaners, these are used for more specialised and heavier tasks, such as removing ('stripping') polishes on vinyl floors. They are also known as 'degreasing agents'. Alkali detergents contain more alkali than neutral detergents, and are corrosive and can damage most surfaces including skin. If used too often, they may destroy the surfaces being cleaned, so it is important to follow manufacturers' instructions about frequency of use. Once cleaned, the surface should be well rinsed to remove all traces of the alkali. Some

alkali detergents contain abrasives, and these should never be used on surfaces that can scratch, for example plastic baths.

Acid cleaners   These are used for cleaning toilets, for removing bits of plaster and cement from surfaces, such as a new floor, and for removing stains caused by deposits of lime from dripping taps. They are weak or strong, depending on the type of acid used. Strong acids, used for cleaning toilets, are harmful to the hands, and to most surfaces. When using strong acids, it is important to follow the instructions carefully and never to mix with any other cleaning agents, as the combination could produce harmful chemicals and gases.

Other cleaning agents

Solvent based cleaners are a solution of a liquid, for example methylated spirits or white spirit, water, wetting agents and other additives. (The real definition of 'solvent' is any liquid, including water, that will dissolve a solid. But in cleaning, 'solvent' refers to a liquid that can dissolve heavy deposits of grease and oil, which water cannot.) Solvent cleaners are used for removing wax from wooden floors, and also for dry cleaning and stain removal.

Abrasive cleaners, also called scouring cleaners, are mostly used for cleaning enamel and ceramic sanitary ware, such as baths and basins. Abrasives are used in some synthetic detergents. Available in powder, paste, cream or liquid form, they consist mainly of finely ground minerals (such as sand, powdered ash, pumice, dolomite and chalk) which rub away dirt. Abrasives are classified on a scale from 1 to 10, where talc is 1 and diamond is 10. The coarsest abrasives used in cleaning have a rating of around 6. They are potentially the most harmful and damaging to surfaces. Very finely textured abrasives are used for removing tarnishing and surface scratching from metals. But if used too often, they will also remove the surface metal.

Abrasives are not suitable for any surfaces which scratch easily, such as plastic baths or floors. They can also damage the hands, and they leave a deposit.

Using cleaning agents

It is important to follow the instructions on the containers, paying special attention to dilution and safety warnings. Different cleaning agents require different dilutions, so care must be taken to add the right amount of water, or other liquid, to a measured amount of the cleaning agent. Too much, or the wrong dilution, can damage surfaces or at best require additional rinsing. Too little may be ineffective. Hand pumps or automatic dilution tubes, called dispensers, are sometimes used with liquid cleaning agents. Other manufacturer's instructions to follow are:

- how to store cleaning agents when not in use
- whether to wear protective clothing
- how to dispose of used cleaning agents.

Chemical disinfectants
Chemical disinfectants are no longer considered an effective way of dealing with bacteria, except in special circumstances and under carefully controlled conditions (see unit 16). If they are used, the surfaces have to be cleaned with a detergent first.

✔ HOUSECRAFT TIP

When using alkali detergents, always protect your hands with gloves, and make sure that no other part of the body can come in contact with them.

---

pH values
Containers of cleaning agents often indicate their type using the pH scale. This scale indicates the product's acid/alkali content, the lower the value the higher the acidity:

- Toilet cleaners are acid and usually have a pH value of less than 4.
- Soap and neutral detergents come midway on the acid/alkali scale, with pH values of 6 for soap and 7–9 for neutral detergent.
- Hard surface cleaners are alkali and have a pH value of around 10; detergents for stripping water-based polishes from floors are even more alkaline with pH values of around 12.

✔ HOUSECRAFT TIPS

Soap and detergents often form a foam when diluted in water. Remember that the amount of foam is not an indication of how good a cleaner it is, and too much foam can be a nuisance. So do not add extra just because there is no foam.

Most cleaning agents work better at higher temperatures, particularly for removing grease, oils and fats. But over 60°C (140°F) any proteins present on the item will begin to harden and starches to gelatinise, making them more difficult to remove.

 **TO DO**

Make a list of the cleaning agents used in your place of work (or an establishment of your choice), with details of what surfaces they are used for, dilution rates, safety precautions and any other instructions.

Cleaning cloths

Cloths have many uses in accommodation establishments—for washing, wiping and polishing. Sometimes sponges are used instead of cloths.

Cleaning cloths should be:

- absorbent, so they can be moistened to collect the dirt and dust effectively
- soft so they do not scratch surfaces
- lintless so they do not leave fluff behind
- either disposable or capable of being thoroughly cleaned after use.

Cotton or sponge cloths are suitable for most surfaces and chamois leather (genuine or simulated) for glass surfaces.

Disposable cloths, for hygiene reasons, are an increasingly popular alternative.

Some establishments have a colour coding system for cleaning cloths, for example red cloths for toilet areas, green cloths for general purpose use, yellow cloths for surfaces in contact with food. Coloured types of disposables are designed to have a limited life but can be used more than once. Paper disposables, often dispensed from a roll, can only be used for one operation before being disposed of.

Yellow or check dusters are suitable for applying and buffing polish, for example to wooden, copper, silver and brass objects. As their colour will tend to run when they are wet, they are not suitable for damp dusting. (Dry dusting, even with yellow dusters which are very soft, is unsatisfactory as much of the dust gets scattered.)

Mop sweepers

Mop sweepers are used for collecting dust and small items of waste off floors and walls.

Heads which are made of nylon, acrylic or polyester are suitable because they build up static electricity which attracts the dry dust particles. Another option is to use special cotton heads that have been impregnated with an oil.

Mop sweepers have long, horizontal heads which are pushed along, without lifting, from the floor or wall surface. They usually have swivel heads to make it easier to clean around furniture. For cleaning very large areas, double headed mops (also called 'scissor' heads) are used.

Wet mops

There are three basic types of mop heads suitable for washing floors:

- short-tail, sometimes called 'do-all' or 'dolly mops'
- long tail or Kentucky mops, which can usually be detached and sent to the laundry for washing (some have the fingers sewn together with tapes to prevent tangling; these tapes may be colour coded)
- sponges, normally with a built-in device for squeezing out the excess cleaning solution/rinsing water.

A mop bucket is needed for short tail and long tail heads. This has a device for wringing out the head—a press, a roller, or a simple conical strainer into which the head is squeezed.

Mop buckets are made from a variety of materials such as galavanised iron, fibreglass or plastics, and many have castors so they can be pushed or pulled around easily, bumper guards to protect walls, and internal marks to help measure out cleaning solutions.

With double buckets, the operator wrings out the mop head so the dirty water collects in one bucket, re-wets the mop with the clean detergent solution held in the second bucket, rings it out again over the dirty water bucket, then proceeds with the mopping. This overcomes the disadvantage of single buckets, which is that the dirt wrung out of the mop is added to the cleaning solution, which must be changed more frequently.

Mop heads which cannot be removed for laundering have the drawback that the heads cannot be washed or dried easily and the head will become a reservoir for dirt and bacteria, some of which will inevitably be redistributed over the floor.

Brushes

Brooms (brushes with long handles) are suitable for sweeping patios, outdoor steps, paths and similar areas where the fine dust they send up is not going to settle on furniture and other surfaces. Broom heads come with long, stiff bristles (when they could be used for garden paths and other rough exterior surfaces) or soft heads (suitable for smooth surfaces, such as outdoor steps).

Hand brushes and dustpans can be used to gather up the sweepings after using a broom, or for inside use, for brushing up broken glass or china.

Specially designed brushes are used for cleaning toilet pans. Many models have a plastic handle, nylon bristles and a purpose-built holder. To avoid the risk of spreading bacteria, a toilet brush should be used for and stored, dry, in a container by each toilet.

Bottle brushes may be used for cleaning the overflows of sinks and basins.

Carpet sweepers

Carpet sweepers make much less noise than electrically operated suction cleaners (see unit 22). They are useful for removing crumbs and other light, small pieces of rubbish from carpet and hard floors in restaurants, foyers and corridors, where more thorough cleaning is done overnight for example.

Revolving brushes throw the dirt into a collecting box and can be raised or lowered according to the floor surface: high for thick carpets, low for hard floors. The collecting box has hinged lids so that it can be emptied easily.

Cleaning trolleys

Trolleys are useful for carrying cleaning agents and small equipment, for holding rubbish and sometimes soiled linen (these models usually have a rubbish bag at one end and a linen bag at the other end). They also can be used for holding supplies of clean linen, toilet paper, soap and other guest supplies such as shampoo, sewing kits and stationery items.

Many different models are available. It is important that they are well maintained, easy and safe to move around (not stacked so high that short operators cannot see over the top) and cleaned regularly.

Taking care of cleaning equipment

Disposable cleaning cloths should be carefully disposed of in a rubbish bag after use. They should never be used time and time again. They are not made for this type of use and will start to tear and develop holes.

Cotton and sponge cleaning cloths should be washed after use in a neutral detergent solution, thoroughly rinsed and then hung up to dry completely. Alternatively they can be laundered.

Chamois leather cloths are thoroughly rinsed in water (plain cold or luke warm water), then hung up to dry.

Mop heads which are designed to be removed for cleaning are often washed centrally, in the laundry, when boiling temperatures can be used to sterilise them.

Other mops used for washing surfaces should be washed in a very hot, freshly prepared detergent solution (neutral), rinsed thoroughly, then hung up or placed in a rack to dry.

Static mops are washed and dried in the same way. Impregnated mops have to be treated with oil after washing. These too may be laundered centrally.

Brooms and brushes are washed in a warm, neutral detergent solution, then rinsed and left to dry. They should not be stored resting on their bristles (this will cause them to become mis-shapen).

Mop buckets, wringers and dustpans must be washed after use then rinsed and allowed to dry—upside down so they can drain completely.

▶ ▶ ▶   **TO DO**

Obtain information on at least four different models of cleaning trolley (either by finding articles about them in trade magazines, by contacting suppliers, or by inspecting them in a show room or in use in establishments you have access to).

Make up your own list of the advantages and disadvantages of each model and note its cost to buy new. Give an example of an accommodation establishment that each would be suitable for. Discuss your recommendations with your supervisor or tutor.

Suction cleaners

One of the most essential pieces of equipment for cleaning is the electrical vacuum, or suction, cleaner (still sometimes known by the trade name of the first vacuum cleaner in Britain, the 'Hoover'). Few, if any, establishments can do without it.

The suction cleaner is used for cleaning not only carpets, but hard floors and stairs, upholstery, walls and curtains. There are also wet suction cleaners for cleaning liquid spills. Suction cleaners work by sucking up dry dirt, dust and small litter through a hose and into a dust bag or, in the case of liquid, into a canister/container in the machine. When full, the disposable dust bag is replaced, or where there is a container, this is emptied. The air which is sucked up along with the soil passes through various filters. These trap the fine particles of soil and bacteria, so the air that is blown out of the machine is clean.

Most cleaners come with a range of attachments, for example, a hard nozzle for cleaning upholstery, a pointed nozzle for getting into crevices, a firm brush for carpets, a soft brush for hard floors and walls, and a soft round brush for cleaning shelves and high ledges. Tools with squeegees are used to remove water.

There are many models of suction cleaners, both for the domestic and industrial markets, but they fall into three basic types:

1. *Cylinder cleaners*
Suitable for general cleaning of various surfaces and for cleaning in corners and enclosed spaces, they are usually fitted with a carrying handle. A variation of the cylinder cleaner is the back-vac, which is carried on the back, making it useful for cleaning areas that are otherwise hard to reach, for example high walls, ceilings and staircases.

2. *Upright cleaners*
Originally designed to clean carpets, these are useful for cleaning all large, level areas. They have rotating brushes (and some also have a beater bar) which help to release dirt from carpets. They require less bending and stretching than cylinder cleaners but are not as good for reaching corners, confined spaces or under furniture or for cleaning upholstery and curtains. They are also difficult to manoeuvre on stairs.

3. *Canister cleaners*

These have a hose and operate like the cylinder types but are shaped like a can or drum, or sometimes like a bomb. Some models also have a power head attachment, fitted to the hose but designed to clean carpets in a similar way to an upright cleaner.

Some canister cleaners, known as 'wet and dry' machines, have separate attachments for cleaning liquid spillages and dry soilage.

⚠ **SAFETY**

Using electrical equipment safely
1. Never use equipment which you have not been trained to use.
2. To avoid an electrical shock, always switch off the appliance and unplug before cleaning, fitting or removing attachments.
3. Never use an extension cord when shampooing or scrubbing unless all the electrical connections are protected from getting wet. Keep cleaning solutions well away from electrical connections.
4. Wind flex carefully so that kinks do not form, as they may damage the flex.
5. If a machine is faulty (unusual noises, overheating etc.), a plug loose, or a flex damaged, report it immediately, and label the machine 'out of order'.

Suction driers are in fact canister cleaners specifically designed to suck up liquid. They are used along with scrubbing machines to remove wet, loosened soilage from floors. The liquid is collected in a plastic or metal canister and safety devices are incorporated to prevent the motor or any of the electrical connections becoming wet.

Caring for suction cleaners   A disposable paper dust bag (or paper sack) is used with most types of suction cleaners.

If a dust bag is allowed to get too full, its pores will become blocked with fine particles of dust. This restricts the air flow, reducing the machine's suction power. It also means the motor will become overheated (as the motor is usually cooled by the air passing through it). There is also a risk that the bag will burst. So it is important to check the dust bag regularly and change it as necessary.

The full dust bag, once removed from the machine, should not be shaken about, as the dust collected in it will scatter. In many machines, the dust bag is enclosed by a cloth bag, though some have only a cloth bag. This bag becomes soiled over time, and it can be suction cleaned using another suction machine.

Exhaust filters, which are fitted to some suction cleaners, clear the air before it is blown out of the machine and back into the atmosphere. Like dust bags, exhaust filters must be changed or cleaned regularly.

✱ **FOR INTEREST**

Some buildings have a centralised vacuum system. The suction hose, with the appropriate attachment, is plugged into a socket located in the room or corridor.

The dust which is sucked up enters a collection area, usually situated in the basement. From there it is disposed of. Centralised systems are only likely to be found in modern buildings, as they are relatively economical to install during the construction stage.

 TO DO

Ask permission to examine one, or if possible, two types of suction cleaner used in a public building. Classify the machines as upright, cylinder or canister types and identify each of the tools used with them. Establish where the soilage is collected in the machine and how the air is filtered before it passes out into the room again.

Make short notes on what the users regard as the advantages and disadvantages of the machine (if you find yourself with an opportunity to ask such questions).

Rotary floor maintenance machines

These are fitted with a brush or a drive disc and pad which is rotated mechanically. Different machines are designed for different operations. A 'standard speed' machine can be used for scrubbing, buffing and stripping hard floors or shampooing carpets. Higher speed machines can be used for buffing or spray cleaning.

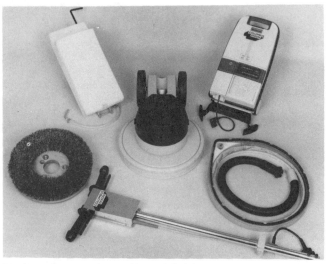

Many machines can be quickly modified for particular uses, coming with a variety of attachments for scrubbing, buffing, polishing, shampooing and (shown right) suction drying

Scrubber dryer with suction drying option

Battery-operated scrubber dryer

Shampooing machines

There are basically four models available:

- *Dry foam* machines dispense the cleaning solution over the carpet. Once the foam has loosened the soil and dried it is removed, along with the soil, with a suction cleaner.
- *Standard speed rotary floor maintenance* machines can be used for carpet shampooing. They are fitted with a tank from which the cleaning solution is released. The brush, or pad, works a shampoo solution into the surface. As soon as a small area has been treated, a suction drier can be used to remove the shampoo and soil. Alternatively they can be used to apply a dry foam shampoo which will be removed by dry suction along with the soilage.
- *High speed* or faster types of *rotary floor maintenance* machines, fitted with a 'bonnet' pad can be used to shampoo a carpet along with a proprietary carpet shampoo spray. The shampoo loosens the soil which is absorbed by the bonnet pad. The bonnet pad will need frequent changing. (This is called *bonnet buffing*.)

Taking care of electrical equipment
Tanks in scrubbing and shampooing equipment should be emptied after use, if necessary rinsed out with clean water, then allowed to dry with the filler cap off. Tanks in wet suction cleaners should also be rinsed out and allowed to dry.

Any tubes that carry cleaning solution, filters and nozzles must be cleaned regularly in a fresh, neutral detergent solution, rinsed, then allowed to dry before the machine is re-assembled.

Brushes and pads should be removed, washed in a neutral detergent solution and then hung up to dry.

The outside of equipment, including the wheels and the electric supply cord, should be wiped over after use with a cleaning cloth and a neutral detergent solution.

Wheels need to be oiled regularly (but with care so that the oil does not drip on to surfaces as they are being cleaned). Check the manufacturers' instructions. |

- *Hot water extraction* machines combine cleaning and drying. The cleaning solution is sprayed under pressure into the surface, sometimes with a power-driven brush to improve the penetration, and sucked back together with the loosened soilage, into the machine. This may be done as one operation or the operator may need to switch the machine to extraction and pass back over the area just sprayed. Two dry passes over the carpet are usually necessary to ensure as much cleaning solution as possible is removed.

City and Guilds

Test yourself: Units 20–23

1. By itself water is generally not a suitable cleaning agent.
   (a) What is the reason?
   (b) What is the main exception?
2. What is the reason soap is not a suitable cleaning agent for surfaces?
3. Give two examples of surfaces which each of the following cleaning agents are suitable for use on:
   (a) acid cleaner (b) neutral detergent
   (c) alkali detergent.
4. Give three qualities that it is important to bear in mind when choosing a cleaning cloth.
5. Name one type of mop head which is suitable for mop sweeping and describe briefly how it prevents the dust scattering.
6. Name two basic types of suction cleaner.
7. State four safety points relating to the use of electrically operated equipment.
8. Many shampooing machines apply the cleaning solution. Describe briefly two ways in which the solution can then be removed.

A particular floor or floor covering is chosen for a number of reasons: its attractiveness, durability, cost, feel, insulation properties and ease of cleaning. As work on floors is one of the most time consuming of all the cleaning tasks, ease of cleaning is a major consideration when selecting a floor covering.

Types of floor coverings

Hard floors fall into three types:

- **Porous** floors readily absorb (suck in) dirt and spills. Examples of porous floors are wood, cork and concrete.
- **Semi-porous** floors absorb some dirt and moisture, particularly as they begin to wear. Vinyl (tiles or sheet) and linoleum are semi-porous surfaces.
- **Non-porous** floors do not absorb dirt and moisture. Non-porous floors include marble (and other stone), epoxy resin (a plastic material which is mixed as a liquid, poured into position, and dries to a hard finish), ceramic and quarry tiles.

Seals for hard floors Both porous and semi-porous floors are generally treated with a seal, which fills in the pores so that the surface can no longer absorb dirt and spills. This makes cleaning easier and it extends the life of the floor. Non-porous floors may also be sealed in order to improve their appearance.

The seals on wood and cork floors look similar to a colourless paint. They are solvent-based and some use polyurethane as the main component. Plastic floors (such as vinyl) and linoleum would be damaged by solvents so water-based seals are used. They are relatively easy to apply and can also be used on almost any type of floor except porous types. Special coloured seals may be used on concrete floors to enhance their appearance.

Polishes for hard floors Hard floors are also sometimes treated with a polish. This helps preserve the seal, assists maintenance, reduces slip hazards and may give the floor a shiny surface.

There are two main types of floor polish:

- solvent-based or spirit-based, consisting of waxes suspended in a solvent and available in a paste or liquid form
- water-based or emulsion, consisting of fine particles of wax dispersed in water.

Solvent-based polishes are suitable for untreated wood and cork floors but cannot be used on vinyl, rubber and other types of floors that are treated with water-based seal. The spirit causes these materials to soften and their colour runs.

Sealing a floor is a specialised task, requiring on-job training and practice if it is to be done well.

Some hard floors

Vinyl asbestos and *thermoplastic* flooring are the least expensive form of plastic flooring of acceptable quality for accommodation establishments.

Vinyl and *PVC* tiles and sheets are more expensive but quieter underfoot, less likely to crack and good for areas which require frequent damp cleaning.

Backed flexible PVC flooring combines a dense, hard wearing surface with excellent resilience. It is also soft and warm to walk on, though may be subject to tearing.

Rubber flooring is quiet, soft and warm underfoot, slip-resistant (especially if it has a raised pattern) but becomes porous with age.

Linoleum is very hard wearing and suitable for use with under-floor heating. Like rubber, it becomes porous with age and requires good maintenance. It is more resilient than vinyl.

Cork floors have an appealing warm, soft finish and provide good sound insulation. Being porous, they require sealing and regular maintenance. They can be easily damaged.

Wooden floors look attractive and are hard wearing if hard wood is used. They are expensive but offer good heat insulation.

Terrazzo flooring (marble or granite chippings, mixed with concrete and ground smooth) is hard wearing and resistant to fire, but cold and noisy.

Quarry tiles are hard wearing and non-porous, particularly where a plastic-type grouting is used.

Vinyl safety floor in a whirlpool spa area

Carpets

Carpets are now more widely used in public buildings. One reason is that people have come to expect higher standards of decor, and carpets usually look better than hard floors. Another is that improved manufacturing processes and materials have meant better quality and lower priced carpeting. Many of the new synthetic fibres used for carpets are extremely hard wearing. The newer processes include treatment against dirt and rot, thus reducing the traditional problem of how to clean stains and spillages.

Carpets have a number of advantages over hard floor coverings. They can be:

- attractive, with many colours, patterns and styles to choose from, to suit a wide range of tastes
- warmer and quieter, helping to insulate a room against cold and noise
- safer than hard floors: this is an important consideration in homes for the elderly, where falls are common, or in areas where spills on a hard floor may make the floor slippery.

✎ HOUSECRAFT TIP

Floor maintenance will be reduced and floors and carpets will wear better if as much dirt as possible is collected before it reaches the floors. Most dirt is brought into a building on people's shoes, so door mats are very important. Mats should be cleaned regularly or changed, otherwise they actually dirty the shoes which pass over them.

➧ ➧ ➧ TO DO

Make a list of all the types of floor coverings in your workplace or an establishment of your choice. Find out as much as you can about how they are cleaned, including how often, and the cleaning materials and equipment used. Make a note of their appearance.

Carpet fibres

Wool is the traditional fibre used for making carpets. It is warm, and because it has a natural 'bounce' it does not become flattened with use. It looks good, and it feels good, but it is expensive. Nowadays, wool is often used mixed with other fibres, such as nylon, to make the carpet more hard wearing, and cheaper. Other natural fibres used are **cotton** and **sisal**.

Synthetic fibres are manufactured from chemicals. For example, nylon, the first synthetic fibre to be produced, is made from benzene in coal, hydrogen, oxygen and nitrogen. Polyester is made from the by-products of petroleum. Among the principal synthetic fibres used for making carpets there are:

Nylon (for example 'Enkalon') which is hard wearing, and does not absorb spillages or moisture. It is therefore suitable for hotel entrances or hospital wards. The best quality nylon carpets feel fairly soft, but cheap nylon carpets can feel harsh. One disadvantage of nylon is that it melts when it burns, resulting in unsightly and irreparable damage to the carpet. It also builds up static electricity (this can cause mild, but unpleasant shocks to users).

Polypropylene (for example 'Fibrite') is very hard wearing, easy to clean and highly dirt and rot resistant, but it has a harsh feel. Other synthetic fibres are **acrylic** (for example 'Courtelle') which is the most wool-like of the synthetic fibres and **polyester** (for example 'Dacron').

Types of carpets

Like all fabrics, carpets start off as fibres, and these are woven, knitted, tufted or bonded to make the final product (see unit 34). For weaving, knitting and tufting, the fibres must first be spun into yarn. For bonded carpets, the fibre is fixed directly on to a backing.

1. **Woven carpets**: weaving is the traditional way to make carpets. There are three types, distinguished by method of weaving:

- Handwoven: for example Oriental or Chinese rugs.
- Axminster: machine made, although it looks like a handmade carpet, often richly coloured (including up to 40 colours) and patterned; each tuft is woven separately with the backing, then cut.
- Wilton: machine made; either plain or patterned; usually only five colours are used; unlike Axminsters, the yarn is woven in continuous strands, and the threads run along the back of the carpet.

Woven carpets are made on a loom, and the **pile** (the upper surface of the carpet) and **backing** is constructed at the same time. The use of synthetic fibres for both the pile yarn and backing has simplified the whole process of carpet making, since natural fibres must first be cleaned and straightened, which is both time-consuming and expensive.

Pile may be *loop pile* or *cut pile*, where the loops are sliced. The tighter and denser the pile, the less likely it is that dirt, spills and grit will go to the base of the pile, from where they are difficult to remove.

2. **Tufted carpets** are common, and are made by inserting yarn into a pre-woven backing of jute, cotton or polypropylene. The backing is then coated with an adhesive so that the tufts remain in position. Stripes and zigzags can be made, but not the elaborate patterns sometimes used in woven carpets.

3. **Bonded carpets** are becoming increasingly common. In this process, the pile is bonded (sometimes with glue, or using an electrostatic process) on to a backing

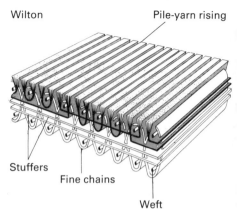

Wilton — Pile-yarn rising — Stuffers — Fine chains — Weft

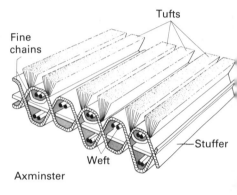

Axminster — Fine chains — Tufts — Stuffer — Weft

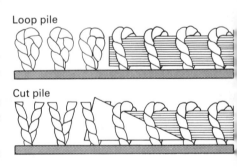

Loop pile — Cut pile

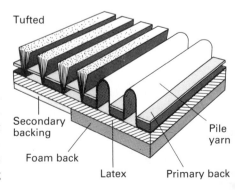

Tufted — Secondary backing — Foam back — Latex — Primary back — Pile yarn

material, and the backing may then be fixed to an underlay called a secondary backing. Some types of bonded carpet use the raw fibre, rather than yarn. The pile is usually shorter than on other carpets. Because they have very little pile, bonded carpets are not soft to walk on. But lack of pile makes them easier to clean, as the dirt cannot penetrate to the same extent as in a carpet with regular pile. For this reason, bonded carpets are often chosen for hospital wards, and other areas where hygienic conditions are essential.

4. Knitted carpets are uncommon. Manufacturing techniques have not yet been perfected, and they tend to stretch out of shape with heavy wear. Also, like tufted carpets, patterns are not easy to make, unless they are printed on in the final stage.

Carpet sizes

Carpets come in many different sizes, but the most common width is 4 metres (13 ft), which is called *broadloom*. *Body*, or *strip*, carpet is a narrower width—usually 90 cm (3 ft) or 70 cm (2 ft 4 inches)—and is more suitable for corridors and stairs. If body width carpets are used to cover a large area (*fitted carpets*), the strips are seamed up (sewn or in some other way bonded together). This is often necessary, for some woven carpets, particularly Wiltons, are only made in body widths.

Carpet tiles are squares of carpets. The edges are either sewn or specially sealed to prevent them from fraying. They are usually made from bonded carpet (though tufted and woven carpet may also be used) and are available in a number of sizes. Carpet tiles are easier to handle when being laid than other carpeting, and sections (rather than a whole carpet) can be lifted, giving convenient access to underfloor services, such as trap doors, plumbing etc. Where they are well laid they can be moved around to shift areas of wear, and if any tile is damaged or dirty, it can be replaced—which is cheaper than replacing an entire carpet.

Carpet underlays

All carpets benefit from protection from the floor provided by an underlay. Some carpets are made from foamback underlays already fixed to them, while others need to be laid on separate underlays.

An underlay is used to:

- protect carpets from rough or uneven floors
- cushion the carpet and help to make it last longer
- help insulate rooms against cold air and noise
- prevent dirt from entering through the floorboards and getting into the carpet.

Types of underlays There are two main types—*felt* and *foam* or *rubber*, but there is also a combination of the two, called *rubberised felt*.

1. Felt underlays may be made from jute, animal hair, man-made fibres, or a mixture. They tend to lose some of their thickness at the beginning of use, but they then settle and wear more slowly. They are usually specially moth proofed during the manufacture.

2. Foam underlays, made from man made materials or rubber, may be 'waffled' (ridged) or flat. They lose their thickness more slowly, but more steadily, than felt underlays. They can perish in overheated areas.

Bonded

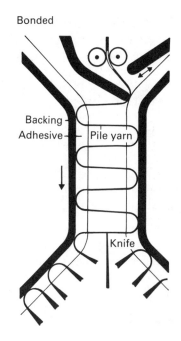

Classification and labelling scheme of the British Carpet Manufacturers' Association (BCMA)

A *extra heavy* wear	for commercial, rather than home, use
B *very heavy* wear	for heavy use areas in the home, such as stairs
C *heavy* wear	home living and dining areas
D *general* wear	fairly busy areas in home, but not heavily used, such as studies
E *medium* wear	bedrooms, and other not heavily used home areas
E *light* wear	only suitable for little used areas

 TO DO

Visit a local carpet supplier and ask to see samples of woven, tufted and bonded carpets used for *extra heavy* wear (A) or *very heavy* wear (B)—this information should be on the labels. Note down what fibres they are made from, how the carpets are made and their prices.

Hard floors can be cleaned using dry or wet, either manual or mechanical, methods. Dry methods will remove loose dust, dry dirt and litter (for example cigarette ends), while wet methods are necessary for removing sticky, greasy, wet or caked (dried on) dirt.

Dry methods

Mop sweeping
The mop head (see unit 21) is kept flat on the floor at all times, moving up and down the area in long, straight lanes. At the end of the lane, or from time to time, any litter, dust or grit which has not held on to the head should be collected using a suction cleaner or dustpan and brush. Mop heads should be suction-cleaned after use and washed regularly.

Suction cleaning
Suction cleaning is probably a more effective method for removing dry soilage than mop sweepers, provided the noise of the suction cleaner is acceptable. Machines must be well maintained, otherwise fine dust will be blown back into the air, only to re-settle later.

Wet methods

Damp mopping
Damp mopping is carried out with a neutral detergent and water. The mops are used in different ways (see unit 21):

- The *short tailed* and *sponge* mop is used with a push and pull action.
- The *long-tailed* mop is used standing upright, and swung from side to side in a figure of eight movement, working backwards.

Scrubbing
A rotary floor maintenance machine is used fitted with a tank, drive disc and scrubbing pad, or a scrubbing brush. The tank is filled with a neutral detergent solution. Most machines are operated from side to side, working backwards. Ideally two people should work together, so that one can operate the suction drying machine which follows the scrubbing machine.

Buffing
After a floor has been damp mopped, scrubbed or re-polished, it may require buffing. Buffing hardens the finish, increases the floor's resistance to soilage and gives it an attractive shine.

A rotary floor maintenance machine with a special buffing brush or pad is used. Like scrubbing, buffing is done working backwards, and from side to side.

Alternatively, buffing can be done with a high, super or hyper-speed buffing machine, which has a buffing brush or drive disc and buffing pad.

Some high speed buffing machines have attached suction cleaners which draw up loosened polish particles. This can also be done with a static or impregnated mop sweeper.

Spray cleaning
Spray cleaning is a way of combining cleaning and buffing of floors. It is sometimes referred to just as 'spray buffing'. A high speed floor maintenance machine is used, fitted with a high speed dry cleaning pad. The machine may have a spray attachment to provide the cleaning solution. Alternatively a hand spray is used, or even a well wrung damp mop.

  TO DO

Collect leaflets of several, different, industrial hard floor seals and polishes. Make a list of their trade names under four headings: water-based polish, solvent-based polish, water-based seal and solvent-based seal, and include details of cost. Discuss with your supervisor or tutor which areas each might be suitable for and why.

✐ HOUSECRAFT TIP

Solvent-based polishes are flammable and applicator pads can be a fire risk. Store polishes carefully, following instructions, and wash out pads with hot water and a neutral detergent to remove all traces of polish.

In spray cleaning, the floor is first mop-swept or suction-cleaned and then a small amount of solution is applied to the floor. The machine passes over the moistened area two or three times, or until the floor has dried. In this way dirt is removed and held by the pad, and the floor takes on a hard shine. As pads become dirty very quickly, they have to be turned and changed frequently. After cleaning, dry deposits are mop-swept, unless a suction cleaner is fitted to the machine.

Polishing hard floors

Floor polishes are either solvent-based (for cork and wood) or water-based (for plastic floors, terrazzo and linoleum). Water-based polishes may also be used on any wood, cork or concrete floor that has already been sealed, and they are used in preference to solvent-based polishes in more and more establishments.

Applying solvent-based polishes   Areas of heavy wear may be touched up where necessary, but occasionally solvent-based polishes need to be stripped completely, and a fresh coat applied.

Stripping is done with a standard speed floor maintenance machine fitted with a scrubbing pad or brush. First a solvent-based floor stripper is applied to a small area of floor—about 5 square metres (6 square yards)—with a mop, and the scrubbing machine, filled with hot water, is passed slowly over the area, loosening the polish. The slurry produced is then removed with a suction dryer. The area is then rinsed using a mop and water, changing the water frequently and suction-dried again.

Once the floor is dry, polish is applied. Paste polish is spread (on unsealed floors) with a lambswool applicator from an applicator tray. Liquid polish used on sealed floors, is easier to apply. It is poured on to the floor and rubbed in well with a polish applicator. Two or three thin coats are required—except at the edges, where one coat is sufficient. Each coat is buffed well before the next coat is applied.

Applying water-based polishes   Old polish is always stripped first. This may be done in one of three ways.

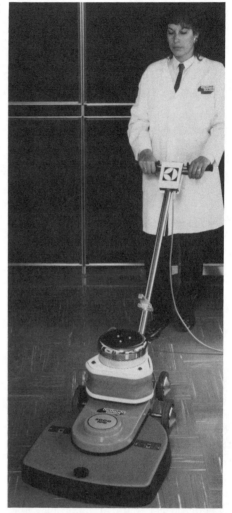

Hyper-speed buffing machine and pad

- An alkali detergent (floor stripper) is diluted in the tank of a standard speed floor maintenance machine fitted with a stripping pad. The floor is scrubbed, covering small areas at a time—5 square metres (6 square yards)—and several passes of the machine may be required. The dirt and polish is then removed using a suction dryer. The floor is rinsed using a weak vinegar solution—28 ml per litre (5 fl oz per gallon)—and applied by a damp mop. This is to neutralise the alkali stripper used.
- A specialist polisher stripper (which does not need neutralising) is damp-mopped on to the floor and rinsed, using a damp mop and bucket. The rinsing water must be changed regularly.
- A specialist spray-stripper is used with a high or super-speed floor maintenance machine fitted with a dry stripping pad. As polish is removed it is absorbed into the pad and the pad will need turning and changing as it becomes clogged. If the machine has no suction cleaner attached, the floor will need to be mop swept to remove loose powder deposits.

The polish is spread on to the floor evenly and thinly, using a lambswool applicator or direct from the can on to the fringes of a clean cotton damp mop. It is allowed to dry, then buffed if necessary. Two or three coats are required over the main part of the floor, but only one around the edges.

All carpets need to be cleaned:

- Regularly (normally daily) to remove light soiling. Suction cleaning is the most effective method.
- As required to remove heavy soiling. Off-site or factory cleaning can produce good results but most carpets are fitted and require cleaning 'in situ' (that is, on site). Wet cleaning methods are used.

Suction cleaning

Suction cleaners (see unit 22) suck up grit and other loose dirt from the surface, and, less effectively, from the carpet pile and backing. The main part of the carpet should be cleaned every day, and the edges weekly, using a crevice tool.

Suction cleaning works less well on carpets which are stuck to the floor, or on carpets with a very dense pile, which is difficult to penetrate. Nor can they remove ingrained grease, oil or other forms of soil which adhere to the pile. For these types of soil, wet cleaning methods are necessary.

Carpet sweepers are useful for picking up crumbs or lint, or any other dirt lying on the surface, for example, small pieces of food left on a dining room carpet after a meal. A carpet sweeper used daily will leave the surface looking neat and clean, but it does not reach deep down to the roots of the pile and so cannot replace a suction cleaner.

Wet methods

Dry foam shampooing   This is an efficient way of cleaning dirt on the carpet surface. The tank of a dry foam shampoo machine (see unit 23) is filled with a dry foam shampoo, and the machine passes over the carpet, feeding the foam on to it. The shampoo makes its way into the pile, and loosens the soil embedded in it. Care must be taken not to release too much foam into the carpet, because if the backing gets too wet it may shrink. The residue containing dirt is removed by suction cleaning once the carpet has dried out completely.

When a dry foam shampoo machine is not available, a standard speed rotary floor maintenance machine may be used to apply the dry foam shampoo.

Wet shampooing   More effective than dry shampooing to remove ingrained dirt from deep pile, this method uses a standard speed rotary floor maintenance machine fitted with a special carpet shampoo brush attachment (see unit 23) and a suction drier. The shampoo solution is released as the machine passes over the carpet, carefully regulated to avoid over-wetting, and then worked into the surface with the machine's brush or pad.

As soon as the shampoo has been applied to a small area, the suction drier is passed over the same area to suck up the liquid and the dirt released from the carpet. Cleaning section by section ensures that the water does not have a chance to soak into the carpet backing, which could otherwise shrink. The area of each section depends on the experience of the operator and the speed of the machine, around 5 square metres (6 square yards) is a guide.

At the end of the operation any remaining shampoo is drained away, the tank washed out and re-filled with clean water. The machine is then passed over the carpet a second time, section by section with the rinsing water. After each section has been completed the suction drier is used to remove the rinsing water. Once the whole carpet is completely dry it is suction cleaned.

HOUSECRAFT TIP

Grit is public enemy number one on any carpet. Door mats should be kept in good condition so they do their job effectively and prevent grit being carried on to carpets near entrances to the building. On wet days, clear plastic carpet protectors can be quickly rolled over existing carpet and taken up as the weather improves.

HOUSECRAFT TIPS

Clear the room as much as possible before using a wet cleaning method. Place plastic around the base of furniture which cannot be removed, and if possible card under metal and wooden legs (to prevent staining).

Work in straight lines up and down the room, taking care to overlap the preceding lane.

If possible open the windows so the carpet will finish drying quickly.

One problem with most wet cleaning techniques is that residues of shampoo are left in the carpet, even after suction cleaning. These residues occasionally build up over time and may in the long run cause even worse soiling. Because of these residues, carpet shampoos should not contain bleach, or any other agent that, over time, may harm or discolour the carpet.

Removing stains

1. Stains should be dealt with as soon as they are observed. When the stain is the result of an accident in a public area or by a member of staff, it should be dealt with immediately. It may not be possible to deal with accidents in guestrooms until the room is next serviced (unless the guest reports the spillage earlier).
2. Solids should be lifted off carefully—how will depend on what they are. Broken glass or china should be brushed into a dustpan with a hand brush, while bits of food can be lifted up by hand or carefully scraped up with a spoon or similar implement (but do not use one with a sharp edge as it may damage the carpet).
3. Liquids should be blotted up with absorbent paper or a disposable cloth.
4. The spill should then be wiped with warm water and this soaked up with absorbent material. Soda water should be poured on wine spillages.
5. If the stain is still visible it will have to be removed with a suitable cleaning agent. If the stain cannot be identified it is best to use a warm detergent solution first. If there is any doubt about the effect of stronger agents on the carpet, they should be tested first on a small area which will not be seen, for example behind a piece of furniture.
6. When applying water or stain removal agents, to the affected area, always work from the outside edge towards the centre of the stain. This will help stop the stain spreading, and for the same reason it is important to avoid over-wetting the area. (Over-wetting is also likely to cause shrinking and damage to the underlay.)
7. After using stain removal agents, blot them up with absorbent material. Rinse the area with clear water (or as directed in the instructions for use of the agent). Blot dry again then, if possible, cover the affected area (for example, by moving a chair or table over it) until it has dried.

Caution: many stain removals contain harmful chemicals. Always:
- read instructions carefully before use
- wear gloves.

If you are not successful in removing the stain, note down as much information as you can about the cause of the stain, how you have attempted to remove it and then consult an expert.

Bonnet buffing

A high speed rotary floor maintenance machine can be used to clean carpets. It is fitted with a bonnet pad which can absorb the moisture.

The carpet is sprayed in sections with a suitable carpet shampoo, then the floor maintenance machine passed over the area to collect the loosened soil and shampoo on the bonnet pad.

✱ FOR INTEREST

To prevent an excessive build up of soil, which could damage a carpet beyond repair, *soil retardant finishes* may be applied to new carpets, or to carpets which have first been cleaned by one of the wet methods. First try out the finish on a small corner section to check that it causes no colour change, or dulling or stiffening of pile. If you are satisfied, then apply the finish to the entire area, in straight, even and overlapping strokes.

▶ ▶ ▶ TO DO

Make a table of the various electrical carpet cleaning machines available on the market for commercial use, and any special attachments that they can use. Incorporate in your table illustrations cut out from sources such as magazines and leaflets supplied by manufacturers. What seem to be the main differences between appliances for commercial and those for domestic use?

Hot water extraction cleaning This technique combines cleaning and drying. It removes embedded dirt and liquid far more effectively than dry foam or wet shampooing. Very little residue is left and the carpet also dries out very quickly. Since specialised equipment is needed (see unit 23), small establishments tend to use a professional cleaning company or hire the equipment.

The hot water extraction machine (which is sometimes called a spray extraction or water injection machine) is filled with the cleaning solution—a low foam shampoo mixed with water (in spite of the name 'hot water' the water may only be warm, depending on the carpet fibre). As it is passed over the carpet, the shampoo is sprayed under pressure into the surface so it penetrates the carpet. It is sucked back up again, together with the loosened soilage. This may be done as one operation, or the operator needs to switch the machine to extraction and pass back over the same area again. This drying stage should be repeated once to ensure as much solution as possible is removed.

Test yourself: Units 24–27

1. State three reasons why floors need to be cleaned regularly.
2. Explain briefly why some hard floors are sealed and polished and some only polished.
3. Give two advantages that carpets have over hard floor coverings for a public room, such as a lounge.
4. Describe briefly the difference between bonded carpets and either tufted carpets or woven carpets.
5. What are two of the uses of a carpet underlay? Give an example of one type of underlay.
6. Hard floors can be cleaned by wet or dry methods. State one example of each and describe briefly how it works.
7. State the name of the machine that, depending on the attachment fitted, can be used for cleaning hard floors and also shampooing carpets.
8. Describe briefly a situation where a carpet sweeper would be a suitable method for cleaning a carpet. What other type of equipment would have to be used regularly?

City and Guilds

Walls and ceilings provide privacy and security, and help insulate rooms and buildings by trapping heat and noise. Some are also load bearing, which means that they support the building by carrying the weight of the structure above it. The most common building materials for load bearing walls and ceilings are bricks or large, grey coloured breeze blocks, which are made of pre-cast concrete.

Others walls are simply used to divide the building into suitable sized areas, while 'false' (lowered) ceilings, constructed a distance below the floor above, may hide such things as electrical and telephone cables, plumbing and insulation materials. In old buildings, false ceilings may also be used to reduce the height of the room. These non-load bearing walls and ceilings are often made of plaster board (plaster sandwiched between two layers of cardboard).

Wall and ceiling coverings

Where bricks are used for walls, these may be painted over direct, or even left as they are, 'fair-faced'. But walls and ceilings are usually coated with a layer of plaster before a final covering of paint, paper or tiles, for example, is fixed on. The final covering or finish has a number of uses, and choice of covering is affected by:

- *Decoration*: certain finishes add interest, make a room seem warmer, larger/ smaller, lighter/darker, and create focal areas. The size, function, and location of a room will determine the choice of decorative finish.
- *Durability*: a hard surface is less easily damaged if it is knocked or scratched. This will be a key consideration for an area that has a lot of heavy wear such as a service area for a conference room or a hospital corridor.
- *Ease of cleaning*: smooth, light coloured and hard surfaces are easiest to clean. Textured surfaces (for example, textured wallpaper) attract dust and small insects, and cannot be cleaned by wet methods.
- *Heat and sound insulation*: some finishes, such as cork and fabric, are more effective insulators than others.
- *Cost*: prices of different materials vary enormously. If a room is likely to be redecorated fairly regularly, there is little point in choosing an expensive surface.
- *Stain resistance*: a non-porous surface, which does not absorb moisture and dirt, is more stain resistant.
- *Area being covered up*: if the existing surface is in poor condition, certain finishes, such as cork, can mask the problem.

Types of covering

1. *Paints*

These may be *emulsions*, which are water-based and water-permeable, or *solvent-based*, which are oil-based and impervious to water. Both emulsions and solvent-based paints come in matt, eggshell or glossy finishes.

Emulsions are cheaper than solvent-based paints, easier to apply and dry faster. They are recommended for areas of less heavy wear, which do not require regular washing (water will gradually remove the paint). Solvent-based paints are more durable than emulsions, and more resistant to stains, water and any surface knocks, and are therefore suitable for kitchens, bathrooms, doors, window frames and skirting boards.

There are also *cellulose paints*, which are sprayed directly on to brick or stone walls and provide a very tough speckled finish. They are very easy to clean, and can even be scrubbed. Textured paint surfaces can be created by spraying a heavy emulsion paint on to a plaster material applied to a wall or ceiling. They are used for decoration, or to mask uneven or damaged surfaces.

In general, paint finishes are durable, and are a relatively cheap and quick way to decorate a room. Most are washable, and if part of the surface is damaged or stained, the damage can be made good by applying a further coat of paint. The main disadvantage of paint is that it may readily show soilage and may also be liable to chipping.

2. Papers

Available for walls and ceilings, papers may be textured (such as wood chip), printed or plastic coated (such as vinyl papers). Many people prefer the decorative finish of wallpaper to paint. Wallpaper is also softer than paint, warmer to the touch and absorbs noise more effectively. It can disguise poor surfaces, but it stains easily and is difficult to clean. It is more expensive than paint, especially if it is the washable type, and may peel off the walls if there is any moisture.

3. Fabrics

Fabrics for walls are usually fixed to a paper backing. A great variety is available, including hessian, felt, wool yarn and silk. Many fabric finishes are luxurious, and they are all efficient insulators.

4. Plastics

A range of finishes is available. The laminated types, such as 'Formica', are hygienic since they do not absorb dirt and moisture, and are easy to clean. Plastic sheets are sometimes used to cover less durable surfaces, such as fabrics, in areas where the fabric is likely to be soiled, for example, above a serving table. Expanded polystyrene, another type of plastic, is used to provide additional heat and sound insulation. However, plastic coverings can catch fire, and this makes them unsuitable for some areas, for example kitchens.

5. Wood

As a covering, wood may be in the form of boards, panels or veneers (a very thin layer of wood glued on top of a cheaper material). It is fairly expensive, but is durable, decorative and a good insulator.

6. Cork

Available in tiles or sheet (rolls), sealed or unsealed, cork is a good insulator. Sealed cork is easier to maintain than unsealed, as dirt and moisture are not absorbed.

7. Metals

Copper and brass are examples of attractive wall surfaces. They may be lacquered or varnished to prevent dulling. But they are expensive, and are not good insulators. Foil may be used as a cheap alternative. Stainless steel may be used instead of ceramic tiles in kitchens and other areas where high standards of hygiene are necessary.

8. Ceramic tiles

Ceramic tiles provide a hygienic, easy to clean, non-absorbent finish, so they are popular in operating theatres, bathrooms and kitchens. However, the grouting (the cement between the tiles) can absorb dirt and moisture, unless a plastic type is used. This is why stainless steel sheets are preferred in some areas.

9. Glass

Glass comes in sheets (for example 'Vitolite'), and blocks, first used in the 1930s in factories and commercial buildings. Blocks are made of two identical moulded pieces which are seamed together—they still let in light but absorb sound, and are resistant to fire and impact. Mirror wall coverings (in sheets or tiles) create the illusion of greater space.

10. Stone

Stone, such as decorative marble, is hardwearing, but it is expensive. (A decorative stone effect can be created by painting plaster finishes.)

Sound and heat insulation

Both sound and heat are transferred by air, water and other mediums. Thick walls and ceilings, particularly cavity walls, are good insulators, but many walls and ceilings are not thick, and heat and sound escape through them. In order to reduce this heat loss and to control noise, many new insulating materials have been developed. On walls, for example, thin sheets of a good insulating material can be used under wallpaper or lining paper. Ceilings can be covered with thermal (heat) and acoustic (sound) insulation tiles.

In problematic areas, insulation can also be improved by covering walls with book shelves filled with books, or with cupboards filled with clothes and linen.

 TO DO

In the building in which you work, or another of your choice, find two examples of each of the following wall or ceiling finishes:

- painted
- papered
- tiled
- fabric or leather or metal or stone.

Note the use of the rooms concerned, the condition of the finishes, and your views on whether the finishes were a good choice in each circumstance. If you think that they are not the most suitable finishes, explain why.

The frequency of cleaning will depend on how often the room is used, and for what purpose. Some ceilings, for example, may never need cleaning, except prior to redecoration. On the other hand, the walls of kitchens are likely to need cleaning weekly.

- *Dry methods*—that is, suction cleaning or mop sweeping—are suitable for most wall and ceiling coverings.
- *Wet methods*, using a solution of water and detergent, are necessary for removing greasy or moist dirt, or dirt which has lodged in the crevices of rough surfaces. However, they are not suitable for some wood finishes, or for most fabric coverings. Some fabric wall coverings can be cleaned with very little water, but it is important to check carefully before proceeding. Stains on fabrics can be removed with neat neutral detergent or a stain removal agent, but the material must not be over-wet. Leather and wood should be cleaned with a suitable cream or polish.

Quick guide to cleaning methods

Type of surface	Mop sweep	Damp wipe	Suction clean	Wash
Smooth paint	*	*	*	*
Textured paint			*	*
Washable paper	*	*	*	*
Ceramic	*	*		*
Glass		*		*
Marble and terrazzo	*	*		*
Plastic	*	*	*	*
Wood	*	*	*	
Cork (if sealed)	*	*	*	*
Metal	*	*	*	*
Brick and stone			*	*
Leather	*		*	

General procedures for cleaning

1. Display a safety sign to indicate that cleaning is in progress.
2. Move all furniture out of the way and cover it with dust sheets to protect it from loosened dust and splashes.
3. Protect floors as necessary.
4. If the ceiling is also to be cleaned, it should be done before starting on the walls.
5. Work section by section, moving around the room in a logical order. Overlap the last area done.
6. Wear protective gloves.
7. When high areas are to be cleaned, use safety steps. Take care that they are properly opened out and will not cause a danger to anyone passing through the area.
8. If the walls are going to be washed they are normally cleaned first with a dry method (mop sweeping or suction cleaning) to remove all surface dust.
9. Mop-sweep or suction-clean walls working from top to bottom.
10. Take special care around electrical fittings. Plugs and switches can be covered with masking tape.

11. Walls are washed starting at the bottom, then working upwards. In this way any water that runs down the wall will run over a clean surface and no water marks will be left.
12. Remove any splashes from floors, fittings or furniture immediately so they cannot soak through the dust sheeting or other protective covering.
13. Rinse after washing, working from top to bottom on walls.
14. If necessary, carefully dry each section with an absorbent cloth or paper, then proceed to the next section.
15. Do not overlook window sills, tops of door frames, ledges, service pipes, radiator panels and similar items. It is usual to clean these at the same time as walls and ceilings.

Dry methods

Suitable equipment (see units 21 to 23) includes:

- mop sweepers—some have extending handles which make them particularly useful for high or otherwise difficult to reach areas
- suction cleaner with a long extension hose
- back-vac (a suction cleaner that is designed to be carried on the back).

Wet methods

Walls and ceilings can be handwashed using a sponge (as it holds more cleaning solution than a cloth). A wet sponge mop is more suitable for high areas which are difficult to reach. An alkali detergent solution is normally used.

Wall cleaning machines include:

- ones with sponge cleaning pads or spray attachments to cover the surface with cleaning solution—the machine creates enough pressure to get the solution to the sponge or spray head
- high pressure cleaners—these are very suitable for sanitary areas, kitchens, operating theatres and other areas where most of the surfaces are non-porous (do not absorb water).

▶ ▶ ▶ **TO DO**

For the two examples of wall or ceiling finish you found for the activity in unit 28, find out as much as you can about how they are cleaned. Cover:

- frequency
- equipment and cleaning agents used
- how long each stage of the operation took (including clearing the room, the cleaning, returning the room to normal use)
- any problems encountered and what solutions were found to them.

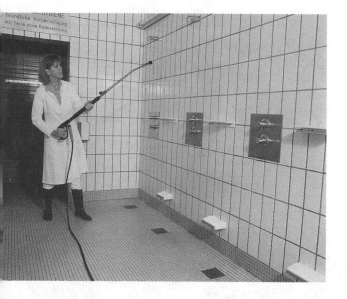

Doors

Materials used to make doors, either on their own or as combinations (for example, glass panels in a wooden or metal frame) include:

- wood (usually painted or sealed), which may be solid or a veneer (wood glued on to another material)
- glass—always specially strengthened safety glass; fire doors also have wire embedded in the glass
- metal—often enamelled, for example, on lifts
- plastic—may be strengthened with fibre glass
- rubber—suitable for service areas where trolleys are used to push them open.

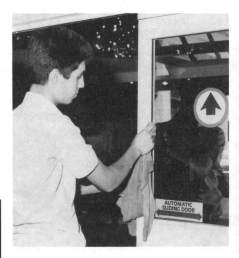

Some types of door:
- conventional solid, side hinged
- up and over (as in some garages)
- revolving (as in department stores)
- folding (may be used to divide up a large space)
- sliding (useful where a door covers a large part of the wall).

Door fittings include:
- hinges and handles
- pushplates and kickplates
- bumpers and protection bars (to prevent damage from trolleys and other equipment)
- security fittings such as locks, bolts and chains
- name and number plates
- purely decorative, such as knocker

Most door fittings are metal (especially brass, wrought iron and stainless steel), but plastic and wood is also used, especially for interior doors.

Cleaning doors Most door surfaces and fittings can be damp-dusted as part of the routine cleaning schedule. Periodically, or if they become very soiled for some reason, non-porous surfaces can be washed with a neutral or alkali detergent solution. Abrasives should never be used.

After damp dusting, surfaces of unsealed wood can be polished occasionally with wax (but very little wax should be used), or oiled (in the case of teak).

Wax polishes must never be used on plastic or painted doors.

Kickplates and bumper bars should be cleaned with an alkali detergent (cream or liquid) if they are very soiled, and then rinsed. For particularly stubborn marks on metal surfaces, use a nylon abrasive pad.

Pay special attention to:

1. Areas around handles, pushplates, kickplates, door frames, which are dirtied through contact with people and equipment.
2. The tops of doors and upper ledges, which collect dust.
3. Squeaky hinges and handles and any fittings which are loose or damaged. Any faults should be reported to maintenance staff.
4. The tracks fitted for sliding or folding doors where dirt and rubbish can collect. A suction cleaner will usually remove such items effectively.

Uses of glass

Glass is widely used in buildings. Most glass surfaces are windows, but glass is also used for walls, ceilings and doors (either as panels or the entire door), for partitions, shower cubicles, roof or sky lights, and to cover large enclosures, for example, swimming pools.

'Hollow' glass is for bottles and containers, while 'flat' glass is for windows, walls and door panels.

✎ HOUSECRAFT TIPS

Doors, like walls, should be washed starting from the bottom and proceeding upwards. This is because dirty water running down clean surfaces will not leave any marks.

Remember the top of the door and the floor under the door when it is closed.

 TO DO

Make a list of the materials and equipment required to clean three different types of doors, bearing in mind the material from which they are made. Write down your order of work and discuss your conclusions with your tutor or supervisor.

✎ HOUSECRAFT TIPS

Work carefully when polishing metal fittings. Metal polish is abrasive and it will damage the surrounding areas if it gets on them.

Metal polishes should not be used on door fittings which have been treated to prevent tarnishing (usually this involves coating them with a plastic-type substance, and this gets damaged by metal polishes).

The types of flat glass for *general use* are:

1. *Tinted glass* has colours added, either for decorative reasons, or to protect a room from sunlight.
2. *Patterned glass* has raised patterns on its surface. It may also be used for decoration, or to provide privacy (as in door panels), as it cannot be seen through easily.

The following flat glasses are for *vulnerable areas*:

3. *Toughened* (or *tempered*) *glass* is used where extra strength is needed for safety, for example, for revolving doors. If the glass does break, it disintegrates into small granules, which are less harmful than the large jagged pieces of ordinary glass.
4. *Laminated glass* consists of a tough plastic layer sandwiched between two sheets of ordinary glass. If the glass is broken, the pieces remain stuck to the plastic layer. It may be used for doors or partitions. Thicker types of laminated glass are very secure. They help to prevent break-ins. Laminated glass may also be tinted or patterned.
5. *Coated glass* has a layer of plastic (or similar material) on one or both surfaces which reduces the risk of injury if the glass is broken. It also helps provide greater security.
6. *Wired glass* is ordinary glass with a wire grid embedded in it. If it is broken, either on impact or due to the heat of a fire, the wire still holds the glass in place. It is used in fire doors and sky lights.
7. *Plastic glass* is not really glass at all. It is made from various sorts of plastics, including acrylic and polystyrene. Resistant to breakage, it is used in public buildings likely to be vandalised or exposed to street riots.

Cleaning glass Glass may be cleaned by an outside firm of window cleaners, by the works department of an establishment, the housekeeping or domestic department, or by a combination of these methods. It is usually cleaned by hand, although there are machines designed to clean the glass outside tall buildings. (Most tall buildings have a cradle system to provide access for cleaning.)

The following cleaning agents are used:

- A neutral detergent solution is suitable for most general purposes. The glass should be rinsed for best results.
- An alkali detergent solution is more effective on greasy dirt. Rubber gloves should be worn and the glass must be rinsed.
- A solution of vinegar and water is suitable for less dirty glass, and it produces a shine.
- An ammonia solution also produces a shine, but it can darken putty round window panes.
- Some proprietary brands of glass cleaners are suitable for moderate dirt, for example, on mirrors, but not for heavy dirt. Directions should be followed carefully. Using too much can leave smears, which take time to remove. Some cleaners require one cloth for application and another for buffing, while others require just one cloth.
- Methylated spirits is sometimes used for display cabinets, table tops and other smaller items to give a good shine. It will also remove hair lacquer from mirrored glass. It is not suitable for very dirty glass, and great care must be taking when using it, as it is highly flammable.

Cleaning equipment

1. Cloths used for buffing and drying must be 'lint' free (that is, they should not leave fibre particles on the glass). For this reason, chamois leather cloths (or imitation versions) are often used.
2. Squeegees may be used for larger areas of glass, but floors must first be protected from splashes. The squeegee is used from side to side or in an up and down movement. The squeegee blade must be wiped free of dirt regularly and water that collects at the bottom of the glass should be wiped away.

✔ HOUSECRAFT TIP

Abrasives should never be used on glass: they will leave fine scratches on the surface which will spoil the appearance and trap soil, making cleaning more difficult in the future.

✔ HOUSECRAFT TIP

Chamois leather, used with water, must be squeezed and not wrung out. Rinse well after use and store in a plastic bag. If chamois is allowed to dry out it will become brittle. Do not use chamois with detergents as they remove its natural oils. Man-made imitation chamois leather can be used with detergents.

⚠ SAFETY

1. Only use ammonia in well ventilated areas. Wear rubber gloves.
2. Methylated spirits is highly flammable, so make sure that containers are tightly shut to prevent leakage or evaporation. Wash and dry cloths after use, or dispose of in a flame-proof bin. Dirty cloths stored in closed places can actually catch fire spontaneously.
3. A step ladder may be required for cleaning windows and other items such as glass partitions. Climbing on chairs or other furniture can be dangerous and may cause an accident. Step ladders should always be used correctly (see units 51 and 54).

Sanitary fittings are appliances fitted to a drainage system, and are used for collecting and disposing of waste. They fall into two categories:

- *soil appliances*, which collect excretory matter (faeces or urine): toilets, urinals, sluices, bedpan washers
- *waste appliances*, which collect dirty water: baths, bidets, wash hand basins (correctly named lavatory basins), sinks and showers.

Sanitary fittings must be made from hard-wearing materials that will not absorb moisture or be damaged by chemicals used for cleaning. Suitable materials include:

- *ceramic* (pottery)—commonly used for sinks, lavatory basins and toilets, it is glazed (coated with a glass-like material) so that it will not absorb moisture
- *cast-iron* or *steel coated with enamel*—used for baths and shower trays
- *stainless steel*—used for lavatory basins, sinks, toilets or urinals
- *plastic*—a recently introduced material, fairly widely used for baths and wash basins as it is cheap, light and easy to fit, and also warmer than the other materials. But it scratches easily, so cleaning agents which contain even fine abrasives must not be used.

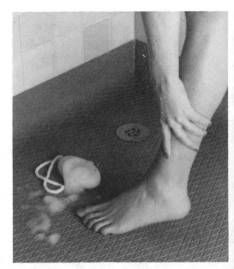

Why the cleaning of sanitary fittings is so important

1. Sanitary fittings are designed to collect waste: dirt from the hands and body, dead skin, hair, excreta or dirt collected from the cleaning of buildings (in sluices and slop sinks). All this dirt contains harmful bacteria, which will multiply in unclean conditions (see unit 45).
2. Sanitary areas in a building are used by many people, and it takes just one infected person to infect many others who use the same bath, basin etc.
3. Sanitary areas that are not regularly cleaned begin to smell, and blockages can occur and leaks may go undetected. A blockage or leak can severely damage the rest of the building.
4. Dirty or damaged toilets are extremely offputting, perhaps even more so than a rundown entrance foyer. If customers find the toilet area dirty and badly maintained, they are likely to become anxious about the standards of cleanliness and hygiene in the rest of the building, including the kitchen, and decide to go elsewhere.

Cleaning agents and equipment

1. *Neutral detergents* can be used on all sanitary surfaces, including the toilet bowl. They remove most types of dirt, and, used regularly, will get rid of bacteria. They will not harm the skin or surfaces, and are safe to use on plastic. A nylon scouring pad should be used on badly soiled areas.
2. *Alkali detergents* (also called hard surface cleaners) are also used for cleaning sanitary fittings. They are more effective on greasy dirt than a neutral detergent, for example deposits of body fats which leave tide marks on a bath.

   Prolonged regular use of hard surface cleaners is not recommended, because they may eventually cause damage to all surfaces and irritate the skin. In general, they should only be used about once a week, and regular daily cleaning should be done with a neutral detergent.
3. *Strong acid cleaners* (this includes most proprietary brand *toilet cleaners*) are acidic, extremely corrosive, and over time build up a deposit. If a toilet is cleaned

See video.

▶ ▶ ▶ TO DO

Carry out a survey of the sanitary areas in your workplace, college or a local public building. Note what materials the sanitary fittings are made from, any special design features, and where cleaning problems exist or could occur.

daily with a neutral detergent and intermittently with an alkali detergent then there should never really be a need for a strong acid cleaner. They are only necessary for cleaning very dirty toilets, or toilets in public sanitary areas that are used a great deal, or where there are water marks in the toilet bowl caused by a build up of lime (alkali), and urine and faecal stains.

Strong acid cleaners must never be mixed with other cleaners as the resulting chemical reaction will form a dangerous gas.

They should never be left unattended, as they are both dangerous to the skin and to other surfaces. Store in the correct place with the lid secure when not in use.

 REMEMBER

Special cleaning points (see also unit 45)

When cleaning toilets:
1. Always wear gloves and an apron to protect clothing and skin from harmful bacteria and contact with cleaning agents.
2. Only use cloths reserved for toilet cleaning purposes. Many establishments use a colour coding system to distinguish the use of different cloths.
3. Pay special attention to flushing rims and crevices (for example seat hinges) where bacteria can multiply if dirt is left.
4. Never transfer a toilet brush and holder from one toilet to another. This could spread bacteria.
5. Once a week (or as instructed) use an alkali detergent and every few weeks a strong acid cleaner. Leave to act.
6. After cleaning a toilet, it is useful to check under the rim of the toilet with a mirror (kept for this purpose!). If you see a build up of dirt and stains, then a thorough clean with a strong cleaner must be undertaken.

When cleaning baths, wash hand basins and bidets:
1. Clean the overflows because they trap dirt and bacteria. The outlets can be cleaned with a bottle brush.
2. Check plug holes for hairs and other waste, and remove with bottle brush or tweezers where necessary.
3. To remove greasy dirt from a bath, spray or wipe over the area with an alkali detergent, and leave for a few minutes before rinsing off.
4. Remove water marks from a bath with an acid descaler. (Never mix descalers with other cleaning agents and always follow instructions.)

Note: Always wash your hands after cleaning sanitary wear.

Test yourself: Units 28–31

City and Guilds

1. Consider the final covering or finish of a wall or ceiling:
   (a) State four factors which would influence the choice of finish.
   (b) Give four examples of a suitable finish for a wall in a hotel bedroom and describe briefly the advantages and disadvantages of each.
2. Describe briefly the general cleaning procedure for non-porous walls and ceilings.
3. (a) Name one type of machine that would be suitable for a wet method of cleaning a non-porous wall (for example in a kitchen or sanitary area).
   (b) Name one item of equipment suitable for a dry method of cleaning (for example the wall in a stair well).
4. When doors or walls are washed, what section should be washed first: the top or bottom? Explain briefly why.

5. Flat glass is used in doors and windows. Name one type suitable for general use and three types suitable when the door or window has to provide security.
6. State two suitable cleaning agents for glass and describe briefly their particular use.
7. State one of the qualities that any material used to make a sanitary fitting should have. Give two examples of suitable materials.
8. Give one reason why each of the following cleaning agents might be used on sanitary fittings, and one precaution that should be taken when it is used:
   (a) alkali detergent
   (b) acid cleaner.

Furniture is used throughout the day and night for such purposes as eating and sleeping, working and relaxation, storage and security. Some of the basic items that meet these needs—tables and chairs, beds, desks, drawers, cupboards and shelves for example—also serve a decorative purpose. Others only serve a decorative purpose—for example an antique wash stand in a bedroom or an old chest in a hall. Yet others serve a particular purpose—for example a piano so that a musician can play music, or a display cabinet so that a hotel can display souvenirs it offers for sale to guests.

Furniture is made in a range of styles to suit different tastes and budgets and in varying quality. Some items, for example, will look beautiful, provide a high degree of comfort but require careful looking after, while others will look plain, provide the minimum acceptable level of comfort but be able to withstand rough use over very many years.

Design of furniture

Furniture can be:

- Freestanding, which means that it can be moved about and arranged in a different way at any time.
- Fitted or built-in, when it is often possible to make better use of space. For example, a free standing cupboard or set of shelves may not occupy the full width of an alcove, whereas a built-in unit can be designed to use all the space.
- Cantilevered, that is made without legs and fitted to the wall. This leaves the floor space underneath clear.

It is usually important that each item of furniture fits in with the decor of the room it is being used in and with the rest of the furnishings. A moulded plastic chair will look out of place in a restaurant with a formal style of decor, polished wooden table tops and a luxury carpet.

It is also important that the furniture suits the function for which it is required. For example, a chair must be stable and strong enough to support the user, the right height for most people to sit in comfortably (see units 7 and 8), and if it is to be used for working at a desk or eating at a table, there must be enough room for the user to get his or her legs underneath the desk or table. The chair must also be easy to move back and forth and if it is likely to be used by elderly or physically disabled people, arm rests will be a helpful feature so the person can lift himself or herself into and out of the chair.

Items that are suitable in a private home may get damaged quickly by the rougher treatment and greater wear and tear they receive in a building used by the public. People rarely treat other people's property with as much respect as they do their own. Hotel beds, for example, are often used to sit on, even if a chair is provided, and this means they must have firm sides.

Some items of furniture are designed for specific uses. For example a hospital bed can usually be raised at one end so that patients who need to, can lie at an angle. Some cabins on overnight ferries and compartments on long distance trains have a couch which is comfortable to sit on during the day and at night converts into a bed. Seats on aircraft used for long flights recline slightly so they are more comfortable for sleeping. In first class cabins the seats are usually wider, spaced further apart and able to recline to a near-horizontal position. Chairs used in large conference or meeting rooms are often made so they can stack one on top of the other in a tall pile.

Design features of furniture: some examples

1. Hygiene—this is particularly important for hospital furniture, which should not absorb spills, and must wipe clean easily to remove dirt and bacteria.
2. Strength—furniture in a school must be able to withstand rough treatment.
3. Compactness—on a boat, train, in a prison or dormitory, space is usually very limited and furniture has to fit into as little space as possible, while still being easy and safe to use.
4. Appearance—in an 18th century country house which has been converted into a hotel, the style should suit the period.
5. Firmness—in a hospital or old people's home, furniture must be stable, so that people may hold on to it when getting out of a chair, or walking.
6. Economy—a consideration in a hall of residence and in many types of institutions, where costs must be kept down.
7. Comfort—in theatres, people may spend a long time in one position. The furniture should fit their size and provide support.

Furniture made from wood

Wood is still one of the most important and popular materials in furniture making, although in conditions which are very moist it is liable to warp and swell and in very dry conditions it may shrink and crack.

The so-called softwoods, which come from the fast growing evergreen trees such as spruce, pine and fir, are less expensive than the hardwoods such as oak, walnut and mahogany, which come from slow growing deciduous trees. But softwoods are not as strong as hardwoods, do not provide such a wide range of colours and finishes, and are more likely to be attacked by insects such as the common furniture beetle. (Woodworm is the general term often used to describe the various insects that attack wood.)

Plywood (sheets of wood glued together), block board (blocks of wood glued between sheets) and chipboard (compressed sawdust and woodchips sandwiched between two sheets of wood) are some of the less expensive options to using solid wood.

Wood tends to absorb dirt and moisture and look dull unless it is treated in some way. (Cleaning methods are covered in unit 33).

- The most durable finishes for wood are applied by the manufacturers of the furniture, for example polyurethane on cabinets and table tops to give the wood an attractive appearance and polyester on television cabinets to give them a very high gloss. These finishes will not be affected by water, coffee, tea, alcohol and similar liquids that might be spilt on them. Some finishes are also heat resistant so a hot dish will not cause any damage.
- Paint also forms a strong finish but it will scratch relatively easily and does, of course, completely change the appearance of the wood.
- French polish gives a high gloss but requires great skill to apply so it tends to be regarded as too expensive. The finish can also get damaged easily, showing scratches, water and heat marks.
- Wax produces a less striking finish than French polish but the soft lustre it gives wood can be just as appealing. Unfortunately it does not give the wood much protection. Water, alcohol and heat will cause marks.
- Oil brings out the natural beauty of wood, particularly teak. It provides some protection but has similar drawbacks to wax.

Other materials used in furniture making

Stone (including marble) is not much used for furniture, except for decorative purposes, and certain specific uses, for example marble table tops.

Wicker and **cane** make attractive, but not very strong, furniture. Back in fashion in recent years, it is a popular choice for outdoor and conservatory furniture.

Metal (steel and chrome) is widely used for office furniture, and for the frames and legs of chairs, tables and couches. It is also used to provide decorative features, such as beaten copper for table tops. Metal can be treated with chemicals or plastics to prevent tarnishing (becoming discoloured).

Plastic has been popular since the 1960s, mostly for smaller items of furniture, such as moulded chairs, tables, benches and desks; or as a veneer on chipboard or metal. It looks attractive and bright, and is easy to maintain although it scratches easily. Plastic builds up static, so it attracts dust and bacteria.

Glass is used for table tops and for the doors and sides of display cabinets (so the items on display can be seen). Glass fibre (fibreglass) is often combined with plastic to strengthen moulded plastic furniture.

Upholstered furniture
Consists of a frame made from wood, cane, metal or plastic, a base, a filling (natural or synthetic), and a covering. Fabrics such as dralon, cotton, wool tweed and leather are popular coverings.

 TO DO

In your workplace or a public building of your choice, see if you can find one example of each of the following:

- fitted furniture
- cantilevered furniture
- furniture made partly or entirely with: plastic, stone, chipboard, and glass.

Make a note of what each example is used for, the condition it is in (including any damage you see), and why you think it was chosen. If possible, discuss the reasons for its choice with someone who would know the background to the original decision.

Damp dusting

Damp dusting is suitable for removing soilage from most types of furniture. It is not suitable for any parts of furniture that are upholstered with a fabric (see unit 35), or for wood which has not been sealed (so wooden furniture which is waxed or oiled should not be damp-dusted).

A neutral detergent is used for routine cleaning. For periodic cleaning an alkali detergent may be required—if this is necessary, the furniture must be rinsed with plain water to remove the alkali before it causes damage to the furniture.

Cleaning cane and wicker furniture

Cane and wicker furniture will soon look neglected if the soil which collects between the strands of cane and other uneven surfaces is left to accumulate.

A suction cleaner should be used on a routine basis with a small brush attachment. Damp dusting will remove finger marks and similar soilage.

Cane and wicker furniture can be washed provided there is no plywood in the structure and care is taken not to over-wet the furniture. A neutral detergent is used, then the furniture is rinsed with cold salty water and left to dry in a well ventilated room (but never near a radiator or in strong sunlight). The salt stiffens the cane. It can then be polished with a liquid wax if it has been varnished or painted, or a paste wax if it has not been sealed in this way.

♪ HOUSECRAFT TIPS

The 'unseen' parts of furniture should be cleaned periodically, for example suction cleaning or damp dusting as appropriate the inside of drawers, backs of cupboards, underneath shelves and chair seats and emptying bookshelves so the areas normally covered by the books can be cleaned effectively.

Furniture will be damaged by constant sunlight or the warmth produced by a nearby radiator. Move furniture that is in conditions likely to be harmful. In some rooms the only practical way of doing this may be to swap the position of one piece of furniture with another—so, for example, all the chairs have a turn at being in front of the window (a popular position because the view is so good).

If one chair or a bed, for example, is being used more often than another because of its position, then swap the items regularly so that they wear at about the same rate.

Polishing furniture

There are various polishes available as liquids, pastes and aerosols, both for cleaning furniture and replacing the wax or oil:

Oil polishes are only suitable for certain types of wood, for example teak. The oil (teak oil or linseed oil) is applied sparingly, using a clean dry cloth and rubbed over the wood. Oil is not meant to provide a high gloss, but it is absorbed into the wood, preventing it from drying out.

Paste waxes can be used on any wood previously treated with a wax or French polish and will be good for the wood. They should not be used on wood surfaces which have been oiled or sealed, for example with a polyurethane seal used on modern furniture. Paste waxes are applied with one cloth, and then rubbed to a shine with another. This can be time consuming and even then the surface produced may be soft, attract dust easily and lose its shine.

Liquid waxes can be used on wood which has been sealed and on wicker or cane (see box). They are unsuitable for wood which has been oiled, or French polished, because of their high solvent content. Liquid waxes, which come in a bottle, spray or aerosol, are easier to apply than paste waxes. They clean surfaces well, but they do not penetrate very deeply. For some liquid waxes, the same cloth may be used for applying and polishing.

Furniture creams do not contain a lot of wax, but they clean well, especially spillages and sticky marks. Creams may come in bottles, sprays or aerosols, and only one cloth is needed. They can be used on sealed wood, metal (particularly enamelled metal, as on refrigerators), glass and plastic.

✱ FOR INTEREST

Vinegar may be used periodically on polished furniture. It helps to remove old, soiled polish and greasy marks. It is mixed with an equal quantity of water, and the solution is applied with a chamois leather cloth, and wiped off with a dry cloth.

A cloth wrung out with undiluted vinegar will get rid of the musty smell of old furniture. Care must be taken not to overwet the wood, as this may soften the glue and cause the wood to smell.

Leather or hide furniture can be wiped with a damp cloth (wrung out in a neutral detergent) if it has been soiled with a liquid spill or greasy hands or hair. After the mark has been removed, the area should be rinsed, dried thoroughly, then polished with a polish recommended for the purpose.

△ SAFETY

Apart from furniture creams, most furniture polishes may be flammable, so after use store them carefully and either wash or throw away the applicator and polishing cloths in a fire-proof container.

Aerosols, when empty, must also be disposed of carefully, as instructed. If incinerated, they will explode, and at the least cause damage to the incinerator.

TO DO

Look for an example of as many different surfaces as possible on items of furniture at your workplace or in your home. Find out how they are usually cleaned, how often and what is used.

Ask if you can clean at least two of the surfaces, if possible choosing an example which can be polished with a paste wax and another which can be polished with a liquid wax. Time how long each task takes and note what the finished effect looks like.

Fabrics are cloths or materials produced by weaving or combining in some other way cotton, nylon, wool, silk or other threads together. Textiles is another name for fabrics, used especially in association with the manufacturing process—as in a textile factory. The many different fabrics can be put into two broad categories according to the source of the thread (more precisely called the yarn):

- wool, cotton, linen, silk and asbestos are *natural fibres*
- rayon, nylon, polyester and acrylic are *man-made fibres*.

The traditional manufacturing process falls into two categories:

1. The fibres are spun together to form a **yarn**. The yarn or thread may contain only one type of fibre or consist of a combination of fibres, chosen because of their different qualities. For example, for bed linen, cotton, which is cool to touch and absorbs moisture readily, is mixed with polyester, which does not crease and is stronger than cotton, to produce cotton-polyester, which has the qualities of both fibres.
2. The yarn is then woven, knitted, laced, crocheted or bonded together to form the **fabric**.

Production of fabrics

The enormous variety of textures and finishes available in table linen, upholstery and curtaining material, fabrics for overalls, are examples of what the different processes of combining the yarn can achieve.

The traditional weaving methods can produce:

- The plain weave typical of sheets. The lengths of yarn are woven over and under each other (holes in blankets may be darned using a similar technique). The result is smooth in appearance but liable to tear.
- More interesting appearances and a stronger fabric. This is done by altering the pattern by which the lengths of yarn are threaded together as in the twill weave of denim, the figured weave of brocade and the damask weave of pure linen tablecloths and napkins.
- A very open structure, created by twisting the lengths of yarn together, as often found in net curtains and tablemats.
- The deep pile effect of velvet and corduroy. This is created by weaving extra lengths of yarn through the cloth, so they stand out from the base, either as loops or cut to form short lengths.

These methods all require skill and even the most advanced weaving machines are relatively slow compared with new processes such as:

- Tufting: the yarn is punched into a base cloth and held in position on the reverse side by an adhesive. This is the way in which many candlewick bedspreads are made and it has become a very important method in carpet making.
- Needle punching: punching barbed needles repeatedly into a thick layer of fibres until a tangled, but strong web is created. Some blankets are produced by this method and so are many carpet tiles.
- Bonded fibre: soaking the fibres with an adhesive so they are bonded together. The fibres are laid in a pattern for interlinings and similar materials, but may be left completely random, as in some cleaning cloths.
- Stitch bonding: the lengths of yarn are held in place by machine stitched rows of a second, strong yarn. This is much faster than traditional weaving and many furnishing fabrics are made in this way.

USEFUL TERMS

Natural fibres may be *vegetable fibres*, for example cotton, linen, jute and hemp, or *animal fibres*, for example wool or silk, or *mineral fibres*, for example asbestos.

Man-made fibres may be *regenerated fibres*, such as viscose rayon, which are made from various raw materials, such as wood pulp, cellulose and cotton waste, or they may be *synthetic fibres*, such as terylene and nylon, which are made entirely from chemicals, for example from the by-products of coal, oil, petroleum.

✳ FOR INTEREST

The small, but unpleasant shock experienced sometimes when metal is touched—a door handle for example—is caused by a build-up of static electricity. The electrical charge is created every time there is friction between two surfaces, so walking over a carpet will create static electricity.

Normally the charge is safely carried or 'conducted' to earth. Cotton, wool and wood are examples of good conductors, which is why shocks are not felt after walking over a wool carpet.

Many of the synthetic fibres are poor conductors, however, and a build-up of static electricity will occur. If the atmosphere is dry, as in a centrally heated room in winter, the build-up is significantly increased. Air-conditioning usually keeps the atmosphere sufficiently moist to prevent a build-up, natural ventilation also helps.

Fibre and some of its common uses	Advantages	Disadvantages
Wool carpets, blankets, upholstery	Warm Does not flatten or crease easily Does not soil quickly Does not burn easily Does not hold static electricity Has a natural bounce	Has to be dry cleaned, or if washing is possible only low temperatures can be used Is attacked by moths Not particularly strong
Cotton bed and table linen, towels, curtains, uniforms	Cool to touch in hot weather Can be washed at hot temperatures for hygiene purposes Absorbent, holding water (for example, towels) or moisture (for example, perspiration) Does not hold static electricity Will not cling to the skin if it burns	Creases easily Will shrink up to 9% unless pre-shrunk Not fire resistant Not as strong as many synthetic fibres Attacked by mildew
Viscose rayon uniforms and (when mixed with other fibres): table linen, towels	Soft, hairy texture Moth proof Slow to build up static electricity Blends with other fibres Colour fast	Flattens and creases easily Soils easily Can stretch and loose structure when wet
Nylon or polyamide often mixed with other fibres to give extra strength to carpets, upholstery fabrics and uniforms	Cool Does not crease easily Not affected by fungi or insects Does not hold much water and dries quickly Very hard wearing and strong	Holds static electricity Low heat resistance: melts at low temperature
Polyester uniforms, bed linen	Will not crease, shrink or stretch Very strong and blends well with other fibres (cotton-polyester bed linen lasts 3 or 4 times as long as the pure cotton equivalent) Does not absorb much water	Fades with constant washing Cannot be washed at very high temperatures

The type of finish

A fabric may be smooth or roughly textured, heavy or light, coarse or fine, depending on the yarn and the methods used to make it. It can then be dyed, printed, crimped or brushed to give it a particular appearance. It can also be treated in a number of ways to make it more suitable for its intended use, for example:

- made resistant to soiling or static electricity
- made water repellent
- pre-shrunk or given a shrink-resistant finish
- made fire resistant
- made crease resistant.

 TO DO

Make a list of different fabrics used in a hotel and catering establishment of your choice. Divide your list into three categories of fibre: natural, regenerated and synthetic. Try and find at least two examples in each category.

Against each item, describe what the fabric feels like to the touch, its appearance, how absorbent it is when wet and how readily it creases.

Find out as much as you can about the cost of each fabric, how well it wears, and how resistant it is to soiling and fire.

Most accommodation establishments contain items made from a fabric of some sort, for example:

- curtains and pelmets from velvet
- fabric wall covering from hessian
- cushions from cotton
- lampshades from silk
- bedspreads and valances from cotton/polyester.

These can all be usefully classified as 'soft furnishings'. Furniture which is upholstered or covered in a fabric requires similar care, especially when it is cleaned and so it is also dealt with in this unit.

Soft furnishings can provide an attractive finish to a room, adding colour, pattern and texture. Most fabrics will help absorb sound and some are good for trapping heat inside the room (or keeping the hot air out). However they do trap dirt and dust more readily than hard surfaces, so they are not suitable for areas such as treatment rooms or operating theatres in hospitals. They also absorb moisture which makes them unsuitable for kitchens and small bathrooms.

Cleaning soft furnishings

Fabrics which are in direct contact with people, such as bedspreads and upholstered furniture, are often cleaned weekly, while those which are not, such as lampshades and pelmets, are cleaned every few months. A typical schedule would be:

routinely
- damp dusting of any surfaces not covered by fabric
- suction cleaning (probably weekly)
- stain removal (as soon as possible after the staining has occurred)
- laundering of bedspreads and valances

periodically
- shampooing
- laundering or dry cleaning of curtains and loose covers.

Damp dusting   Any non-upholstered parts of chairs, stool, settees, bedheads and so forth should be damp-dusted. A neutral detergent solution is used on most surfaces. The principal exception is wood which has been waxed or oiled—this is only likely to be the case with certain styles of antique or country furniture (see unit 32).

Suction cleaning   This is a very effective method for removing the dirt and dust that settles on soft furnishings, even when they are hanging vertically, as in the case of curtains.

An upholstery tool is used for most surfaces and a crevice tool for reaching difficult edges and down the sides of chairs. A back-vac suction cleaner is particularly suitable for cleaning curtains and high surfaces like pelmets.

When the fabric being cleaned is hanging loose, such as a curtain, then a lower suction strength should be used, otherwise it will be difficult to move the head of the cleaner evenly (or at all if the fabric is relatively thin). Some suction cleaners have controls connected to the motor which can regulate suction strength, with others, the air inlet slot on the suction hose has to be opened up in order to reduce the suction power.

 TO DO

Choose either a living room or sleeping area, and make a note of the soft furnishings and, where possible, the fabrics they are made from. If you cannot identify the fabrics, first discuss these among your colleagues or fellow students, and then ask the housekeeping department for advice. Also discuss and note down the appropriate cleaning methods for every item, and how often they should be carried out.

Stain removal   If stains occur as a result of spills or other accidents on a bedspread or cushion, for example, then the best procedure may be to remove the item and send it off for dry cleaning or laundering with any information that is available on the nature of the stain. But if it is a relatively small stain, or a stain on one of a set of cushions, for example, and it is not appropriate to send all the cushion covers for cleaning, or if the stain is on a piece of upholstery that cannot be removed from the furniture, then the stain will have to be dealt with on site, using a stain removal agent (see unit 39).

Laundering or dry cleaning   Curtains, bedspreads, valances and loose covers on chairs and settees are examples of items that can be sent for laundering or dry cleaning (see unit 40).

What method is selected and how it is carried out will depend on whether the fabric is likely to shrink, if it is affected by high temperatures, whether it is colour fast and whether a soil retardant or other special finish has been applied. Bedspreads and loose covers will often have a textile care label indicating how to clean the fabric (see unit 40).

Shampooing   Upholstered furniture, pelmets and bedheads usually have to be shampooed on site, either because they cannot be removed or because they are too heavy to move easily. Heavy curtains are often cleaned where they hang for the same reason.

Before the items are shampooed they must always be suction-cleaned (to remove as much dirt and dust as possible—see above) and any stains dealt with (since special stain removal agents are likely to be necessary).

Small items of furniture can be shampooed by hand if no machine is available or only one or two items have to be cleaned. A dry foam carpet shampoo is used, mixed according to the instructions and gently rubbed into the fabric with a soft nail brush. It is then left to dry and then the fabric is suction-cleaned to remove the loosened soil and residue of the foam.

In most cases, however, a dry foam carpet shampoo machine or a hot water extraction machine is used, fitted with an upholstery tool.

The procedure followed is similar to that used for shampooing carpets (see unit 27). The shampoo is applied to a small section at a time (taking care that the previously treated area is just overlapped), using a long straight stroke—if possible in the direction of the pile.

Safety of bed linen

Hospitals, old people's homes and other residential establishments run by the National Health Service, the Department of Health and other government departments use fire-resistant bed linen as a matter of policy. Most hotels and other commercial establishments also place this aspect of safety high on the priority list when choosing sheets, blankets, bedspreads, pillows and so forth. There are basically two options:

- To choose fabrics which have good fire resistance properties: 100% polyester, for example, for sheets, pillow cases and bedspreads, modacrylic for blankets.
- To choose what is termed a *durably treated fire resistant material*, a fabric such as cotton and wool which is not naturally resistant to fire but which is given a special finish (this will be known by a brand name, for example Proban and Pyrovatex).

The specifications for fire resistance are laid down by the British Standards Institution. They are complex because no two fires are the same—they will be affected by environmental conditions as well as by the characteristics of the material, how it is being used and how much of it there is.

✳   FOR INTEREST

Some lampshades can be cleaned using a warm water and neutral detergent solution. The shade is removed from the light fitting, totally immersed in the cleaning solution and if necessary rubbed lightly with a soft scrubbing brush. It should then be rinsed in cold water and left to dry.

However if the fabric is likely to shrink, or there is a danger that the adhesive and/or stitching used to assemble the shade will be weakened, then the shade should be wiped with a cloth that has been dipped in the cleaning solution and well wrung out. It should be rinsed in the same way with clean water.

For any type of residential establishment, the comfort and appearance of the bed is a major consideration. The more luxurious the establishment, the more comfortable the bed will be expected to be. There is likely to be more space available so the bed will be bigger than the standard sizes considered necessary for sleeping. The quality of the materials used to make the bed, its mattress, the sheets, pillows, blankets and so forth will be higher. It is even possible that a touch of the exotic may be introduced with silk or satin sheets and a waterfilled PVC mattress!

Bed bases

Beds have to be strong as well as comfortable. For this reason the frame and base of the bed is usually made of wood or metal. With some beds the mattress is supported on a solid panel, or on slats of wood, or on metal bars. These provide a very firm support and can be comfortable when combined with a good quality mattress. Solid bases are used when the base of the bed provides storage space, with drawers or a hinged top.

The base for the mattress is sometimes a wire mesh attached to the frame. This is neither firm nor particularly comfortable, but such beds are inexpensive and unlikely to harbour bacteria, so they are often found in hostels and similar establishments.

The wire mesh system is more comfortable when springs are used at each of the points where the mesh is connected to the frame.

Coil springs mounted on metal bars or wooden slats make the bed much more comfortable. In many divan beds, the springs are contained within an upholstered base similar in many respects to a mattress. In some beds the base has fewer springs and a wooden frame to provide a very firm edge.

When the legs of beds are fitted with castors, the bed can be easily moved for cleaning and to change the bed linen. Hospital beds can usually be tilted at either end and can also be raised or lowered.

Mattresses

The simplest mattresses likely to be used in a residential establishment nowadays are made of foam. The better quality foam mattresses use latex foam, or a mixture of latex and the less expensive polyurethane foam.

Foam mattresses should be placed on a slatted base so the mattress is well ventilated (solid bases can cause condensation to build up, creating favourable conditions for the growth of bacteria). Even the thicker foam mattresses—between 10 and 15 cm (4 and 6 inches) is the usual range—will not provide the degree of comfort that mattresses with interior springs can offer.

The spring mechanism varies considerably in different quality mattresses. Generally:

- the gauge and quality of the metal used to make the spring will affect how firm or soft the mattress is
- when springs can operate independently of each other, they offer better support, catering for the different contours of the body (and if two people are sharing the mattress, each person's body shape and weight will be accommodated without affecting the other person)
- the greater the number of springs, the better the quality.

Bedding

Pillows, duvets and eiderdowns are stuffed with various natural or man-made fillings.

The best natural fillings are the down and feathers of ducks and geese; goose down is the softest and fluffiest of all, durable too, but very expensive. Some natural fillings can be laundered but dry cleaning is usually recommended, and even then some of the natural 'bounce' is likely to be lost.

Man-made fillings are comparatively inexpensive and easy to care for. They can be laundered and there is no danger of the contents poking through the cover (this can happen with natural fillings, even though the cover is usually thicker).

Blankets have been in use to keep the occupant(s) of a bed warm for far longer than duvets, and so it is not surprising that similar advances have been made in producing man-made fabrics that are as effective as the best natural product (wool) for retaining heat, almost as light and soft and significantly cleaner. Furthermore good quality man-made products can be washed without fear of shrinking or damage to the finish. They can also be stored without any risk of moth damage. One disadvantage of some man-made fabrics is that they build up static electricity. Another is their feel. Acrylic blankets—which are the closest in appearance to wool—have a slight metallic feel.

Other natural products besides wool are used in blankets, and some blankets use a combination of natural and man-made fabrics. The so-called 'union blanket' is made from cotton and wool, or from cotton, wool and viscose rayon.

The fabrics used to make sheets and pillowcases should be absorbent and have a smooth texture. Pure linen is an expensive fabric but very smooth and silky and quite cool and strong, so it lasts a long time. Cotton is less expensive and still very comfortable, but like linen it must be carefully ironed (see unit 41) and then will easily crease again.

Cotton-polyester mixtures have an even longer service life (somewhere between 300 and 400 wash cycles compared with about 120 for a cotton or linen sheet sent to a commercial laundry). Their second important advantage (see unit 37) is that they are soil and crease resistant—no ironing at all is required.

✳ FOR INTEREST

Good quality man-made fibres are only slightly less effective at retaining warmth than the best down or wool.

✳ FOR INTEREST

Down is the soft very fine feathers that are found on the breast of fowl. The description of the content of natural fillings is laid down by law. The maximum content (by weight) of the less expensive fillings is specified as follows:

down	up to 15% of very small, fluffy feathers
down and feather	up to 49% feather
feather and down	up to 85% feather

The warmth of fabrics is measured in a unit called a *tog*. One tog is equal to ten times the temperature difference between the two sides of the material. The best quality down duvets have a tog value of between 11 and 14, while polyester fibres (which are among the better man-made products for this purpose) have a tog value of between 8 and 11.

Even if an establishment uses natural fillings to provide the best possible degree of comfort, a small stock of pillows, duvets and eiderdowns filled with a man-made filling should be available for anyone who has an allergy to the natural product.

City and Guilds

Test yourself: Units 32–36

1. Certain furniture is described as cantilevered. Explain briefly what is meant by this and give one other general term used to describe the design of furniture.

2. State five factors which should be considered when choosing the design of furniture for a particular use.

3. Describe briefly why the surface of wood furniture should be treated and state two examples of finishes.

4. If some furniture polishes are not stored carefully there is a particular danger. What is it? Explain what safety precautions should be taken with the applicator and polishing cloths.

5. Give one example of each of the following types of fibres used to make fabrics:
   (a) vegetable   (c) regenerated
   (b) animal   (d) synthetic.

6. State two types of finish that can be given to fabrics to make them more suitable for use in residential establishments.

7. Give two advantages and two disadvantages of using either cotton or nylon as a fibre for making fabrics for a residential establishment.

8. Describe briefly the routine methods used to clean soft furnishings.

9. State two methods used for supporting the mattress on a bed frame: one should give more comfort to the bed's user.

10. Explain briefly what it is about the construction of a blanket or duvet that helps trap heat. Give one example of a suitable material for each.

37 LINEN AND ITS CARE

Sheets, pillowcases, tablecloths, napkins and similar items are known collectively as 'linen'. The term is no longer restricted to pure linen fabrics, but includes those made from cotton and also the synthetics, for example nylon and polyester.

In accommodation operations, 'linen' includes all those items which have to be laundered such as uniforms, curtains and chair covers, as well as any that are made of fabrics which require them to be removed for specialist cleaning (including dry cleaning, when special chemicals rather than water are used to remove the dirt).

Linen items and their selection

The key decisions that have to be made when linen is purchased are:

1. Type: what items of linen are to be used in the building?
2. Fabric: what will be most suitable for the purpose?
3. Quantity: how many of each item will be required?
4. Laundry facilities: will the items be laundered on the premises or at a commercial laundry?

Type and fabric

Bed linen (sheets, duvet covers, pillowcases, under-sheets and valances) should be:

- Comfortable: cotton, for example, is more comfortable than nylon, as it absorbs perspiration and is therefore cooler to sleep in.
- The correct size.
- Practical and suit the laundry system in operation. For example, pure cotton creases quickly so is more suitable for use in establishments where the bed linen is changed daily, while a cotton–polyester mixture will not need ironing at all if it is laundered with care.
- Hygienic: to kill bacteria bed linen in a hospital, for example, needs to be washed at high temperatures, so cotton or cotton–polyester is used, and blankets made of cotton or synthetic cotton blends are used rather than wool. (Wool blankets would have to be dry cleaned to avoid shrinkage, and this would be too costly.)

Towels (hand towels, bath towels, shaving towels, bath mats, face cloths etc.) should be:

- Absorbent: made of a fibre that will absorb moisture, such as cotton, or a cotton-rayon mixture (which helps to increase the bulk and so increases the absorption qualities).
- Strong: able to resist constant rubbing.
- Hygienic: able to stand up to washing at high temperatures.

Soft furnishings (curtains, cushions, bedspreads, loose covers) should be:

- Fire retardant or resistant.
- Colour fast: must not fade in sunlight.
- Strong: able to withstand heavy wear—especially cushions, bedspreads, loose covers.
- Easy to clean. Linen covers and cushions, for example, launder well; velvet is softer but more difficult to look after.
- Selected according to specific use. For example, polyester net curtains provide privacy, while heavy wool curtains help to insulate a room and keep out the light.

✳ FOR INTEREST

Pure linen is one of the oldest fabrics. It is made from the fibre of the flax plant and is very hard wearing (but expensive and cold to touch).

For more details on different fabrics, see unit 34.

✳ FOR INTEREST

In many areas of the country it is possible to hire linen from specialised linen hire companies and the bigger laundries. There is also another option: to purchase disposable items—tablecloths, napkins and even sheets and pillowcases that can be thrown away after use.

Disposable linen

The use of disposable items:

- reduces the amount of laundry work
- simplifies hygiene protection (for example, in a hospital, disposable sheets may be used for particular cases in an infectious diseases ward)
- provides an alternative in case of an emergency (for example, if the normal linen supply runs out).

Disposable items are a fire risk so they must be handled and stored with great care. When they are discarded they should never be put in the same refuse container as cigarette ends or anything else that can start a fire.

Restaurant linen (tablecloths, napkins, banqueting cloths) should be:

- Easy to match, repair and replace.
- Well finished—with good edging and stitching—so that it can withstand frequent laundering.
- Able to absorb food spillages.
- Practical and suit the laundry system in operation. For example, a cotton–polyester mixture may be more appropriate for a restaurant in a hotel or guesthouse where laundry is done on the premises, than pure linen which must be ironed (and probably also starched).

Uniforms should be:

- Comfortable to wear.
- Easy to clean.
- Practical, safe and hygienic: able to protect the wearer from spillages, dirt and so forth, or to protect whatever is being processed, such as food, from the handler.

Size of linen stocks

In any establishment, too much stock might not only be expensive, and use a lot of storage space but it would be both a security and fire risk. Too little, however, would also cause difficulties. For example if the laundry does not deliver cleaned items on time, hospital beds or hotel rooms may have to be kept empty until fresh linen is delivered.

Sheets, pillowcases and towels
The number of items in stock partly depends on how often sheets are changed for guests who stay for several nights. In a hall of residence, this may be weekly, whereas it is more likely to be every day in a luxury hotel. Another factor to consider is whether the linen will be laundered:

- On site, when three or four complete sets of linen per bed are recommended (one in the laundry, one in the central linen room, and one on the bed). If polyester-cotton items are used, it is possible to get by with less. These do not require ironing, and so the laundry process is speeded up.
- At a commercial laundry, when up to eight sets per bed may be needed. While the actual laundering may be done as quickly as in an on-site laundry, delays can occur and time is taken up transporting the linen to and from the laundry.

Soft furnishings, blankets and duvets
A few extra sets of each may be kept, particularly where standard colours, designs and sizes are used. In this way, rooms can be kept in use while, for example, one set of curtains is being laundered.

Restaurant linen
Numbers kept depend on how many meals are served at each table each day, and with tablecloths in particular, on establishment policy about how often to change them. Here, too, allowance must be made for time spent at the laundry.

Uniforms
Staff whose uniforms need frequent laundering, for example chefs, will probably require three or more sets. If laundering or dry cleaning is needed less frequently, two sets are usually enough. Some establishments will issue all uniforms from a central pool every day, keeping a supply of three or more per person, and spares for emergency in a number of different sizes.

 TO DO

Find out from the person in charge of linen in the place where you work (or wherever you are able to make these enquiries) and write down:

1. How many different sets of bed linen, guest towels and restaurant linen are kept?
2. How many beds are there in the establishment, and how many restaurant tables?

With this information, work out the number of sets that are kept per bed and per table.

Also enquire if there are ever shortages and write down how these are dealt with. For example, is there a supply of disposable items available? Is it possible to hire extra sheets, towels and other items in cases of emergencies? Are beds sometimes left empty because of stock shortages?

Most establishments either:

- Buy all linen and instal a laundry on site. (A very large on-site laundry may also have a dry cleaning plant.)
- Buy all linen and send it all to a commercial laundry off the premises (off-site laundry).
- Hire everything or specific items, such as sheets and towels, staff uniforms, from a linen rental company. The company exchanges clean for dirty linen at agreed intervals, and is also responsible for replacing worn out items.
- Use a combination: purchasing some items, renting others; laundering some items on site and others off site.

Some establishments have an 'easy-care' or 'no-iron' linen system, using polyester–cotton bed linen and rayon table linen, which do not need ironing if they are carefully washed and tumble dried and folded when warm. Less equipment, staff and space is required for this system.

Linen control

Whatever system is used, the linen is handled by many people, and passes through various rooms and transporting systems. Housekeeping staff, for example, will strip a bed and take dirty sheets to the linen room; the linen room staff then send them to the laundry (either in-house or an outside commercial firm, in which case it is transported by van); laundry staff do the wash; the clean linen is delivered to the linen room; linen room staff store the linen on shelves; and when needed, housekeeping staff remove linen to make up a new bed.

At each stage in the handling process, care must be taken in order:

- that sufficient, clean linen, in good condition, is available where and when it is needed
- that misplacement and theft are prevented as far as possible.

The four most commonly used methods of control are:

1. *Clean for dirty*

This system operates from a central linen store and is suitable for smaller establishments. No item of clean linen is issued before a dirty one has been handed in as an exchange. In the case of table linen, for example, the restaurant staff will take the dirty tablecloths and napkins to the stores, where the exact number of clean items will be issued in exchange. If the stock of clean linen in the restaurant is then too low, there is no doubt that the items have gone missing there and enquiries can be made.

One drawback to this system is that clean and dirty items may come in close contact with each other, and dirty linen can infect clean linen. Another is that beds cannot be re-made or tables reset, without first going to exchange the linen.

2. *Set amount*

A set amount of linen is issued each day, based on the number of items expected to be used by the guests, patients, residents etc. Any spare stock is returned to the stores at the end of the shift. This method is used in situations where it is difficult to calculate how much will be required, for example in an airport hotel when many more rooms than expected may be used as a result of sudden bad weather, it may become the practice to over-issue, and items could be mislaid or stolen more easily.

The linen room

One central linen room may serve the whole establishment, but in larger buildings there may be one central store and smaller ones at suitable vantage points to serve specific areas, such as one hospital ward, or one hotel floor.

Some large establishments have three separate rooms, one for dirty linen, a store for clean linen and a sewing room for repairs. However, it has become increasingly rare to allocate so much space to linen. In fact, some recently built hotels and most guesthouses store their linen in cupboards.

Requirements of the linen room

1. It should be close to the laundry or if laundry is done off the premises, near the entrance where it is loaded and unloaded.
2. It should not be too remote from the areas where the clean linen is used: the wards, bedrooms and dining rooms.
3. It should be a room which can be cleaned easily, and have smooth non-porous floors, walls and surfaces. (Non-porous surfaces do not absorb dirt or moisture.)
4. Good lighting, ventilation and adequate heating is a necessity: heating provides the best storage conditions (and is necessary for the people working in the room), whereas damp conditions encourage mildew which attacks linen.
5. Strong shelves are required for storing linen, slatted rather than solid so air is able to circulate round the linen.
6. A flat surface is needed for sorting linen, and a counter is useful when issuing linen.
7. The room must be secure, to protect against theft of stock.

The room must be cleaned regularly so that dust does not collect. Any signs of pests, such as moths or rodents, must be reported immediately, as they can cause considerable damage to stock.

3. *Topping up*

In this system, every linen cupboard or trolley is topped up to a certain level each day, based on the number of items usually required. Any unused items are left in the cupboard or trolley, ready to be topped up the following day. This method is common in hospital wards. Its advantage is that some stock is always available for emergencies, and excessive quantities are not stored. However, there is a risk of theft if access to the cupboard or trolley is not carefully controlled at all times.

4. *Requisition*

Here, staff check to see how much linen they will need on a particular day, by looking at the list of departures or table bookings or by first checking and stripping the beds. They will then fill in a requisition note or form.

Tips on control and storage

1. Make sure that the same number of items have been returned from the laundry as were sent out—and note any 'shorts'.
2. Check and put aside any linen which has been stained or needs repair. (Linen returned from the laundry has been carefully folded, so it is not always possible to unfold each clean item for checking purposes.)
3. Store clean linen with all folds facing the same way and all types in their correct place (keeping, for example, single and double sheets apart). Some establishments store linen in packs instead of by item type. For example, a pack for a single bed will contain two single sheets and two pillow cases.
4. Move aside any items already on the shelf, then replace them on top of the new, clean stock. In this way, the stock is rotated and the life of the linen will be extended (it benefits from being allowed to rest before re-use).

 TO DO

Calculate the cost of the following items that might be required in a single bedroom (with a standard size single bed). Base your prices on those paid by your workplace, or if you have difficulty finding out what these are, visit the bedding section of a large department store and use those prices.

List A	List B
• 2 sheets	• 1 underblanket
• 2 pillowcases	• 2 blankets
• 1 bath towel	• 1 bedspread
• 1 hand towel	• 1 valance
• 1 face cloth	

Now work out the cost of equipping 100 bedrooms, and having two spare sets per bedroom of each item in list A and one spare set of each item in list B.

 HYGIENE

Clean linen
1. Wash your hands before handling.
2. Store on clean surfaces (never on the floor!), and protect from dust.

Dirty linen
1. Put in a bag or skip as soon as possible. Do not shake dirty linen about.
2. Send promptly to the laundry, as damp linen encourages the growth of fungi (such as mildew) and bacteria.
3. Wash your hands carefully after handling.

In a hospital, linen soiled by faeces, urine and blood must be bagged separately on the ward. Infected linen (used by patients with an infectious disease) is also separately bagged, often in special bags held closed by a thread which dissolves in the washing machine during the laundry process, so releasing the infected laundry.

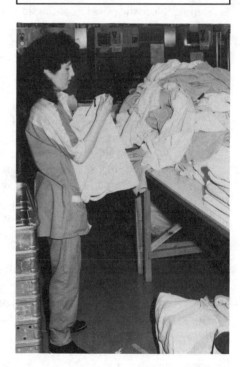

The information in this unit will help you gain certification in the Caterbase module *Handling Linen*.

3 9 LINEN AND ITS CARE

What is a stain?

A stain is not like ordinary dirt which attaches itself to the fabric. It is more like a dye which soaks into the fibres, but because it usually takes some time to soak in, immediate preventive action is often effective.

Some general points to remember:

- No single spot remover will cope with all stains.
- The method used depends on the nature of the stain and of the stained fabric.
- Stains are often very difficult to remove, and some stains may be made worse following attempts to remove them.

Rules of stain removal

1. Deal with all stains as soon as possible. Once a stain has hardened or has seeped into a surface, it will be much more difficult to remove.
2. Try to identify the stain and the surface. Examination of the stain should follow a logical procedure:

   Step A: Note the position of the stain, especially on a garment, as this may give a clue as to the type of stain. For example, a stain on trouser bottoms could be shoe polish.

   Step B: Note the appearance. Stains caused by pastes or thick liquids, such as paint, nail varnish, mud etc., are solid looking and caked on the surface of the fabric. Some stains caused by liquids, such as wine or tea, penetrate the yarn. Compound stains, such as blood and jam, both penetrate the yarn and build up on the surface.

   Step C: Feel the stain. Hardness may indicate lacquer or glue, while brittle stains could be sugar compounds (these often turn white when scratched). Some stains, such as new paint or toffee, are tacky.

   Step D: Note the colour. Many stains have characteristic colours—blood is red but becomes brown with age, and may even look black.

   Step E: Note the odour. Certain stains, such as perfume and salad dressing, have characteristic odours. All odours are more apparent when steam is applied.

3. Remove as much of the stain as possible before using any other treatment, but avoid rubbing it. If the stain is solid, gently scrape away the hardened build-up; if the excess is liquid, use an absorbent cloth to mop it up.
4. Always test the effect of any stain removal agent first, by applying to a part of the surface which cannot be seen.
5. Always use the mildest treatment first. Start with cold water if you are not sure about the type of stain, because hot water or detergent may set the stain and make it impossible to remove.
6. Always treat the stain from the outer edges and work inwards, so as to avoid spreading it and making it larger.
7. If the stain is persistent, then try a harsher treatment, but avoid hard rubbing or using strong stain removal agents.
8. After cleaning, thoroughly rinse the stained area with cold water.
9. Leave the area as dry as possible.

Methods for removing stains include:

Physical methods

1. Soaking up liquid spills with absorbent cloth or paper. Spread it over the stained area and work from the outer edges inwards to the centre to avoid spreading the stain. Remember to use a white absorbent cloth—dye in a coloured cloth may cause additional staining.
2. Using a powder, such as fuller's earth or French chalk, to soak up a greasy stain.
3. Using friction: scraping, brushing, rubbing, or scrubbing dried-on stains. Do not rub too hard as the surface may be damaged by the friction.
4. Using heat to soften the stain and make it easier to remove. For example, remove candle wax with a warm iron and blotting paper (placed between iron and stained item).
5. Freezing to remove stains such as tar or chewing gum which become sticky when warm. When frozen with carbon dioxide spray, they become brittle and can be chipped off.

Chemical methods

1. Using detergents to soften and loosen dirt, making it easier to remove. Use detergents on water-based or non-greasy stains, and also on some greasy stains.
2. Using enzyme powders to remove protein, for example, lipstick, egg and carbohydrate stains.
3. Using solvents to remove persistent greasy-based stains. Examples are methylated spirits, for removing ballpoint stains, and turpentine or white spirit, to remove oil-based paint. Solvents are poisonous and highly flammable, so great care is required when using them: do not work near a naked flame or in a closed room, and do not inhale the vapours.
4. Using bleaches (but they can damage fibres and fade dyes). Follow the instructions carefully, and do not mix bleach with any other chemicals. Rinse thoroughly to remove all traces of the bleach.
5. Using glycerine to soften an old or set stain (it is not always effective).

Stain removal at the dry cleaners or laundry

Stains may be removed at the dry cleaners or laundry. When sending items for cleaning, separate those items that are stained and if possible provide details of the stain. Remember that a commercial laundry will not treat stains unless specifically asked to do so.

Stain removal at the dry cleaners is known as *spotting*. The dry cleaners usually check all items for stains as a matter of course. Stains are usually dealt with before dry cleaning, but items are checked again after dry cleaning, and any remaining stains are then dealt with.

Treating an unknown stain

If you cannot identify the type of stain, try several stain-removing agents until the correct one is found. Rather than treat it once with a strong solution, repeat the treatment twice with a weaker solution. Before trying a different stain-removing agent, remember to remove the first stain-removing agent from the fabric by thorough washing and rinsing, or by neutralisation (that is, if an acid has been used, neutralise it with an alkali).

These are the steps for treating an unknown stain:

Step A: Soak in cold water.
Step B: Dry and use a solvent.
Step C: Use an acid.
Step D: Use an alkali.
Step E: Try a bleach.

 TO DO

By reference to books on housekeeping in your library or home, prepare a chart outlining the stain-removal agents and the methods to be used when removing the following stains:

- red wine spilt on tablecloths
- grass stains on a tennis professional's sports gear
- wine stains on a wool carpet
- tea or coffee stains on cotton–polyester bed sheets
- chewing gum on a synthetic carpet.

The stages in the laundry process are basically the same, whether carried out in an on-site or off-site laundry. These are:

1. Transport to laundry
2. Arrival
3. Marking and sorting
4. Stain removal
5. Weighing
6. Loading
7. Washing and rinsing
8. Drying
9. Ironing
10. Folding
11. Checking and repairing
12. Distribution.

In this unit the first eight points are covered, the rest are dealt with in the next unit.

Transporting and arrival   Dirty linen is transported in skips, baskets, bags, laundry chutes or trucks. When it arrives at the laundry, it is unloaded and stored temporarily until processing begins. It is best to deal with the dirty linen as soon as possible, so as to avoid the spread of infection (due to the likely presence of bacteria in dirty linen), mildew and odour problems. Another risk of stored dirty linen is fire, which can result from spontaneous combustion.

Marking and sorting   Articles not laundered on the premises must be marked with some kind of code so that the owner can be identified and losses prevented. Items can be marked with a stamp, Indian ink, labels or special ultra-violet marks.

Dirty linen is sorted according to:

- type of item (for example single bed linen, double bed linen, towels etc.)
- type of fibre
- colour and dye fastness
- degree of soilage (infected, fouled, ordinary soiled)

Sorting is done so that all dirty items which require the same washing (or dry cleaning) programme, are processed at the same time. For example, colour-fast cotton items will be put into one batch, and wool, silk and other delicate fabrics will be put into a second.

Stain removal   Stains have to be removed from a fabric before it is washed so that they will not set into the fabric (see unit 39).

Weighing   Each bundle of dirty linen is weighed to make sure that it will fit into the machine—the capacity of an industrial washing machine may be 45 kg (100 lbs), 225 kg (500 lbs) and even 450 kg (1000 lbs) dry weight of items.

Loading   The weighed load of items is loaded into the washing machine, either manually or with a machine. If the machine is overloaded, the washing process will be less effective, linen could be damaged, and crease-resistant items may crease. When bulkier items such as towels and blankets are washed, the weight of loads is reduced to ensure effective washing.

Washing and rinsing   The washing process is designed to perform three basic operations:

- the removal of soil from the fabric
- the suspension of soil in the washing solution
- the discharge of soil from the machine to the drain.

Machines can be programmed to different wash and rinse temperatures, and different cycles.

 TO DO

Assume you have been asked to recommend suitable bed linen, towels and blankets for a guesthouse a friend will be opening. Your friend wants to be able to launder everything on the premises. Look around a good local supplier of linen (such as a department store), examine the washing instructions on the labels, and draw up a list of suitable items, their cost and how they should be cared for in the guesthouse.

Textile care labelling code

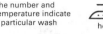 The number and temperature indicate a particular wash

 Household bleach cannot be used

hot · · ·   do not iron The fewer the number of dots the cooler the iron setting

cool · ·   warm · ·

(P) The letter in the circle refers to the solvent which may be used in the dry cleaning process

(A) Can be dry cleaned in all solvents

(F) Can be dry cleaned in white spirit

⊗ Do not dry clean

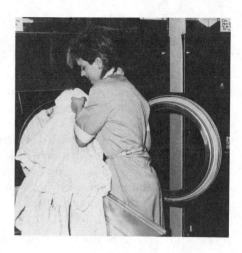

The information in units 40 and 41 will assist you with the Caterbase modules *Laundering of Linen* and *Finishing Linen*.

Drying Washed items are dried in tumble driers. Inside the tumble drier is a horizontal perforated cylinder, through which hot air blows, and the drum rotates so that all the items have contact with the hot air. Items which do not require ironing, such as towels and blankets which only require a 'fluffy', unpressed finish, will be allowed to dry completely in the tumble drier. But those which have to be ironed will be taken out of the tumble drier when they are still moist.

Non-iron fabrics, such as those used for sheets or tablecloths, must be carefully dried if creasing is to be prevented. The degree of loading must be reduced and the load gradually cooled down.

What should the temperature of the water be?
Many chemical reactions will only take place when heat is applied, and most reactions can be speeded up by raising the temperature. The higher the temperature of the wash (up to a certain level), the more efficient is soil removal. But not all washing should be done at uniformly high temperatures. For example, certain types of stains can be removed quite easily at low temperatures but become fixed and almost impossible to remove if subjected to high temperature. Also, water that is too hot may damage some fibres, such as wool.

How should bleach be used?
An ordinary bleach can be used at a temperature below 65° C (150° F). At higher temperatures, bleach begins to destroy the fibres of certain fabrics.

Why are there several separate wash cycles?
With several short wash cycles, more dirt can be removed because new suds and clean water are introduced with every cycle. With only one wash, the solution is not changed, and the soil in the solution may resoil the fabric.

Why can hard water cause a problem?
Hard water contains salts that mix with soap and synthetic detergents to form a sticky substance called 'soap curd', which sticks to the fabric, making it stiff and dirty. Soft water, which lacks salts, is preferred for laundering. In hard-water areas, it is possible to improve results by installing a water softening plant or by using a water softener.

How long does it take to remove dirt?
Even the most effective soap or synthetic washing powder takes time to work, because dirt is removed gradually, over a period of several minutes. But the rate at which it is removed is not constant. It is highest at the beginning of the wash and gradually diminishes until dirt is being removed only very slowly. It is sometimes helpful to extend the final wash to 14 minutes, instead of the usual seven minutes, since extra time may be needed to remove the most resistant dirt.

Are some cleaning agents to be avoided or preferred for certain fabrics?
Do not use alkaline cleaning agents on wool or silk.
Do not use bleach on any coloured items.
Use pure soap flakes for wool and other delicate fabrics.

How should starch be used?
Certain articles are starched in order to give them a degree of stiffness. If an article only requires a moderate stiffness, for example sheets and slips, only a relatively small amount of starch is used, and this is applied in the washing machine following the final rinse. The starch liquor is added to the machine, which is run for a few minutes, after which any liquor not taken up is discarded.

For articles which need to be very stiff, a separate machine, called a starching machine, is used. This is because a large amount of starch has to be used. Starch is expensive, so any not taken up can be re-used for other loads.

81

Ironing Ironing and pressing is generally referred to as 'finishing'. Items are ironed or pressed in different ways, according to their size and shape.

The type of equipment used for ironing or pressing depends on the item:

- Flat items, such as sheets, pillowcases and tablecloths (referred to as 'flatwork') can be finished on calenders (machines with heated padded rollers through which the item passes), or on rotary ironers, which are used in some small establishments.
- Uniforms, coats, shirts (called non-flat items) are finished on various kinds of presses. Some consist of heated padded plates, and the items to be pressed are placed on the bottom plate and pressed with the top plate. The two main types are rotary and scissor presses. Others hold the garment in shape while hot air is blown through it to complete the drying process and remove the creases.

A few items have to be finished by hand using a hand iron.

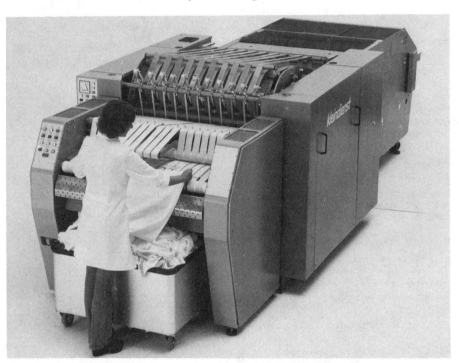

The quality of finish depends on the amount of moisture in the item, the temperature of the calender, press or iron, and the amount of pressure used. If an item is too dry before pressing, it must be moistened first by using a spray containing water, otherwise the resulting finish will be poor. Although very moist items will have an excellent finish, they need a long drying time on the press, and this will slow down the whole process.

Folding As articles of ironed flatwork leave the calender, they must be folded, and flatwork folders carry out this job. A further refinement is to fit a stacking unit at the end of the discharge conveyor from the folder.

Correct folding of each item is important, because the folds will aid the people who have to make the beds or set the tables, for example, and will certainly affect the appearance of finished linen. Folds should be made the same way each time for particular items.

✳ FOR INTEREST

Calenders are used for flat work. The earlier calenders were designed for once-through operations with four or five rollers. The latest type is an upright calender with usually only two rollers, and the items pass through the rollers in a figure of eight action at least twice. It takes up less space than the old calenders.

Keeping the laundry clean

The laundry is the place where dirty linen is delivered, where it is washed, dried and finished, and from where clean items are despatched to other areas of the building. It may comprise a single room or three separate areas.

It is important that the equipment and the rooms are cleaned regularly and well maintained. The heat from the machines, together with the moisture, fluff, and dirt from the linen, provide an ideal environment for bacteria to multiply. Dirt builds up very quickly, so it should be removed often.

The washing materials must be stored according to company rules, and the right level of stock be maintained. If no one is using the laundry, it should be kept locked for security reasons. Only auhorised staff should be allowed to enter.

 TO DO

Visit the laundry of a hotel, hospital or other residential establishment. Find out as much as you can about the equipment used, and about the laundry's special features, if any. Also ask how many items are laundered on average each day.

There are also machines and special folding tables with hinged folding plates for folding non-flat items.

When 'easy-care' or 'no iron' linen is used, it is folded immediately after being tumble dried. (Spin drying is not recommended for this type of linen—although in small guesthouses a short spin may be the only practical option.)

Checking and repairing   At this point, the cleaned linen is inspected for any stains and tears, as many fabrics are damaged or show signs of wear after frequent laundering. Some can be repaired, while others may have to be discarded. Particularly in luxurious establishments, linen which is even slightly torn or worn will be repaired for use only in staff areas or it will be discarded.

Otherwise, dressmakers, seamstresses or machine hands will as necessary:

- repair hems, edges, and seams
- patch any torn or damaged items
- darn holes on worn fabric.

In situations where economy is important, badly worn or damaged articles may be re-made into smaller items. For example, a double sheet can be turned into a single sheet. Any remaining pieces of fabric could be used for patching, or as cloths for engineers or maintenance staff. But before re-making, the original item should be 'condemned', deleted from the records, and a replacement issued. Re-makes are not normally entered on to any stock cards. They are treated as extras or replacements for missing items.

Any stains found on laundered items will be removed where possible, and the item will then be sent back to be washed and finished once more.

Distribution   Finished work is packaged, counted, and sent to the department, individual or central linen room from where it came. It may be wrapped with polythene or polythene-lined paper (which is heat-sealed to close, so protecting the linen from contamination during handling) and loaded into baskets of trucks or individual boxes (which must be spotlessly clean).

City and Guilds

Test yourself: Units 37–41

1. Describe briefly what you understand by the term linen and give six examples of linen which are used in residential establishments.
2. If you had to select the bed linen for a hotel or hospital, give three points you would look out for.
3. Linen storage areas must meet certain requirements. State five.
4. Describe briefly two methods in common use for controlling the use of linen.
5. If an item you are responsible for checking has a stain, what steps can you go through which will help identify the cause of the stain? Describe at least three.
6. Methods for removing stains can be described as physical and chemical. Briefly describe either two physical or two chemical methods.
7. Briefly describe three options which could be considered by the owners of a hotel for laundering the linen.
8. Identify as many of the stages as you can in the laundry process (starting with transport and ending with distribution).
9. Linen has to be sorted before it is laundered. What is the reason? Give three of the ways or criteria in which it can be sorted.
10. What are two things which could go wrong if proper attention is not paid to the weight and bulk of items when they are loaded into a washing machine?
11. What special procedure should be used for foul and infected linen?
12. When linen is found to have been slightly torn or shows signs of wear, what action might be taken (a) in a luxury hotel or private hospital and (b) in an establishment where economy is important?

Organisation of cleaning

The procedure and frequency of cleaning a bedroom will depend on (see also unit 18):

- The type of establishment, for example whether it is a luxury hotel, residential home for old people, student residence, intensive care unit in a hospital.
- How frequently the room's occupant changes, for example in a holiday centre a high proportion of guests may stay for a week, most students in residential accommodation stay for an academic term, whereas some patients may stay in an intensive care unit for a few hours only.
- What the establishment's policy is regarding the frequency of cleaning, for example luxury hotels will change curtains in rooms more frequently than many guesthouses do.
- The room's exposure to dirt and dust from outside, for example some surfaces in an air-conditioned room may require less frequent dusting than those in a room where the windows and doors are kept open most of the time and where it is relatively dusty (as in a city-centre location).
- The amount of use the area is put to.

The cleaning of a group or section of bedrooms can be done:

- By a method known as *block cleaning* when the housekeeping staff move from room to room and complete the same task in every room, for example:
  — strip the beds in all the rooms
  — remake all beds
  — damp-dust all rooms
  — suction-clean all rooms.

This is a suitable method for a business hotel where most guests stay one night only and check out early in the morning.

- By individual room (a method known as *single* or *orthodox cleaning*), when all the tasks are completed in one room before proceeding to the next room.

This method is used in establishments where the length of stay and time of departure varies.

- Or by a combination of both procedures, block cleaning all rooms which have been vacated, and then individually cleaning the rooms of people staying for one or more extra nights.

In general, one member of the housekeeping staff can clean and service between 6 and 15 bedrooms depending on:

- what other duties he/she has to perform
- what his/her hours of duty are
- how experienced he/she is
- the type and size of room
- the amount of furnishings and fittings, the materials they are made of and the condition they are in
- when and how thoroughly the room was last cleaned.

✎ HOUSECRAFT TIPS

Remember that you will be leaving the cleaned room in the same condition as the next (or returning) guest will find it. So the final check is very important!

Remember also that just as you can learn something about the personality of guests from the way in which they leave their rooms, so too the guests can learn about *your* personality from the way in which *you* leave the room.

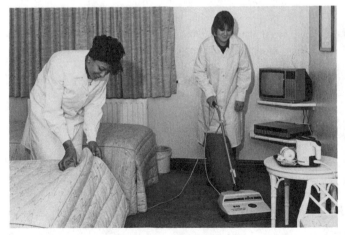

Bedroom cleaning procedures

The basic steps in room cleaning vary from one establishment to another, and even some of the bigger hotel chains allow housekeeping staff to develop and follow their own procedures. What is important is that:

- The minimum amount of time and effort is wasted. For example, when leaving the room with the rubbish, it makes sense to try and return with some of the cleaning equipment that will be required. Thinking ahead will also save time, for example, by cleaning the bathroom while the dust settles in the bedroom after making the bed.
- The risks of spreading bacteria and dust (which may contain bacteria) must be kept to the minimum. For example, by placing soiled linen into bags immediately, and by damp-dusting high surfaces before low ones.
- A logical order is followed so nothing is overlooked and the work is thorough. For example, by damp-dusting around the room in a clockwise (or anticlockwise direction), by suction-cleaning back towards the door.

The example of a cleaning procedure given in the box alongside would need to be modified to deal with specific situations:

Departure rooms (guests have left)
The room would be checked for personal property left behind in drawers, wardrobes, and under or behind beds. Items found in this way would be handed to a senior member of the housekeeping or management staff, with a report on where and when they were found.

Stayover rooms (guests staying for at least the following night)
Some of the guest's own possessions may be left lying around and may need tidying—for example, there may be clothes and discarded papers on the floor. Depending on establishment policy, the room may not require suction cleaning and the sheets on the beds and towels may not be replaced. It is obviously not necessary to check for lost property.

Vacant rooms (not occupied the previous night)
A thorough cleaning is not necessary, but a check on the bedclothes (to make sure that no one has used the room and re-made the bed to look as if it has not been slept in) and the bathroom, soap and towels (for the same reason) is needed. The lights should be checked and any not working reported. If the room has been vacant for two or more nights, it is likely to need dusting.

 TO DO

Check the typical bedroom cleaning procedure given alongside with that used in your workplace (or a residential establishment of your choice). Note any variations and the reason for them.

Typical bedroom cleaning procedure

1. Place trolley with room cleaning equipment, clean linen, stocks of soap, stationery etc. outside the room. (In some establishments the bedroom door is kept open while the room is being cleaned.)
2. Pull back the curtains and open the window(s) to ventilate the room (this may not be possible with air-conditioning or double glazing).
3. Remove any refreshment/meal trays and return to the service area (or leave to be collected).
4. Empty ashtrays and waste bins (including those in the bathroom). Many trolleys have bags for rubbish, but ashtrays should be emptied into a metal bin—never among paper or other material which might catch fire.
5. Flush toilet, put in alkali detergent or strong acid cleaner (if one is being used—see unit 45).
6. Strip bed(s).
7. Remove all soiled linen (including towels from the bathroom). Place in the bag provided on the trolley or down the linen chute.
8. Re-make the bed(s).
9. Leave dust to settle in the room and clean the bathroom (see unit 45).
10. Damp-dust all the furniture. Do this in such a way that nothing is missed, for example by starting at the door, then moving in a clockwise (or anticlockwise) direction, dusting everything in contact with the wall, then all furniture in the centre of the room.
11. Check and replace guest supplies (see unit 44).
12. Close window(s) or adjust air-conditioning.
13. Check that all electrical fittings, television, radio etc. are working, and note and report any that are not.
14. Replace ashtrays and waste bins.
15. Suction-clean the floor and (weekly) upholstered furniture.
16. Check the room's appearance: straighten as necessary any pictures, curtains, pillows, and remove any smears on mirrors or furniture.
17. Leave the room locked, notify your supervisor/other departments that it has been cleaned.

Knowing when to clean

Normally the housekeeping staff responsible for cleaning a number of bedrooms in a hotel or similar establishment are issued with a daily cleaning schedule or worksheet by their supervisor. Based on information supplied by the front office/reception staff, this deals with the rooms in a particular floor or section of the building that have been allocated to a specific member of staff (or two or three members of staff if team cleaning is in operation). It will usually indicate:

- *Departures*, that is the rooms which are due to be vacated during the day. Usually this means by a set time in the morning, for example by 11 am.
- *Stayovers*: in other words the occupants have reserved their room for the following night(s). In some establishments where the beds are not re-made with clean sheets every day, the schedule may indicate that re-sheeting is due.
- *Arrivals*: rooms which must be prepared for occupation on that day.

Any special requests will also be noted on the schedule, for example that a bed board should be put in a particular room, a cot in another, flowers for a VIP in one of the suites, handicapped guests will be occupying a room near the lift.

There may be standing instructions that all departures are cleaned before stayovers—this is likely in a hotel where guests generally spend most of the day out of their room, and/or arrivals are expected quite early in the day. Otherwise special instructions of this sort will also be made on the day's schedule.

Weekly and periodic cleaning tasks may also be specified on the schedule:

- In some cases this may be for a section of rooms which have been taken out of operation for periodic cleaning (sometimes referred to as 'taking' or 'putting' a room 'off'). Wherever possible, this will be done during the off-season or during a quiet period.
- Where establishments are busy throughout the year, periodic cleaning of specific items may be undertaken as part of the routine cleaning as are weekly cleans. For example, staff may be required to suction-clean or damp-dust the tops of wardrobes every Tuesday, or to wash the frames and glass of pictures on the first Tuesday of every month.

Some flexibility is always necessary about the order in which rooms are cleaned. If for example there is a 'do not disturb' notice on the door, or nó notice but the guest is still in the room, the cleaning should be left until it is convenient for the guest. On the other hand a notice which requests the room to be cleaned can mean it should take priority (depending on the policy of the establishment).

Bed making

The procedure for making beds varies between different establishments, particularly when a duvet is used instead of blankets.

There are some general rules which should be considered in any situation:

1. When stripping the bed, avoid flapping the bed linen about, as this will scatter dust and bacteria through the room. Each item can be folded towards the centre of the bed from the four corners, then folded in half and half again to form a neat bundle.
2. Never place blankets or clean linen on the floor. Put soiled linen directly into the dirty linen container (often a bag attached to the cleaning trolley).

> **‼ REMEMBER**
>
> **Some typical periodic cleaning tasks in a bedroom**
> Shampooing carpets and soft furnishings—*see* units 27 and 35
> Laundering or dry cleaning curtains and loose covers—*see* unit 35
> Mop-sweeping or suction-cleaning and washing walls and ceilings—*see* unit 29
> Damp-wiping polished furniture with a solution of vinegar and water to remove polish and sticky marks—*see* unit 33
> Suction-cleaning/damp-dusting inside drawers of furniture and replacing drawer linings—*see* unit 32
> Cleaning back of furniture and floor under heavy furniture—*see* units 26, 27 and 32
> Cleaning doors and windows (inside and outside)—*see* unit 30
> Cleaning ledges and frames of doors and windows—*see* unit 30
> Cleaning lamp shades and bulbs—*see* unit 35
> Suction-cleaning or dusting bed bases—*see* unit 36
> Suction-cleaning and turning mattresses—*see* unit 36

3. Take care to ensure the occupant of the bed will be sleeping between the right sides of both sheets. The bottom sheet is placed right side up and the top sheet with the wrong side up.

4. To ensure the occupant is comfortable and warm, the large hem of the top sheet is usually lined up with the head of the bed, and the top of the blanket placed about 10 cm (4 inches) lower down. The top sheet is usually turned over the blanket edge, then both the top sheet and the blankets are folded over to form a band of top sheet just in front of the pillows, about 20 cm (8 inches) wide.

5. Fold pillows in half lengthways to insert them into their case. Then open out the pillow and ensure that it is tucked under the flap of the case at the open end.

6. It is usual to position the open end of pillows so they are least likely to be seen (away from the door, or on a double bed, both ends face the middle).

7. Mitre the folds which are made at the foot of the bed (see below.)

?? HOW TO

Mitre a corner

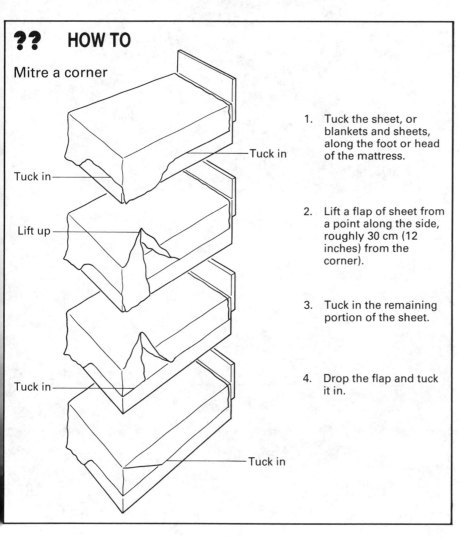

Tuck in

Tuck in

Lift up

Tuck in

Tuck in

1. Tuck the sheet, or blankets and sheets, along the foot or head of the mattress.

2. Lift a flap of sheet from a point along the side, roughly 30 cm (12 inches) from the corner).

3. Tuck in the remaining portion of the sheet.

4. Drop the flap and tuck it in.

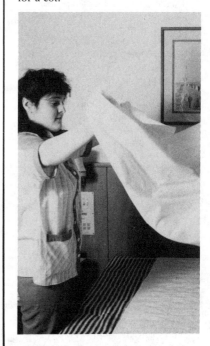

➧ ➧ ➧ TO DO

The procedure for making beds varies. Write down the steps in a procedure you are familiar with—as clearly as possible—then see if a friend can follow them.

‼ REMEMBER

On security

1. Keep service keys on you at all times, and return to the person in charge after work. Never lend keys to anyone else and report losses immediately (see unit 59).

2. Do not admit other staff to guest bedrooms unless they have been given authority (and you are sure this is so). Never unlock rooms for guests who claim to have lost their key. Check with reception or obtain some other proof that it is their room. Report anyone acting suspiciously.

3. Make sure that guest room doors are locked when you leave the room.

4. If you find any lost property, hand this immediately to the housekeeper, or deal with it according to establishment procedures (see unit 59).

5. If you leave your cleaning trolley placed across the open door it will discourage unauthorised people from entering a room you are in the process of cleaning.

6. If a room that was meant to have been occupied according to the cleaning schedule, but has not been, or the opposite has occurred, or two people appear to have slept in a room booked for one person, report the matter immediately.

7. Check that fire notices are in place (usually on the inside of the bedroom door) and not damaged or covered by anything (see unit 57).

On conserving energy

1. Switch off lights which are not being used.

2. Check that air-conditioning/central heating is set at an appropriate temperature for the weather conditions. If the room is not in use, turn the equipment off.

3. Keep curtains closed during winter to conserve heat, and during summer if the sun makes the room very warm (when the room is air-conditioned).

4. Make sure that no heat is escaping through open windows or doors.

5. Report any dripping taps.

Replenishing guest supplies

In all but the most basic accommodation, various items are placed in bedrooms for
the convenience and comfort of the occupant:

- coathangers
- ashtrays (unless the room is a non-smoking one)
- Bible
- information on the room charges, meal times, other guest services, telephone
  numbers for reception, bar, restaurant, housekeeper etc.
- door notices to indicate room ready for service/do not disturb and breakfast/
  early morning tea/coffee orders, newspaper requirements etc.

Sometimes the items are designed in such a way that they cannot be removed from
the room as 'souvenirs', for example coat hangers are often fixed to the hanging bar
of the cupboard.

In many hotels, however, various items are left in rooms for the use of the guest,
ranging from those which are re-usable and are not intended to be removed, such as
hairdryers, tea/coffee making equipment, cups and saucers, to those which guests
may find useful during their stay, and if not, may wish to take away as reminders.
These include sewing kits, shoe shine cloths, stationery and magazines (many of the
larger hotel chains produce their own).

Some hotels also place food and beverage items in bedrooms for the use of guests:
tea bags, sachets of coffee and sugar, baskets of fruit, packets of biscuits, bottles of
mineral water and complimentary bottles of wine or champagne, for example.

Where a selection of alcoholic drinks is provided in bedrooms, guests are usually
charged for what they consume during their stay. Some 'mini bars' automatically
record what has been taken and transmit the information to reception, adding it to
the guest's account. Others have to be checked manually by the housekeeping staff.

Units 42 to 44 will help you gain the
Caterbase modules *Daily Replenishment
of Guest Bedrooms* and *Bedmaking*.

Bathrooms and toilets are two of the most abundant sources of harmful bacteria in a residential establishment (see units 16 and 56). If the sanitary fittings are not cleaned regularly and thoroughly, the bacteria present in

- faeces and urine
- semen, saliva and vomit
- sores, cuts and blood
- and even on healthy skin

will multiply rapidly (warm, moist conditions are ideal) and spread

- from one user to another
- to the staff responsible for servicing the bathroom.

The second danger is that the harmful bacteria will be spread to another fitting in the same room, perhaps, or to an adjacent bedroom, or a 'clean' tea cup, or to another bathroom. This can happen:

- If cleaning equipment is used carelessly. For example: a cloth used to clean the handle of a toilet door is later used to wipe the mouthpiece of a telephone.
- If staff neglect their own personal hygiene. For example: forgetting to wash hands after cleaning the bidet.
- If safety measures are ignored. For example: a used razor blade is picked up off the floor of the bathroom, cutting a finger.
- If working procedures are not followed. For example: a bathroom glass is rinsed under the tap then polished with a used hand towel.

Typical procedure for cleaning *en-suite* bathroom and toilet

Two of the stages in cleaning an *en-suite* bathroom and toilet should have been carried out already (as one of the initial steps in servicing the bedroom, see unit 42):

- removing soiled linen
- removing rubbish and emptying the waste bin and sanitary towel bin.

1. Clean the sanitary fittings other than the toilet (bidet, bath, shower, wash hand basin):
   - Put any soap and personal property on one side.
   - Clean the fittings, the surrounding wall area, door handles and such things as bath safety mats and shower curtains using a neutral detergent applied to a dampened cloth. (Stronger cleaning agents are only necessary when there are marks or stains—see unit 31.)
     The cloth should be rinsed in warm water in a bucket, or, when the hand basin is being cleaned, by half-filling the basin with warm water.
   - Rinse with clean water.
   - Polish mirrors, taps, sanitary and tiled or panelled surfaces with dry paper towelling.
   - Replace personal property and soap.
2. Clean the toilet:
   - Flush the toilet.
   - Using the toilet brush, pump the water out of the toilet pan. Apply neutral detergent and brush all round the pan, including the rim. (A long handled mirror can be used to check that it is clean.)
   - Clean the wall immediately surrounding the toilet, the outside of the toilet (cistern, handle and pipes) and the seat with neutral detergent.

⚠ SAFETY

Always wear a suitable apron and gloves. They will protect your uniform and hands from harmful bacteria and contact with cleaning agents.

Avoid any risk of spreading bacteria:

- Begin with the least dirty areas, moving on to the dirtier.
- Do not move toilet brushes from one bathroom to another. (Every bathroom should have its own toilet brush and holder.)
- Keep a set of cloths specifically for cleaning sanitary fittings. Many establishments use a colour coding system for cloths, for example red cloths are for toilets, wash hand basins, showers etc., blue for general purpose cleaning, such as damp dusting.
- Never wash bathroom or drinking glasses, cups, saucers, tea spoons, coffee/tea pots etc. in an *en-suite* bathroom. Where these items are made available for the use of guests in their rooms, they should be removed for cleaning to a central service area. Not only should they be washed and rinsed in very hot water, but they should be left to air dry and this is not possible in a bathroom.
- Wash hands thoroughly after completing each task.
- Regularly rinse cloths and brushes in clean water. Renew detergent solutions before they become too dirty (and ineffective).

Never mix cleaning agents (see units 16 and 31). For example, if an acid toilet cleaner has been used and left to soak, and a bleach is then added, dangerous asphyxiating gases may be produced.

Pay particular attention to the accessories, such as taps, plugs and chains, to overflow outlets, and to the underpart, pipes and wall surrounding the fittings. Hairs and other waste caught in the outlet pipe can be removed with tweezers. A bottle brush can be used to clean overflow outlets.

Do not step into a bath to clean it and to avoid back strain, bend your knees not your back.

Take special care of used razors, razor blades and hypodermic needles (see unit 56). Dispose of them in a metal or hard plastic container (they may cut or poke through paper or plastic rubbish bags). Beware of such sharp objects when emptying waste bins.

- Flush the toilet, rinsing the brush at the same time.
- An alkali detergent (also called a hard surface cleaner) may be used instead of neutral detergent in the toilet pan, probably once a week. Where stains are a problem or hard water causes lime deposits, an acid cleaner may be used in the toilet pan weekly (see unit 31).

3. Renew linen and guest supplies (see below and unit 44).
4. Inspect the room and make a note of any faults or damage. These should be reported to the supervisor or maintenance department, according to establishment procedure.
5. Clean the floor: damp-mop hard floors (see unit 26), suction-clean carpets (see unit 27).
6. Wash, rinse and leave to dry cleaning cloths, brushes, gloves, apron etc. Store cleaning agents correctly (see unit 20).

Bathroom supplies

Towels and bathmats
Usually a bathsheet, medium-sized towel, hand towel, and sometimes a face cloth are provided for each person occupying the room. A bath mat is also provided: either one that can be laundered regularly with the towels or a disposable one is best for hygienic reasons (foot infections, such as verrucas, can be spread if rubber or cork bath mats are provided).

Toilet paper
To ensure that the supply of toilet paper does not run out, it is the procedure in many establishments to leave two spare rolls by each toilet. In some luxury establishments a choice of toilet paper is provided: one hard and one soft.

Soap
Usually at least one tablet or bar of soap is provided per guest, sometimes extra tablets are provided for the wash basin (perhaps a smaller size than the bath soap).

It is usual to replace all used soap on a guest's departure with new tablets but luxury hotels provide new soap every day. (The used tablets may be used in the public toilet areas or staff toilet areas.)

Sanitary towel bags
To discourage guests from flushing sanitary towels down the toilet, (where they may cause a blockage) either sanitary towel bins are provided, or special bags in which they can be discreetly and hygienically disposed of.

Other supplies
Many hotels place sachets or small bottles of hair shampoo in bathrooms, boxes of tissues, disposable shower caps etc., with the hotel's name or logo printed on the container. Bath robes are provided in some high class hotels, but good quality bath robes are expensive and desirable—so some guests take them as souvenirs!

Other smaller supplies are made available on request, when they may also be given away or charged for. These include razors, toothbrushes and sanitary towels. Hair dryers, heated rollers, electrical adaptors and converters are sometimes available on loan, and irons and ironing boards if there is no valet service available. It is even possible that the housekeeper may be able to help out the male guest who is going to a formal event but finds at the last moment that he has forgotten to pack his bow tie or cuff links!

▶ ▶ ▶ TO DO

Make a list, for an establishment you are familiar with, of:

- the cleaning agents and equipment
- the supplies

you would need to clean and replenish a guest bathroom. Check your list with your supervisor (let him or her know the name of the establishment that you have chosen).

This unit will help you gain the Caterbase module *Daily Cleaning and Replenishment of Toilet and Bathroom Areas.*

In hospitals, the cleaning routines are designed to prevent infection spreading from one patient to another and to reduce to the minimum the risk of introducing new problems from bacteria present in dirt and dust. Most patients are weakened by their illness, which means they are much more likely to catch new infections.

A colour coding system is used in many hospitals for cleaning equipment and cleaning cloths (cloths are also usually disposable) (see unit 21).

Typical cleaning procedure for low risk areas

Corridors, offices, sitting rooms etc.

Routine cleaning
Daily:

- suction-clean or mop-sweep hard floors
- damp-mop hard floors
- suction-clean carpeted floors
- damp-dust all surfaces (except high surfaces)
- empty all bins and ashtrays.

Weekly:

- buff hard floors
- suction-clean or use a high dusting tool to clean all high surfaces.

Periodic cleaning

- scrub hard floors
- strip and polish hard floors
- strip and re-seal hard floors
- shampoo carpets
- wash walls and ceilings
- wash doors, windows and other glass surfaces including light fittings
- shampoo upholstered furniture
- launder or dry clean curtains.

Some periodic tasks might be carried out monthly, such as stripping hard floors, others will be carried out less frequently, for example washing ceilings.

Typical cleaning procedure for medium risk areas

Wards etc.

Routine cleaning
Nursing staff always make beds occupied by patients (they are trained to move sick persons with the minimum of risk and pain). The bed linen is normally changed every day, or in some hospitals, every second or third day, but if a patient vomits or is incontinent it will be changed as soon as possible.

The other cleaning operations will be timed to start after bed making has finished (this always creates some dust and will disturb other dust) and to avoid meal times, doctors' rounds, visiting hours and so forth. They are carried out by the hospital domestic staff and include:

1. At each bed space, remove the rubbish bag from the side of the locker, plus any other items such as empty bottles and old newspapers. Using a neutral detergent solution damp-dust the outside of the locker including the wheels, the bed frame including the wheels, the over-bed table, the chair(s), the bed light, head phones and control panel. Attach a new rubbish bag to the locker.
2. Suction-clean the floor area, making sure that dust and fluff lying under furniture is also removed. It may be necessary to wheel out the patient's bed very gently to do this. Lockers and chairs can be moved easily.

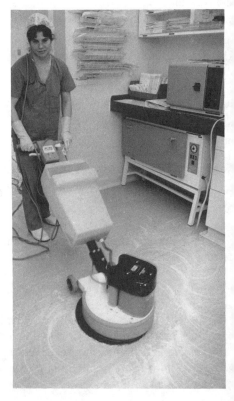

3. Remove the water jug and glass from every locker, wash them in the ward kitchen using very hot water and detergent. Rinse (again in very hot water), dry, then refill the jugs with cold drinking water and return to the lockers, with the clean glasses. In some cases, water jugs and glasses may be machine washed on the ward or sent to a central service area.

When a patient leaves, the cleaning procedure is very thorough. All the stages are usually carried out by the domestic staff:

1. Strip the bed completely, and send all bed linen including blankets and bedspread to the laundry.
2. Damp-dust the bed frame, mattress and pillow (which are both encased in tough polythene covers) with neutral detergent solution. The mattress will need to be moved aside so the frame underneath can be properly cleaned.
3. Remove any rubbish from the locker. If any of the patient's property has been left behind, it should be handed to the appropriate person with a note detailing what ward it was found in, when, by whom, and the location of the bed.
4. If necessary, suction-clean the inside of the locker to remove fluff and bits, then damp-dust the whole locker, inside and out.
5. Damp-dust the chair(s), bedlight and other items that are done in the normal daily clean.

Periodic cleaning

Tasks include floor maintenance and regular changing of cubicle curtains. Window cleaning, wall and ceiling washing, and the cleaning and maintenance of lights, are often carried out by maintenance staff or contractors.

Some hospitals may close a ward for a short period for cleaning and wall washing in one year, and in the following year for slightly longer for cleaning and redecoration. All these jobs may be carried out by contractors.

Other hospitals never close wards, and periodic cleaning is scheduled, over a period of time, around the patients.

High risk areas

Isolation and intensive care units, operating theatres etc. A number of special precautions are taken when high risk areas are cleaned, designed either to protect the cleaning staff from infection and to prevent bacteria from spreading to other areas of the hospital, or from one unit or room within the high risk area to another; or to protect the patient from outside infections (or both).

- Gowns, caps, gloves, overshoes and masks (to cover the mouth and nose) are worn. Gloves and masks are usually disposable, and gowns are either disposable or made of a fabric that can be washed at high temperatures every time after use—cotton for example.
- Hands must be washed very frequently and always before entering, before leaving and after leaving a high risk area.
- Cleaning equipment may only be used within the high risk areas. (Generally it will be colour coded and labelled so that this procedure can be enforced.) Mop heads are either disposable or can be washed at very high temperatures and heat sterilised.
- Waste and soiled linen from within the high risk area are placed in colour coded bags which are sealed before they leave the area (see units 38 and 56).
- Routine cleaning procedures include washing walls and ceilings, scrubbing floors and cleaning lights.

✱ FOR INTEREST

Hospitals have special procedures for cleaning beds which have been occupied by an infectious patient. If this involves the use of a chemical disinfectant, very careful control will be exercised.

Some hospitals have special bed bays where beds are taken for cleaning once a patient has departed.

 TO DO

Either
Arrange to work with a domestic assistant at your local hospital for a day. Produce a diary of the day's activities and a list of equipment and agents used. Discuss the way in which nursing staff and domestic staff work together.

Or
Arrange with the hospital administrator to visit a local hospital at visiting time. Walk around some of the areas where visitors are allowed access (for example the entrance foyer, reception and corridors to wards). Make a note of the different surfaces that have to be cleaned, how you think they are cleaned and how often. Note also any points which you feel could be improved on, and any special problems that seem to exist. Finally make a list of any repairs and maintenance work that you feel should be carried out and discuss your observations with your tutor/supervisor.

In halls of residence, boarding schools, hostels, old people's homes and similar establishments, the sleeping accommodation provided is often quite basic and ranges from individual bedrooms to units shared by two or more people and dormitories for as many as 50. In some cases, cleaning resources may be limited, and the occupants may have to do some of the cleaning tasks themselves, for example making up their own bed.

In accommodation which is occupied throughout the year, the cleaning procedures will be similar to that of a bedroom in a hotel, except that the furniture and fittings are likely to be more basic and the floors are less likely to be carpeted.

When the accommodation is unoccupied for periods of the year (for example, during school/college/university holidays/vacations or during the winter) then special routines are usually followed in the period immediately before the accommodation is to be occupied and as soon as it has been vacated.

Routines also have to be adapted if the establishment is occupied by a different group of people during the holidays or off-season.

A number of typical cleaning procedures to deal with these situations are given below.

Routine cleaning (during term time)

In most student halls of residence the bedrooms are only cleaned once a week, when the domestic staff will:

- empty the waste bin and ash tray
- clean the wash hand basin
- damp-dust the furniture
- clean the floor as appropriate.

In some establishments the bedrooms are checked on a daily basis (Monday through to Friday), when limited cleaning may be carried out, for example emptying the waste paper bin and cleaning the wash basin (if there is one).

A rota is usually organised, so that in addition to the daily cleaning tasks (which cover public areas, bathrooms, toilets, kitchens, laundries etc.) a set number of bedrooms are given their weekly clean on a certain day.

Most students are expected to make their own beds every day, and also to change and re-sheet them. A linen exchange system is used: clean sheets are left in bedrooms on one day, and soiled linen collected the following day, or the students exchange dirty for clean bed linen on a specified day, usually once every two weeks. In this way, stock can be carefully controlled.

Students typically clutter their rooms with personal belongings and books, which can make them very difficult to clean. Some rooms are also very untidy and dirty. Students often keep irregular hours, and may be sleeping or working when staff call to do the room, so it may be necessary to agree a day and time convenient for both parties.

✱ FOR INTEREST

A few student halls of residence also put up conference delegates during Christmas and Easter, when rooms are still technically occupied by students, although they are away on holiday. In such cases, students are requested to pack up and move their belongings to another room for the holiday period.

Routine cleaning (during conference use)

At some conferences, delegates' rooms are cleaned and their beds made for them every day, as in a hotel. The routine followed is similar to that described in units 42 to 44.

Periodic cleaning (during vacation/off-season)

Every bedroom is stripped completely, and bed linen, bedding, and curtains sent to the laundry or dry cleaner (whatever is appropriate). The walls are washed, the windows, furniture and light fittings cleaned and the floors washed, polished/re-sealed as appropriate.

A maintenance check is made to make sure that everything in the room is in good working order, and any faults are reported.

Before the new term or the start of the season, the rooms are damp-dusted, the floor suction-cleaned, the bed made up, and curtains re-hung.

Periodic cleaning (before arrival of conference delegates)

Special routines are called for when there is no time for a thorough periodic clean of the bedrooms (as in the above example), because the conference delegates are arriving a day or so after the end of term.

Extra staff may be called in so that thorough cleaning can be completed in the time available, or bedrooms may be thoroughly cleaned on a rota basis in the week before the end of term. In many establishments, different bed linen and curtaining is used for conference delegates and this will be placed in the rooms immediately the students have departed.

Test yourself: Units 42–47 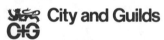 City and Guilds

1. Give two of the general principles that should be followed when a bedroom is cleaned.
2. What sort of rubbish container should be used to collect the cigarette ends and ash left in ashtrays?
3. Give three examples of the sort of information that would be put on a daily cleaning schedule or worksheet for the housekeeping staff of a medium-sized hotel.
4. Nowadays, hotel guests expect to find certain supplies in their bedrooms and be able to borrow other items if necessary. Give examples of:
   (a) two items that would be found even in a hotel offering a basic level of service
   (b) four items that might be left for guest's use in a more expensive hotel
   (c) two items that might be available for loan in a city centre business hotel of medium standard.
5. Describe three ways in which bacteria can be spread from sanitary fittings in the bathroom. Also describe three working practices which will reduce the risk.
6. Describe briefly the cleaning procedure for:
   (a) a wash hand basin in a hotel bathroom or bedroom
   (b) a hotel bedroom which has been vacant the previous night
   (c) an occupied bed space in a hospital
   (d) a bedroom in a student hall of residence during term time
   (e) periodic cleaning of a bedroom in a student hall of residence.
7. Give four special precautions that are taken when cleaning in a high risk area in a hospital. Include at least one example that relates to equipment and one that relates to personal hygiene/uniforms.
8. Describe briefly why cleaning equipment is often colour coded.

 TO DO

Find out which of the colleges or universities near you offer accommodation to conference delegates or holiday visitors outside term time. Try and find out as much as you can about the standard of accommodation offered to the delegates/visitors. Write a cleaning routine to cover the preparation of the bedrooms for them.

The well-cared-for entrance and reception area give a good first impression to anyone entering the building. When corridors, staircases, lifts and sitting areas also look pleasant and properly maintained, the work that goes into keeping the bedrooms, wards, leisure areas and so forth clean will be all the more appreciated—so will every service offered by the establishment, from the food prepared in the kitchens to the medical treatment.

Cleaning procedures for public areas

In general, the cleaning procedures for public areas will take into account three factors:

1. They are used by a greater number of people than any other room or area. This means surfaces and furnishings get soiled more quickly. Wear and tear will be considerable, but even more rapid if soil is not removed effectively and regularly.
2. They should always look attractive and inviting and be safe to be in. (On the other hand, hygiene considerations are not as important as they are in sleeping, washing and food preparation areas.)
3. They have to be accessible at all times. This is particularly true of the entrance and circulation areas such as corridors and staircases. Fortunately there are usually times when all the building's users are asleep, or out, or it is possible at quiet periods to close parts of the area temporarily (for example, by roping off half the foyer, corridor or staircase) or shut a room altogether (for example, a lounge) or take one facility out of service (for example, a lift).

Frequency and method of cleaning

The heavy use that public areas receive and the importance attached to their appearance means firstly that weekly cleaning routines will include items that in a bedroom, for example, might only be cleaned periodically , such as:

- damp-dusting picture frames, skirting boards, tops of door frames and high shelves
- suction-cleaning carpet edges
- cleaning backs of furniture.

Secondly the more intensive cleaning methods will be used more frequently, for example:

- upholstered furniture may require suction-cleaning daily
- alkali detergents may need to be used weekly on metal and glass surfaces of main entrance doors
- windows, mirrors and picture glass may need to be cleaned weekly
- carpets may have to be shampooed every month, curtains and upholstered furniture every six months
- hard floor surfaces will need to be suction-cleaned and damp-mopped daily, scrubbed or spray-cleaned weekly, and stripped and polished every 3 to 6 months
- walls may need to be washed every six months.

Points to watch during routine cleaning

1. Follow carefully all safety procedures (see box in unit 49, and units 53 to 55).

2. Think of the needs of guests and other staff on duty and keep to the minimum any disturbance or inconvenience to them.

3. Follow as far as possible the general procedures for reducing the movement of dust and dirt. Start by collecting rubbish, emptying ashtrays and waste bins, then damp-dust surfaces, then suction-clean floors.

4. Keep the area free from unpleasant odours. If there is no air-conditioning system, this will mean opening windows and doors for a short time.

5. Check thoroughly for:
   - damaged, faulty or missing items: report these in the appropriate way
   - stains on carpets, furniture and soft furnishings: deal with as soon as they are noticed (see unit 39)
   - lost property, particularly between cushions and under furniture in sitting areas: hand this in with a note of the circumstances in which it was found (see unit 59).

6. Pay attention to areas and items that will get soiled more quickly as a result of heavy usage, for example door handles and armrests on furniture.

7. Consider carefully the appearance of items:
   - keep brass plates, knockers, handrails and stairrails looking bright and tarnish free (see unit 30)
   - keep notices, direction signs and such things as menu display panels free of finger marks, smears and accumulated dust
   - where possible remove graffiti written or drawn on walls, signs, posters etc. or report it so that the defaced item can be replaced or re-decorated.

8. Pay particular attention to areas where rubbish might be dropped or accumulate or be deliberately hidden by a naughty child, for example:
   - behind curtains
   - down the backs of chairs and under cushions
   - in flower vases and ornamental pots.

9. When cleaning has been completed, check carefully that:
   - all furniture is in its proper position
   - cushions are plumped up and attractively arranged
   - fittings are left as they should be, pictures level, lamp shades straight with the seams out of sight
   - electric cables to light fittings are not caught under furniture or tangled and plugs are properly pushed into sockets
   - sufficient ashtrays are available
   - flower arrangements and indoor plants are looking their best (see box in unit 49)
   - curtains are hanging straight.

10. Follow specific cleaning procedures as necessary for door mats, lifts, staircases and corridors. (Guidelines are given in the next unit.)

 TO DO

Visit two contrasting establishments such as:
- an old people's home and a business hotel
- a leisure centre and a luxury theatre or cinema
- a NHS hospital and a private medical clinic

and write a brief report on the appearance and standards of cleanliness of the public areas in each.

Suggest when these public areas could be cleaned with the minimum inconvenience to the building's users.

The information in this unit and unit 49 will help you gain the Caterbase module *Daily Cleaning of Furnished Areas*. (See also units 41 to 44 for points relating to bedrooms.)

Specific cleaning procedures

Doormats
To prevent dust, grit and mud from being carried into a building on people's shoes, there is often a mat or grill of some sort outside entrances and a second mat immediately inside the building. These should be suction-cleaned daily.

Corridors and staircases
Corridors and staircases must be cleaned in such a way that anyone who has to use them while cleaning is in progress can do so safely (see box) with the minimum of inconvenience and without spoiling the appearance of the cleaned surface:

- Divide the corridor or staircase in half (lengthways) and clean one half first. This means people can proceed safely down the other half and their footmarks will not spoil the appearance of wet floors.
- If the corridor or staircase is a long one, divide it into sections and clean one half of each section first (see illustration).
- Start at the highest point of each stair landing and work down.

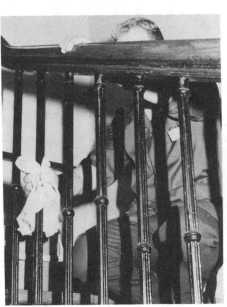

Lifts
The call button panel and outside lift doors should be damp-dusted as part of the corridor cleaning programme. Check that no finger marks remain.

The door track at each floor should also be suction-cleaned to remove rubbish and cigarette ends which have collected in it. Call the lift, then turn it off with the doors open (see steps 1 and 2 below).

1. Place a notice on each floor to warn anyone wishing to call the lift that it is out of service for cleaning.
2. Turn off the lift using the control key.
3. Remove any rubbish and empty ashtrays.
4. Damp-dust the control panel, any pictures, mirrors, display cases and the walls of the lift (unless they are upholstered or carpeted).
5. Suction-clean the floor (and the walls if they are carpeted). Damp-mop hard floors.

✳ FOR INTEREST

Door mats at the entrances of public buildings are usually sufficiently large for both feet to come into contact with their rough surface at least once when a person walks across them at a normal speed.

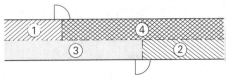

To *clean a very long corridor with doors leading off it, first divide it into half (lengthways) then divide each half into sections. The cleaning order (1, 2, 3 and finally 4) means that it is always safe for someone to come out of one of the doors and proceed in either direction down the corridor*

△ SAFETY

- Put up warning signs and cordon off work areas where necessary.
- Never touch electrical sockets with wet hands.
- When using electrical equipment such as suction cleaners and floor maintenance machines, work backwards towards the socket you are using to get power.
- Run power cables from equipment over your shoulder from the point they connect with the equipment. (This will reduce the risk of getting the cable caught up in the machine.)
- When cleaning corridors, lay the power cable down one side of the corridor and try and avoid it running in front of doors.
- Never work so far from the plug socket that you are stretching the cable: move to a closer socket.
- If you cannot reach a high surface, use the correct equipment and procedures (see units 52 to 55). Never stand on furniture.
- Report any damaged fittings such as loose handrails or broken electrical sockets.
- Do not leave fire doors wedged or propped open (see unit 57).
- Check that fire extinguishers are in their proper position.

6. Close the lift doors and damp-dust the inside of the doors.
7. Return the lift to service and remove the notices.

Periodic cleaning

Periodic cleaning of public areas will include all the tasks that are appropriate for the surfaces concerned. From time to time, for example, carpets will be shampooed (see unit 27), while hard floors will be scrubbed and buffed (or spray-cleaned), stripped and polished (see unit 26).

It is possible in most establishments to close off a lounge for periodic cleaning, particularly if alternative sitting areas are available, but it is more difficult to organise the periodic cleaning of corridors, foyers, lifts, staircases etc. Sometimes the only solution is to carry out the work at night, possibly using a cleaning contractor.

Typical procedure for periodic cleaning of a furnished public room (closed for the purpose)

1. If necessary, inform reception that the room has been closed for cleaning and give an estimate of when it is likely to be available for use again.
2. Remove all rubbish.
3. Clear the room of as much of its fittings and furniture as possible. Send curtains for dry cleaning or laundering.
4. Cover any furniture that cannot be removed with protective sheeting. It may be possible to move some furniture to the centre of the room.
5. Mop-sweep and/or suction-clean walls and ceiling. Then wash (see unit 29). Do not overlook skirting boards and radiators.
6. Wash doors and windows, including the sills (see unit 30).
7. Damp-dust fixed light fittings and light bulbs. Glass light covers should be removed and washed in a neutral detergent solution, then allowed to dry thoroughly before being refixed.
8. Suction-clean and shampoo upholstered furniture. Polish non-upholstered parts and items of furniture (see unit 33).
9. Suction-clean floors then shampoo carpets, strip, seal, polish and buff hard floors as appropriate (see units 26 and 27).
10. Wash accessories such as pictures, mirrors, ornaments, ashtrays etc.
11. Replace all the fittings and furniture in their original/proper position. Check that everything is working correctly and report any faults or damage.

▶ ▶ ▶ **TO DO**

Look at the arrangements of fresh flowers offered by your local florists. Choose three, one suitable for each of the following:

- the centre piece of a buffet table
- the top table of a banquet-style table arrangement (see next unit)
- a small reception desk.

Draw a rough sketch of each arrangement indicating the approximate dimensions. Note what flowers and foliage might be included in the display, the type of container or vase which would be used, how the flowers would be kept in position and the cost of each arrangement.

Discuss your findings with your tutor or supervisor.

The information and that in the cross-referenced units will assist you gain the Caterbase module *Periodic Cleaning of Furnished Areas*.

 FOR INTEREST

Fresh flower arrangements are often placed in foyers, reception areas and public rooms to provide an element of colour and beauty, helping to provide a relaxed atmosphere or perhaps a touch of luxury.

Flower arrangements can also be a very effective way of welcoming important guests to their suites or bedrooms.

In the restaurant a simple arrangement of a few carnations on each table, for example, can make a major contribution to the decor,

while more elaborate arrangements can make effective centrepieces for buffet tables or mark special occasions such as weddings and anniversaries.

Fresh flower arrangements need care to keep them looking good:

- the water should be checked daily and topped up as necessary
- water which is more than two or three days old, or which smells unpleasant, should be replaced with fresh water
- wilting or dead leaves and flowers should be carefully removed without disturbing the arrangement.

Plants have become a popular form of indoor decoration—the green providing a cool, fresh and natural look.

In many hotels, indoor plants and sometimes fresh flower arrangements are supplied and looked after by a specialist firm on a contract basis.

Dried flowers and silk flowers make attractive displays, provided they are kept dust free. (Some local authorities insist that dried flowers are treated with a fire retardant.)

Hotels, student halls of residence, even hospitals, often have rooms which are suitable for conferences, dinners, banquets, meetings, exhibitions, sales force briefings, and other, similar, occasions involving a number of people getting together. In some cases the room may normally be used for another purpose, for example in a hospital or hall of residence the staff restaurant may provide the venue for the annual Christmas party, in a hotel, one of the bedrooms may be converted into a small meeting room. However many residential establishments have *function rooms* designed for these sorts of events, and more and more towns and cities have purpose-built centres, sometimes very large, specifically for conferences, meetings and exhibitions.

Cleaning function rooms

The schedule for routine and periodic cleaning tasks will be adapted to the use which is made of the particular function room, and the nature of its surfaces (walls, floor, doors, furniture and fittings etc.).

A room must be clean and tidy before it can be set up for any function.

- If it has been cleaned recently, but not used, all the furniture and fittings should be damp-dusted.
- If it has been used, the procedure is:
  — remove rubbish
  — dismantle and remove any furniture which will not be required
  — damp-dust remaining furniture and surfaces
  — suction-clean carpets and hard floors (or mop-sweep hard floors)
  — check and report any damage, burnt-out light bulbs etc.

If the room is used three times a day for three different events, then this procedure will have to be followed before each event. This requirement to fit in with the bookings made for the room may mean cleaning very early in the morning, in the evening or late at night on some days. Periodic cleaning tasks can be carried out on the days when there is no scheduled function.

Sometimes two different types of functions may be held on one day in the same room. This necessitates setting up the room in one way and then having a different arrangement later on. For example, what served as a conference room in the afternoon is transformed in the evening for a dinner dance.

✳ FOR INTEREST

There has been a big expansion in conference, meeting and exhibition facilities available not only in Britain but throughout the world. The organisers of any particular event usually have a wide choice of suitable venues, especially if they can organise the delegates to travel as a group and stay overnight, either at the venue or at local hotels.

In many cases, the decision on venue will take into account what leisure and entertainment facilities are available in the area—theatres, ski-ing, golf courses etc.—but the organisers almost always expect certain basic services (see unit 13):

- comfortable seating
- suitable lighting and good ventilation (preferably air-conditioning)
- enough power points to supply any special electrical equipment which is required: overhead projectors, videos, computers, sound amplification systems, slide projectors, tape recorders etc.

and they may be persuaded to use a venue because it has sophisticated international communications systems, simultaneous translation facilities, microphones and earphones at each delegate's seat, in-house technicians to operate sound and visual systems.

Setting up the function room

Once a room is clean, the furniture and equipment can be arranged for the next function. The organiser's requirements would have been discussed and agreed some time in advance and the details noted for all concerned with the smooth running of the function.

The procedure for the housekeeping staff will usually include:

- Fetching the required furniture from stores, assembling and arranging. (Often conference porters are expected to help out.)
- Damp-dusting the tables and chairs (or suction-cleaning where appropriate).
- Placing tablecloths or baize on tables if required.
- Making sure that all the items requested by the function organisers have been laid out—these may include flower arrangements, bottles of mineral water, pencils, paper etc.
- Finally, checking that the room is clean and tidy and that lights are all working.

Servicing a function room

Most meetings and conferences, whether they last just one day or run over several days, are divided into a number of sessions, with breaks in between for refreshments and meals. These are made available in the function room itself or served in an adjacent area or even another room.

These breaks provide an opportunity for the room to be serviced. This usually involves:

- emptying and cleaning ashtrays
- removing other rubbish
- removing dirty coffee or tea cups
- replenishing water jugs or mineral water and replacing dirty glasses with clean glasses
- replenishing pads, pens etc.
- generally tidying the room.

◆ ◆ ◆ **TO DO**

Find out as many details as you can about the capacity of a function room of your choice. Either obtain or draw rough plans showing at least three different types of seating arrangements.

Suggest what sort of event each arrangement might be suitable for and if possible, indicate how many people the room could hold.

Finally, for one of the functions make a list of any special requirements that you think its organisers might require.

USEFUL TERMS

These are four basic styles of laying out furniture for functions:

Schoolroom style: chairs and tables are arranged in straight lines, or chairs are arranged in lines facing a table at the front of the room.

Theatre style: tiered or semi-circular arrangement, facing a raised platform.

Banquet style: top table with rows of tables leading from the top table.

Dinner/dance style: tables and chairs arranged around the room and the dance floor.

Commonwealth Suite: Specimen Dinner/Dance Layout

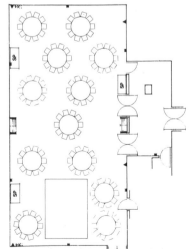

Commonwealth Suite: Specimen Theatre and Banquet Layout

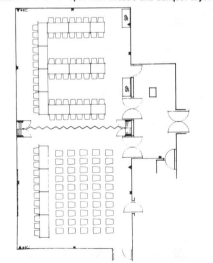

An increasingly sophisticated range of leisure facilities is made available to the guests of health clubs and many hotels (see unit 14 also): swimming pools, spa pools, saunas, solariums, steam rooms, jacuzzis, massage showers, gymnasiums, mini-gyms, fitness rooms, squash courts etc. The leisure area often includes a relaxation room or lounge, bars and restaurants, as well as beauticians, massage parlours and hairdressing salons.

The swimming pool water is usually heated to a temperature of 28 to 30°C (82 to 86°F) and the spa pool, which may be an integral part of the pool area or in a separate room, to 39°C (102°F).

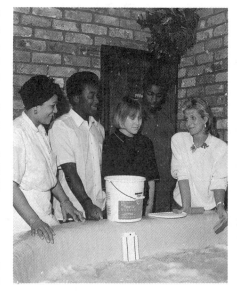

Leisure centres should be staffed at all times and attendants should be able to keep an eye on guests in each of the different areas. They should have a good knowledge of first aid and if they are ever on duty in the pool area, be fully trained life savers.

Cleaning leisure areas

Most of the floors, wall surfaces and fittings in leisure centres will be designed so they can withstand the humid conditions and heavy use. Typical cleaning methods will include:

routine

- damp-dusting fittings and furniture
- damp-mopping floors around swimming pools and spas, in changing rooms, toilets, saunas etc.—areas where water or moisture is present (alternatively, hosing down or using a pressure cleaning unit)
- mop-sweeping other hard floor surfaces
- scrubbing any floors which are heavily soiled
- suction-cleaning any carpeted areas, for example in coffee shops and fitness rooms
- cleaning sanitary fittings.

periodic

- washing walls, ceilings, windows and furniture
- scrubbing all hard floors.

Furniture

Furniture and equipment for leisure areas should be able to withstand the humid conditions and heavy use.

For very strong furniture, lightweight coated steel or polythene coated cast aluminium are suitable materials. The coating protects the metal from corrosion and some manufacturers recommend that it should be re-sprayed every two years (in a different colour if a change of decor is sought). This will give the furniture an almost unlimited life.

Chairs, sun loungers, tables and similar pieces of furniture for leisure areas are also made from weatherproof synthetic resin. Depending on the quality, this type of furniture is guaranteed by the manufacturers to last from two to ten years.

Routine cleaning is straightforward: damp-dust with a neutral detergent solution and rinse.

If the protective coating on steel or aluminium surfaces is found to have been damaged, perhaps because it has received a sharp knock, report the problem. Corrosion will set in unless the coating is repaired quickly.

✳ FOR INTEREST

Spas need very careful maintenance by experts to ensure they are pleasant and safe to be in. The methods are similar to those described briefly in unit 52 for swimming pools (filtration and chemical disinfectants) but three major differences make proper treatment especially important:

- Spas are used by more people at any one time than swimming pools, so there is a greater concentration of body oils, skin flakes and other organic wastes.
- Spa water is kept at a higher temperature, which means that evaporation is considerable and the concentration of dissolved solids can rapidly increase.
- The rapid circulation and temperature of the water reduce the effectiveness of disinfectants and increases the water's pH.

Security in leisure areas

There are two aspects to security in leisure areas.

1. Protecting the safety of the users. This may mean keeping out anyone who is not authorised to be in the area. In a health club, members may be asked to produce their membership card, or in a hotel the guests may be requested to give their name and room number. There is likely to be a restriction on children under a certain age using the facilities, and rules to prevent dangerous behaviour.

2. Protecting the safety of the users' property. Lockers are usually provided for valuables, but in some leisure centres clothes will be left in changing rooms. Any problems with the lockers should be reported, such as lost keys or locks that have been tampered with. Also report anyone you see acting suspiciously.

Safety in leisure areas

- A good standard of illumination is important to safety:
  - external windows should be kept clean
  - lighting should be kept clean and in full working order
  - emergency lights should be tested daily.
- Floors, passages, ramps and stairs should be kept free from obstructions and any substance which is likely to cause a slip or fall.
- Lifebelts must be in place at all times so they are available for use in an emergency.
- Report any broken or missing tiles and sharp edges on floors where people walk barefoot.
- Keep drainage gulleys clean and unblocked.
- The humidity and possible presence of chemicals in the atmosphere will cause metals to corrode faster than usual. Report any signs of corrosion noticed during cleaning of light fittings and roof voids, for example.
- Be particularly careful when using electrical equipment to keep plugs and other electrical connections absolutely dry.
- Never attempt to clean up spillages of chemicals used to treat swimming pool or spa water, but report them at once so they can be cleared away safely.
- Ladders, stepladders, trestles or platforms should only be used if you have received training in their safe use. Check that the ladder, trestle or platform:
  - is fixed securely so it will not slip in any direction or collapse
  - will not sway or vibrate making it difficult to keep your balance.
- Also be careful when working at heights to:
  - have only the equipment you need and can conveniently handle
  - keep a safe hand-hold
  - clean only the area you can reach easily and without stretching or otherwise endangering your balance
  - tie or otherwise secure any equipment which might be dropped accidentally, breaking something below or injuring someone.

▶ ▶ ▶ TO DO

Carry out a small survey of the hotels and conference centres in your area to establish what leisure facilities they offer their guests and when they were first introduced.

If possible, arrange to visit one of your sample and meet with a member of staff who is involved in cleaning the leisure areas. Find out as much as you can about the cleaning procedures that are used.

The information in units 51 and 52 will help you gain the Caterbase module *Servicing Leisure Facilities*.

Swimming pools are complex facilities to look after. The water in a properly maintained pool should contain as few bacteria as drinking water, even when it is heavily used. But if things go wrong, people using the pool could get gastro-enteritis, dysentery or even typhoid.

The problems are caused by:

- sweat, body fats and oils and make-up present on the bodies of swimmers when they enter the water—even if they do shower beforehand
- urine introduced by thoughtless swimmers
- dust and grit, litter, cigarette ends and dead insects which fall or get blown into the water from the surroundings (leaves and grass cuttings will also be a problem if the pool is outdoors).

There is also a danger that the various chemicals used to disinfect the water can cause irritation to the skin and/or eyes, or release dangerous gases.

Maintaining swimming pools

Keeping the water in a swimming pool safe is thought by many experts to be one of the most labour and maintenance intensive areas in a hotel. Almost always there will be a team of trained technicians and maintenance staff as well as pool attendants to look after the safety of people using the pool.

Basically there are six procedures.

1. Removing any debris floating on the surface of the water. A hand-held filter net can be used and some pools have a special skimming device at water level which traps the larger debris on the surface.
2. Cleaning off any build-up of body fats on the water-line. Special pastes or powders are used with a nylon scouring pad.
3. Cleaning the bottom of the pool using a tube linked to the pumping system. Water and debris are sucked up through the hose.
4. Using chemical disinfectants to kill any bacteria introduced into the water from swimmers or the surrounds. The level of disinfectant should be tested every two hours or so (a pool testing kit is used).
5. Maintaining the water's correct pH value (the level of its acid and alkaline content—see box in unit 20). This is also tested using a special kit every two hours or so when the pool is in use and should be between 7.2 and 7.4 (some experts give a slightly higher upper limit).
6. Filtering the water through sand (which is excellent at trapping dead algae and such things as hair and skin flakes) and then a flocculent agent (this forms a gel that traps any remaining particles). In some systems the water is effectively renewed every 4 to 6 hours. The pool is also back-washed regularly (two or three times a week, but more frequently if the pool is heavily used). This involves reversing the flow of water through the filter, so clearing the particles which have accumulated. This water is drained away, so the pool level will drop—typically about 150 mm (6 inches)—and fresh water is used to make up the loss (heated first to the correct temperature). If indoor pools are well looked after, they rarely need a complete change of water, but it is still necessary to drain and thoroughly clean outdoor pools once a year.

Keeping the pool users safe

In addition to keeping a close check on the condition of floors and other areas where hazards can occur (see unit 51), cleaning staff should be aware of the following problems and if they occur report them immediately. They are each

serious enough for the pool to be closed or kept closed by management until the matter is rectified.

- Unclear water: the bottom of the pool should be clearly visible from any position on the poolside and the see-through distance should not be less than 12 m (40 ft).
- A smell of gas.
- Swimmers complaining of sore eyes and/or skin irritations.
- Lifeguards not in attendance at the pool side.
- Chemicals leaking out of their containers. (It is most important that chemicals are kept in their proper storage area and in containers which are clearly labelled as to their contents.)

Keeping the water safe and clear

There is a considerable choice of chemicals suitable for disinfecting swimming pool water and keeping it clear.

Chlorine is one of the cheapest and most reliable of swimming pool chemicals when it comes in powder, liquid or tablet form (in gas form it is regarded as too unsafe to be used in pools). Because of its smell it is not generally used in indoor pools and it can also have a corrosive effect on machinery.

Bromine is widely used in indoor pools as it has no smell at all and will not affect plants growing around the pool area (as part of the decor).

Ozone is a very effective water purifier and disinfectant. However it is highly poisonous so the water is pumped out of the pool for treatment in the circulation plant itself. All traces of ozone are then taken out before the water is returned to the pool. Some chlorine or bromine still has to be used to disinfect the water in the pool itself. In future years, less expensive systems based on the use of ozone are expected to be available.

Other disinfectant systems used include:

- sodium hypochlorite and acid systems
- electrolytic generation of sodium hypochlorite.

Algicides sometimes have to be added to pool water, usually once a week, to prevent algae from growing. Algae, which is a type of plant, reduces the clarity of the water and if it is allowed to grow on a surface may cause a safety hazard (it forms a slimy, green mat).

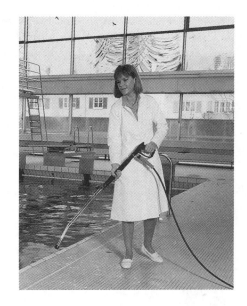

 TO DO

Visit a public swimming pool in your area at a busy time and make a note of:

- the number of lifeguards on duty
- what advice is given to the pool's users for their own safety—on posters, in leaflets and by attendants.

City and Guilds

Test yourself: Units 48–52

1. The cleaning of public rooms often has to be organised at special times or other special procedures followed. Identify the reason and describe briefly what practice might be followed when cleaning:
   (a) a staircase (b) a lounge.
2. Give five examples of checks that should be made in a public room after cleaning has been completed.
3. Power cables to cleaning equipment can present a hazard. Describe briefly two safe practices that should be followed to prevent accidents.
4. What is the procedure for cleaning a lift? Give as many of the steps as you can.
5. Give four of the tasks that should be carried out when a function room has to be serviced during a break.

6. Describe briefly what is meant by the following style of furniture arrangement for a function:
   (a) theatre (b) dinner dance.
7. List four of the facilities that might be provided in a leisure centre.
8. Give five examples of safety practices that should be followed when cleaning a leisure area.
9. Name three undesirable substances that can contaminate swimming pool water and for each give one method that will prevent it causing a danger to the pool's users.
10. What are two problems that should be immediately reported if they occur in a swimming pool or its surroundings?

Accidents are always unpleasant. Even if they are minor and the person or persons involved are lucky enough not to be hurt, there will still be the shock of the unexpected and the awful thought that serious injury or death might have been caused.

Accidents occur too often in the hotel and catering industry—to staff and to customers and guests:

- Some happen because the person involved has done something dangerous and it's entirely that person's fault.
- Some happen because someone else has not done his or her work in the safest possible way.

The person at fault may not know about the safe practices he or she is supposed to follow, or suffered a moment of genuine forgetfulness, or got into careless habits. But whatever the reason for the accident the consequences can be considerable—for the people injured, for the people responsible and for the management and owners of the establishments concerned:

- Hurt and pain are likely to be caused to the people directly involved and to family and friends.
- Medical expenses may be incurred.
- Compensation may have to be paid to the person or people injured.
- Legal costs may result from claims for compensation.
- Time may have to be taken off work until an adequate recovery is made.
- Loss of earnings may result, through absence from work (a particularly serious problem for anyone running their own business).
- A bad impression of the establishment where the accident occurred may be given to anyone who has been or might be a customer.
- Damage may be caused to the structure or decor of the establishment, or to the fittings and equipment.
- Death may result.

Safety at work

Working safely is so important that there are various Acts of Parliament, and Regulations made as a result of these Acts, which lay down exactly what the obligations are of everyone at the workplace.

The Health and Safety at Work Act (1974), sometimes referred to as *HASAWA*, states that everyone at work, whether employer or employee, trainee or contractor brought in to do some of the work has a duty to look after the health and safety of colleagues as well as customers, patients, visitors and members of the general public and anyone else affected by his or her work.

Under the Act *employers* must:

- provide safe equipment and safe ways of carrying out jobs
- ensure that the use, handling, storage and transport of everything is safe and without any health risks
- provide information, instruction, training and supervision in health and safety
- provide a safe workplace, including safe ways of getting into and out of the workplace
- provide a safe working environment with adequate facilities
- write a safety policy.

See: Housecraft video and core book *Health, Hygiene and Safety in the Hotel and Catering Industry*.

!! **REMEMBER**

- Be constantly alert to possible dangers.
- Know emergency procedures.
- Follow safety procedures when carrying out any tasks.
- Wear the correct uniform/protective clothing when at work.
- Take care not to create hazardous situations.
- If you see a hazard that can be easily put right or removed, do so without delay. For example, rubbish that has been dropped in a corridor.
- If you see a hazard that will put anyone in danger and you don't know what to do about it, report it immediately to someone who can put it right.
- Follow safety instructions for cleaning agents.
- Always follow instructions exactly when operating equipment, and leave it in a safe condition after use.
- Do not use or clean dangerous machinery without suitable training and/or supervision.

Every single *employee* at work has a duty under the Act to:

- ensure reasonable care for his/her own health and safety
- ensure that colleagues and other people are not adversely affected by his/her acts or omissions
- co-operate with employers to meet health and safety requirements
- ensure that he/she does not interfere with anything or misuse anything provided in the interests of health and safety (this also applies to employers).

An offence under HASAWA is a criminal offence and can result in an unlimited fine and/or a prison sentence of up to two years. Anyone can be prosecuted.

First aid

The Health and Safety (First Aid) Regulations (1981) require employers to make adequate first aid provision at the workplace. This means that specific members of staff have to be appointed either as qualified first aiders, or as people who can take charge if there is an accident and no first aider is available. Properly stocked and distinctly marked first aid boxes must be provided (they are normally green with a white cross).

Employees must make sure that they know:

- who their first aider is
- where the nearest first aid box is.

Reporting accidents

All hotel and catering establishments have to keep records of certain types of accidents and dangerous occurrences to meet the requirements of the *Reporting of Injuries, Diseases and Dangerous Occurrences Regulations (1985)* usually referred to as RIDDOR. The usual policy is to keep records of all accidents, dangerous occurrences and diseases covering:

- the date and time the incident occurred
- the full name and occupation of the person(s) involved
- the nature of the injury, dangerous occurrence or disease
- the place where the incident happened and a brief description of the circumstances
- names of any witnesses
- details of the person making the report and date and time the report is made.

✱ FOR INTEREST

For most of the hotel and catering industry, environmental health officers or EHOs (who work for the local authority) are responsible for enforcing HASAWA and RIDDOR.

In sports and leisure clubs, factory canteens, theatres and cinemas, health and safety inspectors, employed by a national organisation set up by the government called the Health and Safety Executive (HSE) are responsible for enforcing HASAWA and RIDDOR.

They have the powers to:

- comment on and ask for improvements
- serve an improvement notice which gives a set time to improve specific faults
- serve a prohibition notice closing the premises when the circumstances are so dangerous that they must be stopped immediately.

 TO DO

Make your own list of some of the safety hazards which could occur in an establishment offering residential accommodation. Here are some suggestions to start you off:

- spills not wiped up
- faulty equipment not reported and not labelled 'out of service'
- cleaning agents and equipment left around wherever they were last used
- cables to electrical cleaning equipment causing a tripping hazard
- fire extinguishers left to prop open fire doors
- gloves not worn when cleaning the bathroom/toilet
- heavy object lifted badly.

How accidents can be prevented

Clothing Whether a uniform is provided by the establishment or whether housekeeping staff are expected to wear their own clothes (as they might be in small guesthouses, for example), clothing should:

- be comfortable and practical
- allow for free movement
- be hygienic
- look good to the customer and the member of staff
- have strong pockets to hold such things as keys and note pads.

A change of work clothes is necessary to allow for laundering. Daily washing of washable clothing is desirable.

Footwear Housekeeping staff spend most of their working hours on their feet, so comfortable, practical shoes are a must (see also *How to* box in unit 55).

Cleaning agents Always follow instructions for diluting cleaning agents, measuring amounts carefully and never mix two cleaning agents together (see unit 20).

Change cleaning solutions and rinsing water regularly.

Do not use chemical disinfectants unless specifically instructed.

Cleaning equipment Cleaning equipment will do its job most effectively when it is well looked after and used in the way it is designed to be (see units 21 to 23).

- Replace or empty dust bags and clean exhaust filters in suction cleaners regularly.
- Do not allow the heads of mops or the brushes or pads of rotary floor maintenance machines to get heavily soiled: change as necessary and wash after use.
- Take great care not to spread bacteria from one surface to another. For example, cloths used to clean toilets should never be used for any other purpose.

!! REMEMBER

Safe working is also about:

- preventing the spread of harmful bacteria—see units 19 and 56
- reducing the risk of fire and knowing what to do if a fire occurs—see unit 57
- protecting the property and well-being of all the other people using the building and safeguarding the property of your employers—see unit 58.

?? HOW TO

Push safely

Always keep your back straight and your chin tucked in when using a mop or any electrical cleaning equipment that involves pushing or pulling.

If it is necessary to lean forwards slightly, keep your whole body at the same angle: rear of your legs, back and back of your head.

Use your arm muscles not your back muscles to move the object.

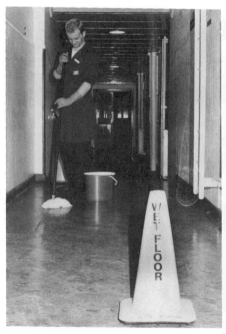

The information in this unit will assist you gain certification in the Caterbase module *Handling and Moving Items*.

- After use, clean all equipment and any attachments to machines such as brushes and pads, and store in the proper place.
- Report any faults and do not use or let others use equipment which is not working as it should be.

When using electrical equipment:

- Make sure hands are dry before touching any switches or plugs.
- Always switch off the appliance and unplug before fitting any attachments.
- Remove plugs from sockets by grasping the plug—never pull by the lead.

Lifting and carrying   Housekeeping staff are frequently required to move heavy bags of soiled linen, mattresses, furniture, boxes of cleaning material and so forth. There are a few simple rules to follow in order to avoid back injury when lifting and carrying:

- If the object is too heavy, do not attempt to lift it without assistance from a colleague.
- Use trolleys as much as possible for carrying things.
- Before lifting an item decide how it will be done, where it will be placed, and if it has to be carried, whether the route is free from any obstruction.
- Never bend or twist while lifting, pushing or carrying.

Using ladders   Ladders or stepladders should only be used by staff who have received training in their safe use or are in the process of being trained and are directly supervised at the time (see also unit 51).

Ladders should always be fixed securely so they will not slip in any direction:

- Single or extending ladders should be placed at an angle of 75° to the horizontal. The top of the ladder should be tied to the scaffolding or platform it is being used to reach, or secured by two guy ropes at 45° to the horizontal. The foot of the ladder should be on a flat surface and staked to the ground. If the ladder cannot be staked to the ground, then it can be held in place while it is being used by a second person—however this is only safe if the ladder is being used at a height of up to 6.9 m (22 ft 8 inches).
- Stepladders must be fully opened out with all four feet resting securely on a flat, sound base.

‼ REMEMBER

- Ask a supervisor or colleague if you are not sure how to do any task, or what it would be best to do in a particular situation.
- Remember at all times that you have a responsibility for the safety of others using the building. If you are doing a cleaning task in an area which others might have to go through, use the warning signs that are provided and wherever possible, rope off the part you are working in.
- Your colleagues will judge you on how tidily and clean you leave equipment when you have finished with it, and how carefully you do the tasks given to you (see unit 61).
- The guests, patients, customers, residents, students—all the people whose needs you and your work colleagues are paid to meet—will judge you on how clean, safe and tidy they find the facilities they use (see units 60 to 62).

‼ REMEMBER

- Don't use a ladder unless you are being or have been trained.
- Fix it securely.
- Only take up the ladder the equipment you need and can safely handle.
- Clean only the area you can safely reach. Don't risk losing your balance by stretching or reaching out—get down and change the position of the ladder.
- Display a warning notice.

?? HOW TO

Lift a heavy object

1. With your feet spread in a balanced position, stand close to the object, if possible facing the direction in which it is to be moved.
2. Always keep your back straight: if the object is on the floor or a low shelf, squat down by bending your knees, not your back.
3. Grasp the object firmly with both hands, holding it as close to your body as possible so the weight is taken by your body not your hands or arm muscles. Keep your chin tucked in so your head does not drop forwards or backwards.
4. Lift with a smooth movement, straightening your legs. In this way your thigh muscles will take the strain, not your (much weaker) back muscles.
5. To lower the object, bend your knees and remember to keep your back straight.
6. If the object has to be lifted above waist level, it is impossible to avoid using arm and back muscles—don't risk straining them, ask a colleague to help!

 TO DO

Make your own list of safety points to remember based on a cleaning procedure of your choice, such as:

- daily cleaning of a bedroom and *en-suite* bathroom
- periodic cleaning of a corridor.

Try and be as comprehensive as possible. Aim to make your list useful to any member of staff asked to clean the same area, even if they have received no previous training.

?? HOW TO

Avoid common accidents

Falls

- Keep floor areas clean and dry.
- Place warning signs when cleaning floors.
- Load trolleys carefully so items will not fall off.
- Remove all hazards from the floor such as containers of cleaning materials, cleaning cloths.
- Report any hazards that you cannot personally deal with. Where appropriate place a warning sign.
- Work tidily at all times, for example when damp-dusting a room, don't clutter the floor with items removed from shelves and other surfaces.
- Take care when cleaning a window not to lose your balance.
- Open and shut doors carefully. Do not leave cupboard doors open.
- Carry things and load trolleys in such a way that you can see where you are going.
- Get help to carry heavy items.
- Always walk, don't run.
- Wear sensible shoes for work so that you will be less likely to slip or trip and less likely to hurt your toes if you should drop something or run over your foot with a trolley wheel.
- Never pile soiled sheets, towels or other linen due to be laundered on the floor of the bedroom or corridor. (See units 38 and 56.)

Cuts

- Clear up broken glass or china with a dustpan and brush, and the very small pieces with a suction cleaner. Never use your fingers.
- Wrap up sharp items such as broken glass or china in paper so they will not tear through plastic rubbish bags, or put them in a metal or solid plastic rubbish container.
- Do not run your hands along surfaces you cannot see without checking first that there are no sharp edges.

Burns or scalds

- Place china, glassware and similar items from guest bedrooms and patients' lockers, for example, into baskets for rinsing (the water should be very hot to help kill any bacteria—see units 16 and 45).
- Take care when running hot water from taps in bathrooms and service areas—it might be hot enough to scald you.
- Never attempt to clean light fittings until they have been turned off sufficiently long to cool down. You might not only scald yourself, but the bulb will shatter as soon as it is touched with a damp cloth.
- Do not use electrical equipment which has loose or faulty connections, or touch leads or cables which are damaged in any way (see Safety box in unit 23).
- Never touch plugs, sockets or electrical apparatus with wet hands.

?? HOW TO

Call for emergency assistance

1. Use any telephone: get an outside line if necessary and dial 999. No money is required if you are using a public call box.
2. Ask for the necessary service:
   - ambulance
   - fire brigade
   - police.
3. When you get through give the telephone number so they can ring you back if the call gets cut off.
4. State the location and give as much detail as can be given quickly.
5. State the nature of the accident, for example a fall down a flight of stairs.
6. If it is a medical condition, such as a heart attack or a child birth, say so.
7. Remain on the phone until the emergency service rings off, to be sure you have given sufficient information.

!! REMEMBER

Treatment in a hospital or medical centre will be required:

- If the cut needs stitching—deep cuts which are longer than 1.75 cm (½ inch) generally have to be stitched together to heal properly.
- If the wound has been contaminated by dirt—bacteria getting into wounds can cause tetanus, a serious and painful disease that makes muscles, especially jaw muscles, go stiff.

 TO DO

Arrange to practise with a qualified first aider:

- opening and clearing the airway
- placing someone in the recovery position.

See *Health, Hygiene and Safety in the Hotel and Catering Industry*.

What to do if an accident happens

Even when all the proper precautions have been taken by everyone concerned, an accident may still occur. It is important to know what to do:

- the effect of an injury can be greatly reduced if prompt first aid is given
- records usually have to be kept of accidents and dangerous occurrences (see unit 53).

Stay calm and act quickly   Make sure the person injured is in no further danger. For example, if an accident has happened with a floor maintenace machine, turn it off and unplug it immediately.

In the case of an electric shock, turn off the power immediately at the plug or the mains switch. Do not touch the injured person until you have done so (otherwise there is a danger that you will get a shock as well).

Call whoever is appointed to deal with accidents at once (normally a first aider or your supervisor).

Reassure the injured person and help him or her to feel more comfortable, but make sure that the person is not moved more than absolutely necessary. Don't allow people to crowd around the injured person because this may increase his or her distress.

Grazes and cuts

- If bleeding is severe, then direct pressure should be applied over the bleeding points and the injured person helped to lie down with the injured part raised slightly and supported.
- The sides of a large wound should be pressed together.
- As soon as a dressing is available it should be applied over the wound.
- If bleeding continues further layers of dressing may be necessary, bandaged more firmly.

Burns and scalds

- Reduce the pain and the spread of heat by running cold water over the burn or immersing it in cold water for at least ten minutes or until the pain stops.
- Carefully remove any jewellery, tight clothing or footwear in the area of the burn (before swelling makes this impossible).
- Burnt clothing should be left on if it is dry (it will have been sterilised by the heat). Wet clothing should be carefully removed.
- Never apply any lotions, oils, ointments or adhesive dressings to a burn.
- Be careful not to infect burnt areas, for example by breathing over them or touching them.
- Dirty wounds should be cleaned before dressing, if possible, either under running water or by wiping carefully with swabs or clean cotton wool.

Difficulty in breathing

Head injury, electric shock, poisoning and obstructed airway can each cause the casualty to stop breathing. If this happens timing is critical, the casualty can die if breathing is not restored within 4 to 6 minutes.

The first step is to open and clear the airway.

1. Lie the casualty on his or her back.
2. Tilt the head back by putting one hand under the neck and the other hand over the forehead and press with both hands.
3. Move the hand from under the neck to push the chin upwards—if the tongue has fallen back, this will bring it forward.
4. Turn the casualty's head to the side and feel inside the mouth with the fingers to locate and remove vomit, dentures or any other obstacles which might block the airway.

The second step is for the casualty to be given resuscitation by a qualified first aider or someone who has received instruction.

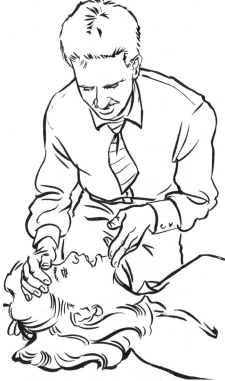

The open airway position: chin up, forehead down. Once the airway is open, the casualty might begin breathing spontaneously. The casualty should then be placed in the recovery position

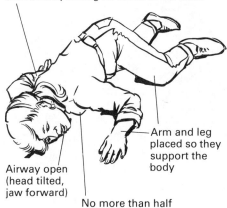

This arm lies alongside the body to prevent the casualty rolling on to his or her back

Airway open (head tilted, jaw forward)

Arm and leg placed so they support the body

No more than half the casualty's chest should be in contact with the ground or floor

The unconscious or recovery position prevents the tongue from dropping to the back of the throat, blocking the airway. It also allows vomit or other fluid to drain from the mouth

---

?? | **HOW TO**

Check a casualty is breathing
1. Put your ear to the casualty's mouth to feel and hear the breathing.
2. Watch the chest and put your hands on it to check its rise and fall.
3. The lips, cheeks and ear lobes of someone who has stopped breathing may go blue-grey.

Cleaning for hygiene

One of the main reasons for cleaning is to remove harmful bacteria (see units 15 and 16) and as bacteria are so small—they cannot be seen without a microscope—a lot of attention has to be paid to the *methods* used for cleaning—*visual* checks are not enough. For example wiping over a surface with a dry duster or sweeping a floor with a broom may produce a reasonably clean-looking result, but no matter how carefully it is done:

- bacteria will be left on the surface
- bacteria and most of the dust will be redistributed elsewhere in the room.

This is why dry dusting or sweeping is not recommended and why throughout *Housecraft* so much emphasis is placed on:

- Good personal hygiene, so that harmful bacteria are not introduced into otherwise clean areas (see unit 19).
- Preventing the spread of bacteria from one surface or area to another by:
  — cleaning equipment thoroughly after use (see units 21 to 23)
  — cleaning sanitary fittings with equipment reserved specifically for that use (see units 31 and 45)
  — changing cleaning solutions regularly.
- Removing 'food' (this is provided in dirt) which bacteria can grow on and leaving surfaces dry (see box).

Pest control

A wide range of pests find their way into buildings, some are carried by people or their pets, others fly in through open windows and doors, others can get through the smallest hole or crack—none is welcome. The sight of a pest will give most people a bad impression, suggesting poor standards of cleaning and maintenance, and many pests are harmful:

- cockroaches, flies, wasps, ants, mice and rats act as carriers for harmful bacteria
- woodworm, moths, carpet beetles, mice and rats can damage furniture, fittings and the building fabric
- mosquitoes, bed bugs, head lice and fleas attack human beings
- spiders and silver-fish are offensive to many people but generally harmless.

Prevention is the most effective form of pest control—see box. In many establishments electric ultra-violet lights are used to attract and kill flies, and poisoned baits are left for mice and rats in food preparation and storage areas, usually under the supervision of a pest control firm. Such firms can also be called in to deal with cockroaches, bed bugs, woodworm and other pests.

Precautions against AIDS

AIDS is a very serious public health hazard, and housekeeping staff should know the dangers and be familiar with the precautions:

- AIDS stands for Acquired Immune Deficiency Syndrome. It is caused by infection with a virus known as HIV. HIV may break down the body's resistance to other diseases with the result that the infected person will eventually die from his or her illness.

✳ FOR INTEREST

Some bacteria are useful, others are not particularly dangerous, but cause moulds and similar food spoilage (see box in unit 15). Those which are harmful are called *pathogenic*.

Bacteria need certain conditions to grow and multiply:

- food—dirt, dust and grease, particles of food, build-ups of body fats, urine, faeces, spit, vomit, semen, rubbish etc.
- moisture—bacteria tend not to develop on dry surfaces
- warmth—bacteria multiply rapidly at temperatures between 10 and 63°C (50 and 145°F); above 63°C they will die and the higher the temperature the faster they are destroyed
- time—in the right conditions bacteria multiply rapidly, doubling in numbers every 10 to 20 minutes.

⁇ HOW TO

Discourage pests

1. Remember clean conditions discourage pests.
2. Report any signs of infestation:
   - droppings, gnaw marks, footprints, shredded paper: a sign of rats
   - small, golden brown grubs with hairy tufts on edges of carpets or in linen rooms where blankets are stored: the larvae of carpet beetles
   - small holes in furniture: a sign of woodworm
   - holes in blankets which have been stored: a sign of moths.
3. Report any defects in the building which might encourage infestation, such as cracks and crevices.
4. Do not leave food uncovered and take particular care with remains of food that is likely to attract pests, such as spilt sugar and jam, biscuit crumbs. Remove or arrange for prompt removal of early morning and meal trays from guest rooms.
5. Remove waste promptly to the refuse area. Do not leave it lying in service rooms where it will attract pests.
6. Keep waste bins tightly covered and rubbish bags closed. Clean waste bins after use.

- In the majority of known cases, AIDS has been passed from one person to another through sexual intercourse, or by taking infected blood into the bloodstream. It is not transmitted in food or drink, nor passed on by shaking hands.
- Special care should therefore be taken when handling or cleaning anything that might have had contact with another person's blood or semen such as razors, used razor blades, hypodermic needles, sanitary towels, soiled sheets and towels, pools of vomit and spills of excreta:
  — wear gloves when handling items or cleaning surfaces that might be contaminated
  — dispose of sharp objects in a metal or plastic bin which they cannot cut through
  — ensure adequate towels are available so that towels do not have to be used by more than one person (warm air dryers or disposable towels are more suitable in public toilets for this reason than roller-towels)
  — dispose of or sterilise cleaning equipment used to clean spills of blood, vomit etc.: check with your supervisor
  — in some cases it will be appropriate to use a chemical disinfectant such as bleach after cleaning surfaces and equipment: check with your supervisor.

Precautions against Legionnaires' disease

The bacteria which cause Legionnaires' disease live in damp, warm conditions. They have been found in large numbers in hot and cold water systems, particularly when the temperature of the water is between 20 and 45°C (68 and 115°F) and stagnant or very slow moving. These conditions occur in:

- hot water systems in which the temperature of the water drops during long pipe runs or through infrequent use
- in cold water tanks which are badly sited or poorly insulated so that the water gets quite warm
- air-conditioning systems which use water to collect the excess heat and then cool the water in special towers.

When the water has been contaminated by algae, rust from metal piping and tanks, or scaling has occurred, the bacteria will grow even more rapidly.

The bacteria cause illness if they are inhaled, for example by breathing in fine spray from a shower, fast running tap, whirlpool or spa. They attach themselves to the inside of the lungs, and after several days the victim is likely to have bad headaches and muscle pains, feel feverish and shivery and become very confused. Legionnaires' disease can be fatal.

Growth of the bacteria can be prevented from reaching dangerous levels by regular cleaning of water storage tanks and cooling towers and treating the water with chemical disinfectants. Both require special expertise and the work can be dangerous so this is a job for experts.

Shower heads should also be dismantled regularly, cleaned and disinfected. This is particularly important if the showers are not used very much because the bacteria will have had time to multiply to dangerous numbers.

✳ FOR INTEREST

Before treating a casualty, cover any cuts or abrasions on your own skin with a waterproof dressing. If this is not practicable, wear disposable gloves and after treating the wound, do not remove the gloves until you have washed them with soap and hot water. Dispose of the gloves, then wash your hands again with soap and hot water.

Mouth-to-mouth resuscitation should never be withheld in an emergency through fear of catching AIDS. No case of infection has been reported from any part of the world as a result of giving mouth-to-mouth resuscitation.

The Hotel, Catering and Institutional Management Association has published two Technical Briefs *Precautions against AIDS* and *Precautions against Legionnaires' Disease* from which the information in this unit has been drawn. Members may obtain a copy by writing to the Association at 191 Trinity Road, London SW17 7HN.

A free booklet *AIDS—What everybody needs to know* is available from the Health Education Council, Department A, PO Box 100, Milton Keynes MK1 1TY.

✎ HOUSECRAFT TIP

The outside of shower heads should be cleaned as part of the housekeeping staff's routine procedure and so should the inside of taps (using a small brush).

Check shower heads for signs of rust and/or blockages which prevent them spraying the water properly. Report any problems.

 TO DO

Design a poster which might be displayed in service areas used by housekeeping staff to remind them of the need for high standards of hygiene.

Most fires result from faulty or misused electrical equipment, carelessly discarded cigarettes and matches, inadequate storage of materials, failure to dispose of or store rubbish safely. Some fires are started deliberately.

The law protects the occupants of most public buildings. In some cases the protection is indirect, for example a licence to sell alcohol will not be given to an establishment where the fire safety measures are poor or non-existent, planning permission will not be given to a new building unless adequate fire exits are provided and safe materials used in its construction.

Many non-residential establishments such as restaurants, pubs, fish and chip shops are covered by the Offices, Shops and Railway Premises Act (1963). The Fire Precautions Act (1971) covers all but the smallest hotels, motels, inns and boarding houses.

Under the Acts it is unlawful for the owners or occupiers of buildings used by the public to carry on in business unless they hold a fire certificate issued by the local fire authority and meet all the requirements. This places a limit on the number of people who can be on the premises at any one time and covers the provision of:

- fire warning systems including notices to guests and staff
- fire fighting equipment
- escape routes
- regular training for staff in fire procedures

✳ FOR INTEREST

Premises not covered by the Offices, Shops and Railway Premises Act (1963) include:

- small establishments in which not more than ten people are working at any one time other than on the ground floor and the total number of employees in the building at any one time is not more than 20.

Premises not covered by the Fire Precautions Act (1971) include:

- establishments where all the bedrooms are on the ground and/or first floor and provide beds for fewer than six people (guests and/or staff).

‼ REMEMBER

1. Smoke only where you are permitted and always use ash trays. Make sure that cigarette ends and matches are properly extinguished.
2. If an electric socket or electrical machine is faulty, report it at once. Adaptors can cause a socket to be overloaded, and this can start a fire. Never overstretch a cable. Place a clear warning notice on faulty equipment or a faulty socket.
3. Movable heaters, such as electric fires, are dangerous. They should not be left near or touching anything.
4. After using irons or presses, remember to switch them off.
5. Collect matches and cigarette ends in non-flammable containers, and keep aerosols separate if rubbish is to be incinerated (as they explode in incinerators).
6. Dispose of refuse from waste bins or compactors in proper containers, for example dust bins or hoppers.
7. Do not leave refuse or greasy cloths lying around, and always store equipment and cleaning agents safely, according to instructions. Spontaneous combustion (when a fire starts without any visible heat source in the vicinity) can occur with rotting refuse, and also when dirty, greasy or oily cloths, such as impregnated mats or mops, are stored in unventilated areas.
8. Report any potential fire hazards that you come across such as faulty heaters.
9. Do not block fire exits or corridors. Don't leave trolleys, cleaning equipment, meal trays from guest rooms, linen, damaged or spare furniture, mattresses, extra beds and so forth where they could get in the way of anyone who has to leave the building in an emergency. Remember it might be very difficult to see in smoky conditions.
10. Remember fire extinguishers should be where they will be needed in the event of a fire, not propping open a door. Mis-used in this way they will actually help spread the fire.
11. Don't attempt to dry cloths by draping them in front of an electric or gas fire. If you see guests' clothes hung over lamps or in front of fires, for example, discreetly put them in a safe place.
12. Some guests insist on smoking in bed, a very dangerous practice. Make sure that there is an ashtray in smokers' rooms—how many and where they are left will depend on establishment policy.

??

Take action in the event of a fire

1. Act quickly! Keep calm!

2. Raise the alarm to call for help. The other occupants of the building must be warned as soon as possible, the fire brigade called and the people in charge notified. Check the fire notices for the exact procedure, as some fire alarms are linked direct to the fire brigade.

3. Help evacuate the building. Remember disabled and elderly guests, children and ill people may need help.

   - Use the nearest escape route.
   - Do not use lifts.
   - Walk, don't run.
   - Do not stop to collect personal belongings.
   - Go to your assembly point.
   - Do not enter the building until you are told it is safe to do so.
   - If you have to go through or evacuate an area filled with smoke:— keep low or crawl (the smoke will be less dense at floor level)
       — keep calm and breathe shallowly through the nose (this reduces the risk of taking gulps of smoke)

HOW TO

   — keep to the walls so you know you are moving in a straight direction—feel your way using the back of your hand, not the palm so you are less likely to cut your hand and cause serious injury if there is broken glass on the floor or a sharp piece of metal sticking out from the wall.

4. Close doors and windows. Fires will spread quickly through open doors. They also need air as they require oxygen to keep burning.

5. Carry out any special responsibilities such as taking lists of occupied rooms, staff on duty. It is vital that there is some means of checking that everyone is safely evacuated from the building.

6. Switch off the power supplies if it is safe to do so. This is important in laundries and other rooms where there is a lot of electrical equipment—the risk of new sources of ignition for the fire from electric sparks will be reduced.

7. Attack the blaze with a suitable extinguisher **if this will not put you in personal danger.**

   - For fires involving solid materials such as wood, paper, fabrics, use a water extinguisher (this will be red).
   - For fires involving electrical equipment use a CO_2 extinguisher (this will be black, or if it is a new model, red with a black band, spot or label).
   - In areas where paint, polishes, oil and other liquids or liquefiable solids are stored or used an appropriate extinguisher will be available, usually a dry powder extinguisher (blue) or a foam extinguisher (cream).
   - A fire blanket will be available in service areas and kitchens where it can be used to smother fires that start in a saucepan on the stove top, or in deep fat fryers.
   - In areas where a fire is likely to involve gas or metals, other special extinguishers will be available.

   TO DO

The damage this house mouse will cause by chewing the electrical cable could result in a fire. Make a list of other examples of fire hazards which could be the result of poor maintenance and inadequate pest control.

How fires start

A fire will start when an electric spark, discarded match, cigarette or similar source of ignition occurs in the presence of paper, refuse, furniture, curtaining or other material which easily burns. A fire also needs oxygen (air is made up of about 21% oxygen).

How fires spread

Fires spread upwards quickly, so fireproof doors closing off staircases, lift shafts and rubbish chutes from adjacent areas and rooms must be kept shut.

Fires will spread horizontally quite quickly, moving through doorways and down corridors, so bedroom doors and fire doors must be kept closed. (Some fire doors can be left open safely—they are linked to the fire alarm system and will be closed automatically in an emergency.)

How fires are put out

A fire will go out if the burning material is removed or cooled down, or if the supply of air (and therefore oxygen) is cut off.

Fire fighting equipment acts by:

- cooling down the burning materials—water hoses and sprinklers do this
- shutting off the supply of air—many fire extinguishers do this by smothering the fire in a foam, powder, gas (for example, carbon dioxide). Fire blankets and fire buckets filled with sand work on the same principle.

How fires are detected

The longer the fire has to take hold, the more difficult it is to put out so the earliest possible detection of fires is of the greatest importance. Sophisticated fire detecting equipment has been developed to catch fires quickly and to safeguard the building and its occupants at night time when few people are about. Systems include:

- Smoke detectors which respond to the high concentrations of very small particles that scarcely anything other than a fire creates. They are suitable for bedrooms, general storage rooms, stairwells, corridors, public rooms and lift shafts. Special versions are available for the ducts in air-conditioning and heating systems (as these will rapidly circulate toxic fumes throughout a building).
- Flame detectors which respond to the radiation given off by a flame. They are only suitable for areas where any fire is likely to involve a flame.
- Heat detectors which respond to temperatures above a pre-set level, or which rise rapidly. These are suitable in boiler rooms, kitchens, laundries and similar areas where the working temperatures are often quite high.
- Manual alarms strategically located so that anyone in the building can strike one very quickly if a fire is observed.

 **TO DO**

Your safety, your colleagues' safety, the safety of the guests, patients, customers and anyone else using the building depend on the care you take to prevent a fire and on your knowledge of what to do if a fire breaks out.

Prepare yourself carefully:

- write down the answer to as many of the following questions as you can
- check your answers with your supervisor or tutor and note any additional information you are given
- find out from your supervisor or tutor the answers to the questions you have not been able to answer and make a note of them.

1. What would be the three most likely causes of a fire in your establishment?
2. Which items in the cleaning stores are particularly flammable?
3. If you discover a fire, what action do you take to alert (a) the fire brigade, (b) the occupants of the building and (c) someone in authority?
4. Where are the exit routes? If you work, study or live in a large building include the areas you might be in.
5. Where is your assembly point if you have to evacuate the building?
6. Who is responsible for checking the names of everyone who should have evacuated the building?
7. What fire fighting equipment is available? Include extinguishers available for fighting particular types of fire.
8. How are the different types of fire fighting equipment operated?
9. When is it safe for you to attempt to fight a fire?

Security

Visitors to leisure centres, patients in hospitals, guests in hotels and guesthouses, students in halls of residence, people in homes for the elderly . . . all expect to be secure, to feel confident that they and their possessions will be safe.

Poor hygiene practices, safety hazards and fire are particular threats (see units 53 to 57) that affect all users of the establishment, customers and staff, and the owners. Other security threats that fall into this category include:

- Theft—of the customers' possessions, of the establishment's property. The thief might be an outsider breaking in to steal as much as possible, or simply an opportunist who takes advantage of a weakness in security. On the other hand the thief might be a guest who packs the bath robe or the towels, or collects hotel ashtrays as souvenirs. Some thieves book in as guests with the intention of robbing other guests of their valuables. And in some cases it is a member of staff who is guilty—perhaps because the temptation was too much to resist, or because stocks of cleaning agents and supplies of soap, shampoo etc. for guest rooms are not adequately controlled.
- Terrorist threats and bomb explosions—a more recent security problem, but one that few establishments can afford to ignore.
- Personal attacks, muggings and rape—by intruders who have gained access to the building.

✱ FOR INTEREST

Housekeeping staff in hotels, guesthouses, students halls of residence and similar establishments may be the first to discover that the occupant of one of the bedrooms has died, or appears to be dead (he or she may be in a deep coma).

A doctor should be called at once and the police informed. Between them, they will take care of arrangements such as informing the next of kin, removing the

body—this will usually be done as discreetly as possible (using back entrances etc.) to avoid upsetting anyone else in the building.

The housekeeping staff may be asked to help gather the dead person's belongings, making a record of them in case of any uncertainty later, and packing them ready for collection by the next of kin.

Controlling the movement of people and goods

When a new building is planned (see unit 8) careful thought will be given to the movement of people—customers and staff—and the movement of goods—customers' luggage and other possessions, supplies to meet their needs and waste materials created during their stay. The objectives will include ensuring that all:

- access points can be observed, either by staff on duty at reception, staff entrances etc. or by closed circuit television systems
- storage areas can be effectively secured and that adequate secure storage is also available for valuables belonging to customers and staff.

‼ REMEMBER

1. If you see anyone in the building whom you do not recognise and who is acting suspiciously, either ask for identification or report the incident.
2. Keep lockers locked and the key in a safe place. If you bring any valuables to work, keep them safe in your locker while you are on duty.
3. Put all equipment and materials in the correct place after use. Storage areas must always be kept locked when unattended.
4. Report missing or broken items found in rooms as soon as possible. A television may well have been taken for repair, but it could also have been stolen. Check to be sure.
5. Report any suspicious-looking items in public places, including bags or suitcases left unattended. Do not handle them yourself.
6. Do not unlock a bedroom door for anyone who does not have his or her own key, unless you are quite certain that it is the person's room. Dishonest people can tell very convincing stories—so point out to the person concerned that you have to check their identity, because it is a rule of the establishment, made to protect their own interests.
7. Always keep keys with you, never:
   - left in the lock
   - lying around while you change into uniform or clean the room or collect something
   - with colleagues, guests or contractors.

✒ HOUSECRAFT TIP

Systems for loaning out towels for the swimming pool or sauna, such as recording names and room numbers of customers, must be treated seriously. If regular customers find that nothing happens if they forget a towel by the pool and don't check it back in, the word will soon spread that the control system is meaningless. Towels could start to disappear rapidly.

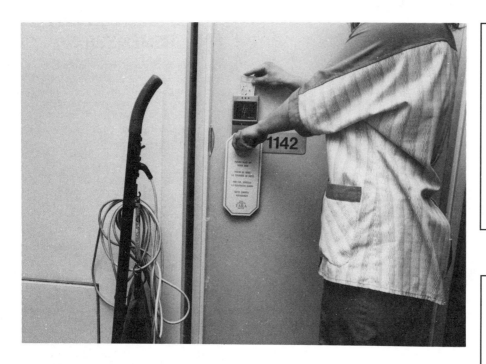

Controlling keys

To avoid the need for housekeeping staff to carry a key for every door, most establishments use a system of master keys:

- The *grand master* will open every lock, even if it has been double locked.
- The *master* will open every lock, but not one which has been double locked.
- The *sub-master* and *floor* or *section master* will open locks on a particular floor or wing of the building, for example, unless they have been double locked. (Sometimes these are known as *pass keys*.)

The master system means that the privacy of guests in a hotel for example can be protected. Anyone not wishing to be disturbed by housekeeping or floor service staff can double lock the door from the inside. The grand master can be used in an emergency.

The control of all keys is important. If a key is lost then the lock will have to be changed (or the barrel of the lock), if a sub-master is lost all the locks which it could operate have to be changed. This is likely to be very costly, so electronic key systems are becoming more popular (see box).

?? HOW TO

Deal with left property
1. Hand the items to your supervisor or the person appointed to safeguard anything left behind or lost by guests, customers, patients etc.
2. Do this as soon as possible as the owner may still be in the building.
3. Make sure you can give details of exactly where you found the item(s), and when.

4. If someone asks you about property they have lost, get a description of it and as much information as possible about when it was last seen.

Lost property is usually kept for between three and six months depending on its value. After this time the person who found it is entitled to have it.

✳ FOR INTEREST

Duplicating keys to hotel bedrooms is one of the professional thief's favourite methods of working. One hotel thief had his own key-making kit with him when he was arrested.

Electronic door locks are expensive to install but do offer guests greater security. The guest is issued on arrival with a keycard, programmed to open a particular bedroom door. The program is unique to that particular guest and will automatically be cancelled when he or she checks out, or the keycard is lost.

?? HOW TO

Deal with a bomb or suspicious-looking item
The most important point to remember is that if you should see a bomb, or a suspicious looking item which could be a bomb, never try to dispose of it yourself. Follow the emergency procedure:

- raise the alarm
- call for help, from the emergency services and from other staff
- evacuate the building.

Deal with a bomb threat made over the phone
1. Keep the caller on the line for as long as possible.
2. Ask the caller to repeat the message and try to record the exact words.
3. Obtain as much information as possible about the location of the bomb.
4. Warn the caller that the building is occupied and that the bomb could result in many deaths.
5. Pay particular attention to background noises, such as engines running or music, which could give a clue as to the whereabouts of the caller.
6. Listen carefully to the voice to see if the person is male, female, young, old, drunk, calm, excited etc., and try to identify the speaker's accent.
7. Immediately after the caller hangs up, inform the police by telephoning 999. Follow any other emergency procedures laid down by the establishment.
8. Inform someone in charge.

Controlling stock

At any one time a residential establishment carries a considerable stock of cleaning agents, linen and such things as new cleaning cloths, mopheads, spare fittings for mechanical equipment, and if it is a hotel, supplies of soap, stationery, shampoo and so forth (see unit 44).

Enough stock is kept to allow the work of the department to be done efficiently, but not so much that unnecessary storage space is taken up.

A control system will usually be in operation to ensure that:

- stocks are re-ordered before they run out
- a calculation can be made quickly of what is held in stock and its value
- a record is kept of what stocks have been issued, to whom and when.

The systems used to issue stocks are similar to those operated for linen (see unit 38):

1. Clean or full items are given out in exchange for dirty or empty ones.
2. A set amount is issued based on the work schedule and past experience of what should be required.
3. Stocks are topped up to a specific level.
4. A written order (usually known as a requisition) is made for the items that will be required. This normally has to be signed by someone in authority.

 **TO DO**

Write a brief report on the system for controlling issues of cleaning materials and guest supplies in an establishment of your choice. Try and get a fairly accurate idea of how much the issues on a typical day have cost. Work out (if necessary with the help of your supervisor or tutor) what the cost per guest, patient etc. is.

‼ REMEMBER

Observant housekeeping staff are one of the best security measures an establishment can have. It's people who:

- are responsible for the proper use of keys and the maintenance of security systems
- have to respond to problems detected by security systems
- can best observe suspicious behaviour
- can notice that something has gone missing or looks out of place
- can cause further security problems by discussing the security systems in operation or the details of how recent thefts have been carried out in places where they can be overheard by outsiders (who may not be as honest as they seem!).

And if the guest in a hotel has been the victim of a theft, the excellent service, friendly staff, comfortable room and good food will soon be forgotten. It is most unlikely the guest will visit the hotel again, nor will anyone else who is told of the unfortunate event—unless it's to take further advantage of the lack of security and rob another guest!

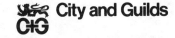 **City and Guilds**

Test yourself: Units 53–59

1. The Health and Safety at Work Act (1974) places obligations on both employer and employee. State six of the requirements (at least three should be for employees).
2. State the name of the regulations which require records to be kept of particular types of accident. Give at least four of the details usually required on an accident report.
3. Describe briefly how a heavy object should be lifted.
4. Give four safety points which should be remembered when using a ladder.
5. Describe some of the safety measures which will help prevent:
   (a) cuts
   (b) falls
   (c) burns and scalds.
   In each case give at least three.
6. Describe briefly how a graze or cut should be treated.
7. Name two examples of pests which might be found in residential establishments and briefly state why they are harmful.
8. Identify three general measures which can be taken to discourage pests.
9. State briefly what it is important to remember about each of the following in the event of a fire:
   (a) lifts
   (b) doors and windows
   (c) the very young, disabled, sick or elderly
   (d) attempting to fight the fire yourself.
10. Describe the procedure you should take in the event of discovering a fire.
11. What is the difference between the following types of key: a grand master and a sub-master?
12. Describe briefly two different ways in which stocks of cleaning materials can be issued to staff.

The importance of personality

Personality—what people are good and not so good at, will affect the way they deal with their customers in just the same way as it affects the way they deal with their family, their friends and their work colleagues.

- Housekeeping staff who deal with *their customers* in a thoughtful, appropriate and efficient way will be playing their part in *keeping the customers satisfied*.
- Housekeeping staff who deal with *their work colleagues* in a thoughtful, appropriate and efficient way will be helping them to play their part in *keeping the customers satisfied*.

This will bring benefits

- to customers through a better quality of service
- to employers through increased business (more patients receiving treatment, more guests staying)
- to individual members of staff through the building-up of their confidence
- to all members of staff through developing teamwork.

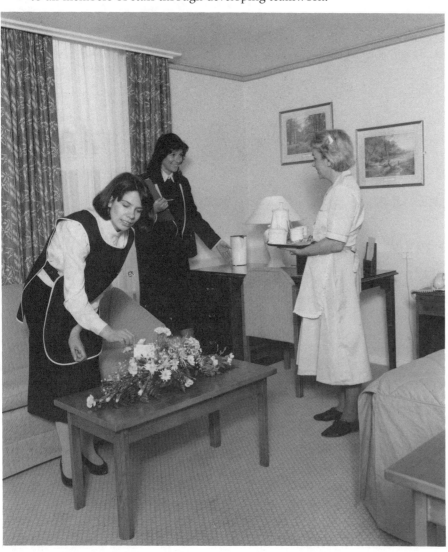

?? HOW TO

Deal with special needs

Many of the special needs of customers will be dealt with by colleagues, for example:

- reception and reservation staff in a hotel who allocate a room with special facilities to disabled guests
- nursing staff who provide medical and personal help to patients.

Nonetheless the housekeeping staff are in a good position to support these efforts and to help provide for other special needs, for example:

- Disabled or elderly guests may appreciate help from a member of staff servicing their room—to hang up some clothes, for example, or to fill in their laundry form.
- The guest in a hotel room who is obviously not well may appreciate being told where the nearest chemist is or the phone number of the local doctor.
- Parents with restless children might be told about the leisure centre in the town or the opening hours of the hotel's pool.
- Business travellers often need to press their clothes or get skirts and blouses laundered very quickly, and would be pleased to borrow an iron and ironing board or know about the express laundry service.
- Students preparing for an exam may know they will be studying long into the night and prefer their room to be cleaned later in the morning, or on another day if the cleaning schedule can be re-organised.
- Some patients enjoy chatting to hospital domestic staff and may in the course of a conversation give some information that would help their treatment—so this must be directly and discreetly passed on to the medical staff.

!! REMEMBER

If you are a cheerful, patient person with a good sense of humour, it is probably quite natural and easy for you to relate well to people, no matter who they are. On the other hand, if you are inclined to be gloomy it will require a deliberate effort to be cheerful, just as talkative people have to be careful not to chat so much they turn into bores or time-wasters.

Knowledge of the services and facilities offered by the workplace

The more staff members know about the establishment they work in and the surrounding area, the more helpful they can be to customers who are not familiar with the services and facilities available:

- When customers ask directly for help—perhaps coming up to a member of staff who is cleaning the corridor.
- When customers would be pleased to be given help—for example after exchanging greetings with a member of staff who enters a lift, they continue in conversation to discuss how nice it would be to go to a film or play.
- When a member of staff has an opportunity to help sell a service or facility which the establishment offers—for example mentioning to a guest in the hotel who happens to say that she is going to the beach for the day that the chef does delicious light packed lunches.
- When a member of staff has an opportunity to help sell a more expensive item to a customer—for example after learning from two young business travellers how much they are looking forward to a drink to mark the signing-up of a new sales deal, telling them that the hotel's roof-top restaurant has just introduced a special celebration dinner menu and the price includes a free bottle of champagne.

Using personality

When expressions such as 'Thank you', 'Good morning', 'Have a nice day' are said in an automatic, robot-like way, they are usually a big turn-off and none of the feelings or character of the person saying them comes through.

To use personality to its full advantage means for everyone:

1. Being aware of the sort of person one is. It may help to write down a list of words like patient, careless, quick-witted, which describe personality, and ask friends and colleagues to help.
2. Making use of all contact with people to develop personality. Experience gained throughout life, as a child with other children, with parents, with teachers, with relatives and so forth, all help shape personality.
3. Knowing what one is good at and not so good at. It is no good being patient and cheerful, for example, unless one is aware of it and can make use of these qualities in dealings with other people. However if someone is inclined to be shy and quiet, he or she can make positive efforts to develop self-confidence.
4. Continually striving to improve what one is good at and still not so good at. The danger of being good at things is that complacency sets in and things are done automatically. It is important to watch for opportunities to become better. Listen carefully to what customers, colleagues and family are saying and how they say it. Watch also how other people do things with you. Find new ways to practise improving customercraft skills.
5. Considering the personality, mood and needs of the people one deals with. Personality should be controlled to fit individual situations in the best possible way. If someone is out-going and bubbly, a customer who is shy or pre-occupied might respond very well to the friendly attitude. On the other hand the customer may not be shy at all, nor wish to be distracted with cheerful conversation, but want to be left alone to think through a problem.

!! REMEMBER

You are important to customers because:

- You help clean and maintain the building, furnishings and equipment.
- You can respond to the individual needs of customers.
- You can pass on how pleased (or displeased) the customers are with the services and facilities provided.
- You can help your colleagues provide a better quality of service by communicating quickly and accurately information they need, by responding efficiently to the information they give you, by making them feel that their well-being is your concern.

Remind yourself why it is important to know your customers and how you can find out more about them by referring back to unit 2.

◆ ◆ ◆ TO DO

In the *Customercraft* book, four examples are given of replies to a guest's question 'Is there a vegetarian menu available in the hotel restaurant?':

1. 'I'm only a room cleaner, I don't know anything about the restaurant.'
2. 'I think there might be, but the receptionist will know for sure. Go down the stairs to the end of the corridor to the ground floor and turn left . . .'
3. 'Yes madam, there is. Our vegetarian menu is very popular I believe . . .'
4. 'There might be, but in any case I don't expect the chef will mind rustling you up something you will enjoy . . .'

Which reply do you think would be acceptable if you know the answer to the question? Which reply would be acceptable if you did not know the answer?

Make a list of any questions you might be asked about the services and facilities offered at your workplace. Tick those you know the answer to, and then find out the information you need to give a helpful answer to the remaining questions.

Get your colleagues to help draw up the list of questions so you can be as comprehensive as possible.

Relating with other staff and departments in the organisation

The housekeeping or domestic services staff belong to one of a number of important departments reporting to the management. They will have responsibility for certain specific tasks to do with the cleaning and maintenance of the building. Many of these tasks will involve co-operation with staff from other departments.

For example in a hospital, the domestic assistants' duties may include cleaning the wards, ward kitchens, offices, restrooms, corridors, stairs, sanitary areas and the fixtures and fittings they contain. However:

- Beds will usually be made by nurses, so it is important that the ward floors are not cleaned until they have finished (so the dust has settled).
- Meals will be served by ward housekeepers or nurses but the washing up will normally be done by domestic assistants unless there is a central wash-up.
- Doctors will not want to be disturbed during their rounds by cleaning activities.
- Equipment will be repaired by maintenance staff.

Similarly in a hotel, it will be the job of housekeeping staff to clean the guest rooms and corridors. However:

- Reception staff will normally provide the information (via the executive housekeeper) of which guests will be departing, whether rooms can be taken out for periodic cleaning, what special requirements new guests have.
- The income the hotel receives will be too low if the cashier does not get told that a single room has been occupied by two guests.
- The maintenance staff can more easily carry out repairs if they are told about damaged fittings when the problem first occurs, not after it has reached a serious state.
- Reception staff will not want to let a room until they know it has been serviced and all the equipment in it is working as it should be.

Team work in the housekeeping department

In all but the very small establishments the cleaning tasks are divided among different members of staff. The work may be organised in such a way that one person is responsible for all the tasks in a particular area or a number of rooms, or it may be organised so that tasks are divided up between different people working as a team and covering a larger area.

Whether the work is allocated to individuals or organised as a team, each member of the housekeeping staff is dependent on others for the successful completion of their job:

- Equipment will be used by a number of different people and it is important that each person keeps it in the appropriate condition for the next user.
- Colleagues will be needed to help with specific tasks, such as turning mattresses, hanging heavy curtains and holding ladders.
- People who do their job badly make extra work for others. This is especially true when the responsibility for cleaning any one particular room or area varies from day to day.
- Housekeeping staff depend on colleagues, usually within the department, for ensuring that the various supplies needed to clean and replenish a room or area are available when needed.

✱ FOR INTEREST

The *executive housekeeper* is the person in overall charge of the housekeeping department in a medium to large hotel, and will report direct to the general manager or to the front of house manager.

The *head housekeeper* is in charge of sections of the hotel, or in a small hotel in overall charge.

The *domestic services manager* is responsible for the cleaning services throughout a hospital.

The *domestic supervisor* is responsible for the cleaning and domestic staff and their duties in specific areas of the hospital.

Some hospitals have *ward housekeepers* who supervise the cleaning and also carry out some of the duties previously undertaken by nurses, such as taking meal orders, serving meals, and the administration work involved in patient care.

The *accommodation officer* or *senior bursar* is in charge of the housekeeping staff of all halls of residence on a college or university campus.

The *domestic bursar* or *housekeeper* is in charge of the cleaning staff in a student hall of residence.

Staff organisation

Occupancy levels of many types of accommodation establishment vary considerably depending on the day of the week, the time of the year and what is going on in the area. Some hotels and student halls of residence even close for periods.

This makes it quite difficult to arrange for all the cleaning and maintenance activities to be carried out to a consistently high standard throughout the year.

Some seasonal hotels get round the problem by employing one or two permanent housekeeping staff who work the whole year around. In the closed period they may be carrying out periodic cleaning tasks and taking their own annual holiday. As soon as the season begins, extra staff are engaged on short-term contracts.

City-centre hotels and other establishments where the level of business is reasonably consistent throughout the year normally engage all their housekeeping staff on permanent or yearly contracts. When the hotel is particularly busy they engage casual or temporary staff, often through an employment agency (in much the same way as 'temps' are called in to help with secretarial work in offices).

Sometimes in large establishments the duties of staff who are on holiday or off ill can be split among their colleagues, otherwise a casual or temporary person will be brought in.

Working methodically

The approach each member of staff has to each task will affect the overall standards of cleanliness but very often the greatest efficiency is achieved when all staff work together as a team.

Good organisation and advance planning, effective stock control and best use of time (see unit 17) all depend on people working well with each other.

Punctuality

Housekeeping staff have a responsibility to other members of staff and the customers to be punctual. If a member of staff turns up late for duty, other staff members will often have extra work to do. This can cause delay and resentment.

▶▶▶ TO DO

On the basis of the following organisation chart for a medium-sized hotel, draw up an organisation chart for an accommodation establishment of your choice. It is suggested that the detail of jobs below department manager level are only given for the housekeeping/domestic services department. Where possible, indicate the total numbers of staff at each level.

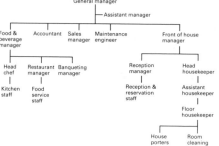

Once you have completed your chart think about the contact the housekeeping/domestic services staff should have with other departments to do their job effectively. Indicate against each job level the degree of contact:

*** close daily contact   ** some daily contact   * occasional contact

---

Housekeeping staff come into contact with many people during their working hours. They will often have to work closely with colleagues from their own department and from other departments, they will receive instructions and have to report to supervisors and they will meet customers—guests staying in the hotel, patients in the hospital (possibly their visitors), members of the club, students living in the residence, conference delegates and so forth.

They will be communicating with these people in one or more ways:

- talking and listening face-to-face and on the telephone
- writing and reading messages, forms, letters etc.
- through their appearance, facial expression, the gestures they use, where they are looking (directly at the person's face, at the floor, out of the window and so forth) and how close to the person they allow themselves to be (a pace or two, using the trolley or the desk as a protection, for example).

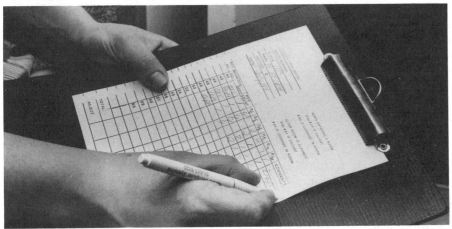

Everyday pieces of information like room cleaning reports need to be clean, accurate and helpful to the reader

Talking

Speech has certain characteristics which affect the message that is being spoken:

- Volume—loud speech may sound bossy, very quiet speech cannot be heard.
- Pitch—an unnatural pitch usually sounds false so it is best for people with particularly high or deep voices not to try and disguise them. Some people's voices get higher in pitch if they become agitated or over-excited, this can turn into an irritating whining.
- Tone—warm tones if overdone can sound grovelling, while cool tones are very unwelcoming.
- Pace—fast speech is not easy to follow, but very slow speech makes the speaker sound stupid, or gives the impression that he or she thinks the listener is stupid.

The effect of speaking in any particular way will be modified or enhanced by the body language the person talking is using. A warm smile accompanying 'Have a nice day' will turn it into a genuine greeting. Looking directly at the person who is being spoken to will indicate a real interest in communicating the message (and make it easier to understand).

The exception is of course the telephone. It is not possible to use body language to help get across messages and distortion sometimes makes speech less easy to understand. The tone of the voice is heightened and the speed exaggerated.

USEFUL TERMS

Body language The form of communication that takes place without words: appearance, facial expression, gestures, gaze (looking directly at the face of the person who is talking or listening) and space (keeping a certain physical distance from the other person, or using other barriers such as dark glasses, folded arms, a table).

?? HOW TO

Deal with complaints

1. Keep calm. Your job is to put things right, not to wriggle out of an awkward situation.
2. Listen carefully. Pay attention to everything the customer says and get all the important details clear. Don't interrupt, it is easy to jump to the wrong conclusion because you haven't heard all the details.
3. Thank the customer for bringing the complaint to your attention. It's worth remembering that most customers don't bother to complain. They just make sure they never have a similar experience again by not returning to the establishment. They also warn their friends off.
4. Apologise to the customer. This is always important even if you don't feel an apology is due. It shows the complaint has been taken seriously and helps calm the customer down.
5. Take action to put things right. If it is not your job to sort out the problem, or you don't feel you can, you should explain to the customer what you are doing and then pass on all details to the appropriate person. Don't pass the buck, or make promises which you cannot carry out.
6. Check that everything has been put right (especially if you have had to pass on the complaint). Take steps to try and ensure the problem will not occur again, if necessary with the help of your supervisor.

Remember customers who complain may well be angry. Don't make the situation worse by getting angry or frustrated yourself. Speak calmly and clearly and try not to forget that it is the situation that is the problem, not you.

Listening

People feel at ease and valued if they know they are being listened to. They will feel more confident and able to make their needs known. The listener gains too, learning more about the person talking—forming better relations with colleagues and providing a better quality service to customers. Considerable time and frustration is saved. Fewer mistakes are made.

Listening involves more than just hearing what someone says. It is an active process:

- Full attention must be given to the speaker. It is no good letting the mind wander, or getting distracted by other goings-on.
- Interest must be shown in what the speaker is saying. Interruptions or attempts to upstage the speaker should be avoided.
- The important things the speaker is saying should be picked out and interesting but irrelevant details ignored.
- Action must be taken on what has been said. If necessary notes can be made, or other staff fetched so they can take action.

Listening also involves taking notice of the body language the person is using. For example:

- yawning might suggest boredom
- looking at the time might also suggest boredom, or else that the person is in a hurry.

How fast or slow, loud or soft, warm or cold the person's voice is and its pitch (high or low) will give further clues to what is being said. For example:

- speaking softly can suggest a desire for confidentiality or nervousness
- speaking hesitantly can suggest unease or indecision.

Test yourself: Units 60–62

1. Give three reasons why housekeeping staff are important to customers.
2. Describe how personality can help or hinder relations with customers and work colleagues, giving four points that it is important to remember.
3. Identify at least one way in which housekeeping staff can use their knowledge of the workplace to help customers, and another way in which it can be used to help customers and increase sales for the establishment.
4. State the purpose of:
   (a) job descriptions
   (b) duty rosters
   (c) arrival and departure lists.
5. Why is good teamwork important? Give at least two reasons.
6. Explain briefly what is meant by body language and give an example which would indicate each of the following:
   (a) warmth
   (b) agitation
   (c) confidence
   (d) concern for the needs of customers.
7. Name four characteristics of speech.
8. Give the steps for dealing with complaints and describe what is involved in each.

‼ REMEMBER

Be brief and to the point. Colleagues won't want you to waste their time giving long-winded explanations. Customers will expect you to be helpful and courteous, but not so chatty they get bored or wonder why you aren't getting on with your job.

Use commonly understood words. Don't try to impress by using long words or jargon.

Time your message appropriately. Pick a time when the person can pay attention to what you are saying. Don't talk at the same time as someone else, or try and deliver an important message when someone's using a noisy machine, or at the top of a ladder.

Pay attention to what is being said in reply. Look at the face of the person directly: it is far easier to understand words if you can also see facial expressions.

Ask for a message to be repeated if you think you have missed important information.

Read back important messages, for example the numbers of rooms you have been asked to service, the quantities of clean linen to be collected, how a function room is to be set up.

Don't shout or wave your arms about in an over-excited way because you think the person you are talking to will find it difficult to understand you. Speak slowly and as clearly as you can to people who are hard of hearing or have only a limited understanding of English. Use controlled, carefully thought-out gestures where you think they will help get the message across.

▶ TO DO

Make your own list of two or three of the greetings and phrases you use on a regular basis at your workplace or college. Practise saying them in different ways, for example:

- at various speeds
- using different tones
- changing the pace
- altering the pitch
- putting the emphasis on different words.

If possible, ask a friend to help by commenting on the effect conveyed by each change.

INDEX